The ideal river

MANCHESTER
1824

Manchester University Press

The ideal river

How control of nature shaped the international order

Joanne Yao

MANCHESTER UNIVERSITY PRESS

Published by Manchester University Press
Oxford Road, Manchester M13 9PL
www.manchesteruniversitypress.co.uk

British Library Cataloguing-in-Publication Data
A catalogue record for this book is available from the British Library

ISBN   978 1 5261 5438 5   hardback

First published 2022

Typeset
by New Best-set Typesetters Ltd

For the Rhine, the Danube, and the Congo Rivers

Contents

Figures

Preface and acknowledgments

People who write about rivers often start their narratives by describing a romanticized clarion call from the river that they simply could not ignore – and off they would go to uncover all the lofty secrets of the river from source to mouth. I arrived at my research on rivers in a much more grounded fashion. As I have often told colleagues and complete strangers who quizzically asked me 'why rivers?', I started my doctoral studies hoping to research international norms and global oceans. I had just spent three and a half years working in the bureaucratic cage of the US government and wanted an intellectual challenge that captured the expansive scope of the global in all its drama and contradictions. However, when I arrived at the International Relations Department at the London School of Economic and Political Science (LSE), my supervisor looked at my ambitious proposal and questioned the wisdom of a largescale historical project on oceans – 'how about rivers?' he asked me.

At first, the move from oceans to rivers seemed like a sensible restraint on the over-eager imagination of a first-year doctoral student. Anchoring my research on the first transboundary river commissions of the nineteenth century whittled down the scope and made the project 'doable' (said one senior academic). But I soon realized that rivers were every bit the fertile intellectual and theoretical playground that oceans represented in my original proposals. The metaphorical and metaphysical richness of rivers astonished me. Once I started looking for it, I found that the dream of taming rivers wove through the history of the modern world like a bright thread. It lurks at the heart of modernity – not just in our ironclad faith in unidirectional progress along the river of history, but in modern society's desire for neatness, predictability, finite boundaries, and a straightened sense of political purpose.

A turning point came when I started to see how this dream of taming the river hung in the air at formal diplomatic conferences of nineteenth-century Europe and in between the lines of international agreements. It led me to reflect on whether the dry, bureaucratic discussion and decrees of these conferences – and the first 'technical' international bodies they created – were actually laden with ideas about how to control not just the political affairs of human society but its relationship with nature. And I grew increasingly disenchanted with accounts of international institutions that seemed divorced from not just a sense of history but a sense of place – as if these diplomatic deliberations and the 'high politics' of international relations occurred in a detached vacuum that sealed them off from prevailing intellectual, social, and geographical imaginaries of their times. Perhaps this is why it is so easy to believe that these institutions are not only technocratic and apolitical but also universal and generalizable across time and space.

All this led me to wonder how environmental history might contribute to a historical sociology of the first interstate organizations established to tame international rivers. Can the history of the river be disentangled from the societies that have dreamed along its banks, bathed in its waters, and engineered its shorelines? Can the history of these societies be disentangled from the river that has watered their fields, cleansed their cities, and carried their ideas and institutions to new shores? Ultimately, my aim is not to capture the 'real' or 'authentic' river (as perhaps those who receive the clarion call might hope to do) but to consider how our entangled human–river histories enabled the political possibilities of modernity. However, studying the co-constitution of human and nonhuman relations as a central theme in the early formation of the current international order also shows us how our modern political order has gone to such lengths to create and reinforce a stark separation between human civilization and nature – an ongoing political effort that informs our troubled relationship with nature in the Anthropocene.

Countless human and nonhuman inspirations have made this book possible. I would like to thank Peter Wilson, George Lawson, Tarak Barkawi, James A. Morrison, and all those at the LSE IR department who saw potential in an unusual graduate project about rivers – in particular, I am very grateful to Peter Wilson for pushing me towards the Danube and George Lawson for his intellectual encouragement, professional support, and no-nonsense advice. Many have, in their own way, inspired me to go on this peculiar intellectual journey including Alexander Wendt, Marco Cesa, Todd Hall, Valerie Morkevicius, Johs Pierce, and my parents Youchun Yao and Qiuping Chen. Many others have contributed to this project by illuminating new avenues and asking provocative questions that have stayed with me – here, I would particularly like to thank Martin Bayly, Klaus Dodds, Andrew Phillips, Tonny Brems Knudsen, Mark Laffey, Meera Sabaratnam, Kim Hutchings, Kiran Phull, and Cameron Harrington.

I would like to thank my friends and colleagues for their untold support in conceiving of, researching, and writing this book – from the LSE gang including Andrew Delatolla, Liane Harnett, Martin Hearson, Heidi NK

Wang-Kaeding, Ida Danewid, Bugra Susler (especially for his insights on Turkish views of the Danube), Marian Feist and Daniel Schade (especially for their help with German translations, place names, and cultural insights), Julia Himmrich, Lukas Linsi, Aaron McKeil, and Andreas Nøhr, to my colleagues at Queen Mary who helped with my final framing and whose trailblazing intellectual brilliance has inspired the concluding chapters. I would also like to thank Ben van Zwanenberg for his unwavering support despite the fact that I don't do a 'real' science. Finally, as I have suggested in the dedication, I would like to thank the main characters of this book – the Rhine, the Danube, and the Congo rivers – without whom this book could never have been written.

Parts of Chapter 4 and 5 were first published in '"Conquest from barbarism": the Danube Commission, international order and control of nature as a Standard of Civilization', *European Journal of International Relations* 25(2): 335–59. I would like to thank SAGE Publishing for permission to reprint this material.

Introduction
The ideal river

Rivers are roads which move, and which carry us whither we desire to go.
Blaise Pascal, *Pensées*, 1670

Historie without Geographie like a dead carkasse hath neither life nor motion at all.
Peter Heylyn, 1652

In the aftermath of an October storm in 1504, Niccolò Machiavelli appraised the collapsed walls of two ditches outside of Pisa. The ditches were intended to divert the Arno River away from the city-state of Pisa, sever its lines of communications and trade, and force its surrender to Machiavelli's Florence. In addition, the surrounding countryside would benefit from flood control and irrigation. If all went well, cutting wide channels to divert the Arno into the sea would transform Florence into a port city and open it up to the possibility of a maritime empire. The engineering plans had been designed by none other than the great artist and polymath Leonardo Da Vinci who had conducted extensive studies of the Arno and surrounding area. However, to save on cost and manpower, the field engineer responsible for implementing Da Vinci's plans changed the depth of the diversionary channels and doomed the project. From the beginning, Florentine military commanders overseeing the siege of Pisa had been skeptical of this newfangled project to control nature for political purposes. Years after its failure, one commander would write to Machiavelli admonishing him for his hubris in playing God since only a divine force could part the Red Sea or divert the Arno for the benefit of human society (Masters 1999: 21).

However, if rivers are meandering roads with surprising destinations, then Da Vinci and Machiavelli's effort to tame the river and bend nature to the will of human society did not end outside of Pisa on that October day. Instead, their experiment represented the beginning of an underlying shift in Western international society's relationship with nature that would not be limited to their ambitions for the Arno and Florence. Between the sixteenth and the nineteenth centuries, the notion that government authorities rather than divine intervention were responsible for taming nature and safeguarding its bounty for society would become a key component of European modernity – and society's faith that scientific advancements could conquer nature took on not only political but moral importance. Likely with the failed diversion of the Arno in mind, in *The Prince* Machiavelli likens fortune to a violent river that rains destruction on an unprepared society. Hence, he advises the wise ruler to build dikes and dams when times are quiet so that when the waters rise, 'either they go by a canal or their impetus is neither so wanton nor so damaging' (1998 [1532]: 98). In this passage, taming the river not only benefits society economically and politically, but it is also a demonstration of moral virtue and prudent governance.

Furthermore, Da Vinci and Machiavelli's project to tame the Arno ultimately looked westward toward the Americas. Since Christopher Columbus's first voyage, Florentine merchants had been interested in the commercial opportunities that America represented, and one of its native sons, Amerigo Vespucci, led the first Europeans to the shores of what is today Brazil. As Florentines celebrated Vespucci's discoveries with fireworks and fanfare, they also wondered how much wealth and power they might gain by becoming a maritime power themselves with access to the world's oceans (Masters 1999: 104–5). Diversion channels on the Arno promised to make Florence a navigable port on the Ligurian Sea. Even more than creating a physical link to the sea, the diversion of the Arno represented the global ambitions of the modern European geographical imagination. Taming and controlling this local river was just the first step to taming and controlling the world.

This book charts how society's quest to tame nature, dismissed by Florentine military commanders as mere hubris in the early sixteenth century, came to shape the modern international order. While Da Vinci and Machiavelli's project ended without success, their overall political project to control the river for the benefit of society would inspire others. By the late eighteenth and nineteenth centuries, Enlightenment confidence in civilized society's ability to tame nature would become a central tenet of legitimate state authority. In addition, like Florentine leaders whose geographical imagination looked to the Americas, the taming of nature as a standard of legitimate rule also spurred colonialism and informed the development of imperial hierarchies. Hence, this book details how the taming of nature shaped not just the modern territorial state and relations between states, but also helped to constitute global hierarchies that continue to underpin modern international politics. Throughout, I use the term 'taming' to capture the multifaceted motivations behind projects to control the river, and in particular, to underscore the moral logics of battling the dark forces of chaos through the use of modern science.

To investigate how the taming of nature shaped the modern international order, I focus on Europe in the late eighteenth and nineteenth centuries as the political moment in which a particular European modernity became the driver of global transformations that reordered international politics and gave rise to early global governance. During this transformation, taming the river was enfolded into a broader liberal economic project that fore-grounded the control of nature as a global standard of economic and political legitimacy. This standard became as applicable to the floodplains of the Arno as to the wetlands of the Danube delta and the megadams of the Indian subcontinent and the American West. Here the ideal river is as conceptualized by Blaise Pascal when he noted that 'rivers are roads which move, and which carry us whither we desire to go' (1670: 5). The ideal river is a rational and reliable highway for the seamless movement of goods, people, and ideas, and hence it enriches the state, enlightens the populace, and brings liberal progress along the metaphorical river of history. This book is about the construction of that ideal river in the European geographical imagination and the ensuing political projects to actualize that vision through the creation of the first international organizations (IOs).

Conceptualizing the river: between matter and ideas

Many characters weave through the story of the establishment of the first IOs – some are scientists and engineers who prepared plans to deepen and straighten unruly rivers; some are explorers and artists whose written and pictorial accounts depicted the wonders and dangers of the river to a mesmer-ized European public; some are bureaucrats, lawyers, and diplomats at foreign offices and conferences who translated the mission to tame rivers into official agreements and international law. But perhaps the most important and understudied characters in these stories are the rivers themselves.

Traditionally, environmental politics has not been a central concern for IR theorizing, with works on environmental policy as either an extension of international regimes scholarship (Young 1994; 2016; Haas 2015) or international political economy (Clapp and Dauvergne 2016; Falkner 2017). This orientation largely treats the environment as a collective action problem for international society to solve, reinforcing an assumed duality between an external nature in trouble and an international human society that must marshal the political will and technological ingenuity to save it. Since the turn of the twenty-first century, the increasing salience of global environmental challenges has elevated consideration of society's relationship with nature into the theoretical limelight (Eckersley 2004; Nixon 2011; O'Neill 2017; Forrester and Smith 2018) – particularly critical reflections that emphasize the interconnectedness and interdependence between human and nonhuman worlds.

To understand the river's role in the creation of the first IOs, it is important not only to examine rivers as material objects that enable or obstruct human endeavors, but as characters with identities taken on through centuries of interaction with human culture and politics. The Rhine flows 1,250 kilometers from streams that empty into Lake Constance (also known as the Bodensee) to the North Sea port of Rotterdam, and cuts across the bloody history of Franco-German contestation over territory, power, and European supremacy. The second longest river in Europe, the Danube flows 2,860 kilometers from Germany's Black Forest region to the Black Sea through ten current European countries and all of European history since Marcus Aurelius stood on its banks and looked dimly across at the barbarian Germanic tribes. The second longest river in Africa and the deepest in the world, the Congo flows in a semi-circle 4,700 kilometers from the highlands of East Africa into the Atlantic Ocean – in fact, the Congo enters the Atlantic with such force that its dark yellow footprint can be seen many kilometers from shore. Despite all its hydrological marvels, however, thanks to Joseph Conrad's chilling prose, the Congo is suspended forever in the Western imagination as the heart of darkness.

Conceptualizing the river in this way draws on a broadly constructivist meta-theoretical framework. I build on Emmanuel Adler's understanding of constructivists as mediativists where 'social reality emerges from the attachment of meaning and functions to physical objects; collective under-standings, such as norms, endow physical objects with purpose and therefore help constitute reality' (1997: 324). The reality of the river is constituted by the social meanings we attach to it. However, while Adler framed mediativists as a 'middle ground' between positivists and post-positivists, I understand this as a different way of analyzing social reality that rejects both the positivist insistence on an objective and pre-social material reality, as well as the post-positivist reluctance to theorize the impact of material forces on social discourses and constructions. Instead, social structures emerge from our entanglement with material forces as much as material forces are constituted and reconstituted by social ones. While the material and social might be analytically distinguishable – the river that flows from source to ocean versus our ideas about what the river should do and therefore what the river means – the political significance of neither can be fully understood without the other.

To put it differently, to understand the rivers' role in the story of the first IOs is also to put the human characters in the context of not only their historical epochs, but also their sense of geographical place. If the river's characteristics are entwined in human culture and politics, then human society has also been intimately shaped by the river. Nineteenth-century Romantics floating down the Rhine might gaze up at the imposing cliffs and wax poetic about the river's 'natural' beauty, but local communities along the river have actively engineered its bends and flows since Neolithic times. And the social fabrics of these local communities have always been shaped by the evolving materiality of the river and the political, economic, and spiritual meanings attached to the vivacity of its flow, its violence during storms, and its placidity during moments of quiet contemplation.

Indeed, the physical attributes of rivers – as a life-giving force, as a boundary that separates spaces, and a conduit that connects them – are rooted deep in human cultures and frame international society's longstanding narratives of water wars and water peace. Water holds a central place in all world religions – the term for Islamic law, *shari'a*, originates from a term that means 'the path that leads to water', while in Daoism, to resemble water is the highest virtue. Talmudic, Christian, and Islamic traditions all recognize the 'right to thirst', *chafa*, as a thirsty person's right to drink water no matter who owns the well or water source. At the same time, the term 'rivals' comes from the Latin *rivalis* or 'one who uses the same stream' and reflects a sense of Malthusian competition. The iconic Persian garden, reproduced in universally familiar carpet designs, has four channels symbolizing the four rivers of paradise dividing the quadrants of the earth and all meeting in a central fountain (Thacker 1979: 28–9). Flowing water not only denoted boundaries between earthly kingdoms – the River Styx famously separated the land of the living from that of the dead, and Julius Caesar's Rubicon separated the past to which we cannot return from a future of our own making. The river's ability to divide, connect, and transform make it more than simply a passive backdrop to human politics.

Environmental historians, perhaps because of their unique analytical focus, have long contemplated this co-constitution of social and natural worlds – indeed, environmental history is the record of that co-constitution. As David Blackbourn eloquently wrote, 'what we call landscapes are neither natural nor innocent; they are human constructs. How and why they are constructed (many would say "imagined", even "invented") belongs to the stuff of history' (2006: 15). In telling this entangled story of human society and the river, Blackbourn and other environmental historians not only wear away at the stark divide between human civilization and nature, but build the case against the purity of either. They do so by articulating the ways in which both nature and society 'are at once material and discursive' (Pritchard 2011: 17).

They remind us, as Count George Buffon did in the eighteenth century, that an untouched nature is a human fantasy: 'the state in which we see nature today is as much our work as it is hers. We have learned to temper her, to modify her, to fit her to our needs and desires' (quoted in Ferkiss 1993: 56). Equally, human civilization has always been actively shaped by nature. Peter Coates's environmental history of six rivers begins with the provocation that he intends to write not only about what societies do to the river, but also what rivers do to society. A nod to new materialist thinking, Coates's rivers are not merely objects in a human story but subjects and agents that act upon societies (2013: 26–7). For much of human history, the movement of people and ideas has depended on the directionality of rivers. Kinshasa emerged as a prosperous trading post long before Europeans arrived in central Africa due to its position at the head of a series of cataracts that made this inland city, rather than a coastal city, the center of Congo River trade. In the mid-nineteenth century, the Danube delta was thrown into the geopolitical limelight due to a hydrological quirk – rather than flowing with force into the Black Sea, the Danube turns and slows down, losing its way in wetlands and causing silt to obstruct international shipping. Lauren Benton shows how waterways acted as conduits for European power projection and colonial control, creating an uneven texture in their overseas empires – 'a fabric that was full of holes' – based on spatial distance from these arteries of imperial control (2010: 39).

While human society and nature are entwined, it is important to emphasize that they are also not reducible to one another. Environmental historians write against a natural world that is entirely collapsible into human constructs as they write against a human world determined purely by material – and some would say biological – forces. Environmental historians challenge a Galtonian biological determinism and Karl Wittfogel's environmental determinism (1956)[1] as much they contest a river that came into being purely from the human imagination. To view the world from either extreme would be to do violence to both nature and society. Indeed, one of this book's main themes is to examine how the materiality of the river reinforces, pushes back against, and reconstitutes the ideal river to create international politics.

Navigating the binary: liberalism, imperialism, and progress

Focusing on human society and the river as entangled, embedded, and inseparable allows me to make two overall interventions into the study of international politics. First, it foregrounds the problematic binary between civilization and nature and an implicit assumption behind ideologies of progress that the advancement of human civilization depends on the subjugation of nature. Here, my reflections revolve around Scottish philosopher James Dunbar's invocation: 'let us wage war with the elements, not with our own kind' (1780: 338). This quote suggests an opposition between a conflictual international society that engages in internal fratricidal violence and an idealized and progressive international society with a united purpose in the struggle against nature. In this way, the creation of the first organizations along transboundary rivers reflects Dunbar's call to forge international cooperation through the common aim of taming nature – a solidarity developed in the conviction that scientific and technical expertise will benefit humankind by rendering the nonhuman world less threatening, more predictable, and more profitable. Indeed, the liberal mantra that cooperation produces a 'win-win' scenario depends precisely on this wager that working together will allow us to extract more utility from our environment. Therefore, international institutions help us redirect our efforts from fighting our own kind to a common struggle against the elements.

Framing the relationship between civilization and nature as one of binary opposition and inevitable conquest by the former over the latter is also problematic in that the line between what is considered 'civilization' and 'nature' is not fixed. Once civilization's dominance over nature is established, moving the boundaries between the two can be an incredibly effective tool for social exclusion and political subjugation. Dunbar's call above was made in the context of praising colonialism in the Americas as essential to improving the climate: 'by opening the soil, by clearing the forests, by cutting out passages for the stagnant waters, the new hemisphere becomes auspicious, like the old' (1780: 338). Here, Dunbar elevates the control of nature based on European models as not only key to making the land more economically valuable, but also to recovering 'our patrimony from Chaos' (1780: 338). This moral framing also implies that indigenous populations' inability or unwillingness to 'improve' the land placed them firmly on the side of Chaos – a framing that continues to hamstring indigenous peoples as they confront capitalist forces and the state over rights to land into the twenty-first century.

Hence, casting a group as 'closer to nature' and therefore 'barbaric' and 'uncivilized' legitimates, first, treating that group as inferior and less worthy of normative consideration, and second, engaging in projects to tame and civilize that group in order to control and perhaps breed out those 'natural' impulses. In other words, the project to tame nature has not been confined to rivers and forests but also extends to 'untamed' elements in human society – indeed, to civilize the savage beyond the pale has long been a central aim of and justification for colonial and imperial practices. The political story this book tells shows how the ambition to tame the river seamlessly dovetails into the mission to master the 'darker' side of human nature and subdue the unruly elements of society. By draining the Prussian swamps in the eighteenth century, Frederick the Great not only made useless land useful, but also hunted down army deserters hiding there. In the twentieth century,

Saddam Hussain's project to drain the Mesopotamian swamps between the Tigris and Euphrates echoed Frederick's efforts by taming the rivers at the same time as hunting down rebels who sheltered in the reeds. By emphasizing how attempts to reorder nature also imply the reordering of society, I contend that liberal accounts of economic and moral progress likewise involve projects to rationalize 'untamed' peoples and places.

Second, and relatedly, the entangled human–river history in this book also cautions us against drawing simplistic lessons on institutional success and failure. It is all too easy to tell a narrative of institutional success in which the first fledging interstate body established along the Rhine developed into an effective international institution and inspired a cooperative model replicated first along the Danube and then across the globe in contexts as diverse as the Nile and Mekong rivers. Perhaps we can even draw a progressive line from the 1815 Rhine Commission to the League of Nations, the United Nations, and all subsequent global governance institutions. Equally, it is just as tempting to tell a narrative of institutional failure in which the first interstate commission along the Rhine was stymied by political conflict between riparian states, the second along the Danube only achieved temporary and limited success because of British hegemony, and the complete failure to establish a third commission along the Congo resulted in one of the worst tragedies of the colonial era. The first narrative reinforces the triumph of international society over untamed nature while the second reverses the story as one of human hubris. But both narratives envision nature and civilization as opposites engaged in conflict and miss a more complex story that resists the alluring simplicity of this duality.

While it is tempting to want the story of the first IOs to be either a liberal tale of progressive triumph or a realist tragedy, the historical wrinkles behind the story of each river commission thwart such a telling. To borrow from Blackbourn, framing history this way would be to 'tell a one-eyed tale', but 'even in our age of sound-bites and simple story lines, with its inbuilt biases against complexity, it is surely still possible to hold two contradictory ideas in our heads' (2006: 11). Here, I suggest it is not only possible but useful to steer between the ideological banks and acknowledge that whether an international organization or an international order is considered a success or failure largely depends on where in history we stand. At the turn of the twentieth century, as a seat of the Danube Commission, the small Danube delta town of Sulina bustled with cosmopolitan life as visitors marveled at the success of the commission in bringing nations together. Half a century later, the Iron Curtain bisected the river and the commission as a beacon of liberal progress seemed all but extinguished. Surely being able to see both stories enhances our understanding of the current international order and the complex dynamics behind envisioning and building that order. But perhaps more fundamentally, being able to hold both stories in our heads dispels the myth that either story is natural or inevitable. One of the goals of this account, then, is to resist and denature simplistic narratives about the inevitable success or preordained failure of international institutions and the global governance projects they represent.

Historicizing the first international organizations

IR scholarship has long debated the role of IOs in facilitating cooperation and advancing international peace and security. The proliferation of IOs since the late nineteenth century seems to fly in the face of realist skepticism toward their efficacy as independent actors in international politics. As of the early twenty-first century, there are an estimated 330 IOs and 37,500 international nongovernment organizations (INGOs) (Rittberger et al. 2019: 1).[2] IR often captures the growth in IOs and INGOs under the designation of global governance, a term used to describe the increasing networks of actors and processes that produce international order in the absence of a central world government. In other words, global governance is about enabling global problem-solving without a powerful central authority to coordinate and enforce collective action.

However, given all the intellectual effort IR scholars have put into theorizing international cooperation and critically assessing the formal institutional structures designed to achieve that cooperation, there is curiously little analytical attention paid to the establishment of the first IOs. Created in the aftermath of the Napoleonic Wars, the 1815 Central Commission for the Navigation of the Rhine is often catalogued as the first intergovernmental organization (Reinalda 2009). This first commission was followed by the first 'international' organization:[3] the 1856 European Commission of the Danube, established in the aftermath of the Crimean War. As the nineteenth century progressed, such organizations multiplied and became an accepted way of deliberating issues of transnational concern and formulating collective policy (Murphy 1994; Murphy and Yates 2019). International bodies sprang up to address issues as diverse as coordinating postal services and telecommunications and collaboration between secret police. While some early twentieth-century thinkers such as Leonard Woolf were interested in the 1856 European Commission of the Danube as a prototype for a world government based on functionalism (Woolf 1916; Wilson 2003), these early organizations have largely been passed over in current debates. Instead, global governance scholars in general and environmental governance in particular focus largely on the United Nations system and its accompanying institutions such as the UN Framework Convention for Climate Change (UNFCCC).[4]

Limited reflection on the origins of global governance beyond the post-World War II moment has several important consequences. First, to begin the story of global governance in the mid-twentieth century obscures the impact of nineteenth-century transformations on the development of the first IOs. The long nineteenth century[5] saw the globalization of a core–periphery international order with western Europe at its intellectual and geopolitical center. Alongside the forces behind industrialization and rational state-building practices, this order also rested on a totalizing ideology of progress rooted in 'Enlightenment notions of classification, improvement and control' (Buzan and Lawson 2015: 3). Situating early global governance among these forces highlights how this core–periphery order, and the imperial logics that underpinned this order, shaped the early development of key global governance structures such as international law and organizations.[6] Extending the timeline back to the nineteenth century frames IOs not just as an outcrop of the post-World War II liberal order but as implicated in a nineteenth-century imperial one. It forces us to theorize the continuities between the two rather than accept the premise that the mid-twentieth-century international order constituted a clean break from the past.

Second, a historical sociology of the first IOs confronts a temptation to conceptualize these bodies as neutral, rational, and technocratic tools to resolve functional international problems. Rather than just a straightforward response to material and economic impediments, I maintain throughout this book that these first transnational and international bodies were shaped by social and intellectual forces expressed through an idealized understanding of what each river meant – what I call 'geographical imaginaries' that are amalgamated through an interpretation of historical texts and cultural artifacts about each river. Importantly, these imaginaries were informed by the materiality of the rivers and centuries of human engagement with that materiality. They are part of what rivers 'do' to society. I argue that despite the common ambition to tame the river, each river held a different inflection in the popular imagination – the Rhine as an internal European highway, the Danube as a connecting river from Europe to the near periphery, and the Congo as the imperial river of commerce, Christianity, and civilization.

These imaginaries operated as ideational frames that enabled international actors to make political sense of the circumstances in which they found themselves and the interests they believed they must protect.[7] In this book, I investigate how geographical imaginaries interacted with context-specific configurations of geopolitical power and, at times, individual agency to enable the establishment of the first IOs. In creating interstate bodies to tame these three transboundary rivers, nineteenth-century European diplomats intended to address a moral problem of international order as much as they aimed to solve river navigation as a technical conundrum. By tracing these geographical imaginaries and how they shaped political processes, I also expose IOs as instruments of a given political order and challenge the notion that a one-size-fits-all model organization might be designed that could be readily transplanted as a functional fix to a host of global problems.

Finally, and relatedly, the absence of a broader historical trajectory has a tendency to present current systems and institutions as a constant through time and imbue current characteristics of international order, such as Western dominance or anarchy, with a sense of permanence or inevitability. This critique questions an ahistorical interpretation of the international system as perpetual and unchanging – an understanding of IR in which the Peloponnesian War and the Cold War might be treated as two case studies of the same general phenomenon. History, then, becomes a large databank of cases to be cherry-picked for testing IR theories that somehow stand 'outside history' in their universal explanatory power (Lawson 2006: 404; Hobson 2007). This treatment of history naturalizes the present as the only logical conclusion of past societal developments. As environmental historian Sarah Pritchard notes in her work on the history of technology, 'to study and recount only what was actually built risks naturalizing technological change' (2011: 5). The same can be said for IOs – to focus solely on the large UN organizations of today constrains us from thinking beyond current global governance institutions and (re)imagining the world otherwise. My examination of three key diplomatic moments in nineteenth-century international politics highlights the interplay between ideational frames and historical contingency at the creation of each river commission.[8] The aim is to challenge the sense of inevitability we might have if we only examined the history of IOs through the rear-view mirror.

In this book, I go back to the very first IOs established to govern the Rhine and Danube rivers – and to the failure to create a similar organization to manage the Congo – to understand the social and intellectual forces that enabled and drove the creation of these first IOs. Doing so allows me to demonstrate that the taming of nature rests at the ideological foundations of the current international order by showing how it informed the consolidation of the territorial state, legitimated imperial hierarchies, and enabled the creation of early global governance organizations. The historical work aims to challenge functional accounts of IOs and ahistorical theorizing of the current international order. Furthermore, examining these first organizations also alerts us to the ways in which the tension between nature and society informed the beginnings of interstate cooperation, and that environmental politics, rather than a peripheral concern in international politics, has always been at its heart.

The structure of this book: following the ideal river

To begin, the next chapter outlines the three main theoretical contentions that frame this book. It shows how the impetus to tame rivers emerged from Enlightenment confidence in science's ability to control, order, and improve on nature. It details how, in the nineteenth century, this confidence became a standard of rational governance that informed the consolidation of the territorial state as the main normative unit of international politics at the same time as it helped to legitimate imperial hierarchy between the core and periphery. Finally, I argue that these forces came together in the creation of the first IOs.

The next six chapters trace the history of three nineteenth-century European diplomatic conferences that aimed to create international commissions to govern three transboundary rivers: the Rhine Commission established at the 1815 Congress of Vienna; the Danube Commission established at the 1856 Paris Peace Conference; and the abortive Congo Commission discussed at the 1884–85 Berlin Conference. Two chapters are devoted to each river. The first of each pair constructs the geographical imaginary surrounding the river – the Rhine as an internal economic highway, the Danube as a commercial road that connects the European center to its near periphery to the east, and the Congo as a colonial river that spread civilization and commerce to the global periphery. These imaginaries reflect an entanglement of the river's physical characteristics, local myths and histories, and an overall Enlightenment confidence in the ability of science and technical expertise to tame nature. The second chapter of each pair relies on primary and archival sources to investigate the diplomatic activities that led to the creation of each river commission in the context of wider European geopolitical concerns. At each conference in 1815, 1856, and 1885, I show how the geographical imaginary of each river shaped the meaning and assumptions that underpinned diplomatic discussions. At the same time, I highlight how the tension between the legal definition of the transboundary river as states' private property and the river as international commons open to all revealed the interplay of political fissures, personalities, and historical contingency that shaped the outcome of each diplomatic encounter.

Chapter 2 examines the taming of the Rhine in the European geographical imaginary and contends that the early nineteenth-century ambition to transform the Rhine into a frictionless commercial highway reveals the double moral and economic logics behind the political project to tame nature. Controlling the river's unruly flows would bring both economic and moral gains – a straightened and disciplined river would minimize economic loss from flooding, reclaim swamps for agricultural production, and create the ideal highway for local and international trade, but it also represented a moral conquest from the barbarism of swampy disuse. This double economic and moral logic not only informed the development of legitimate state authority along the Rhine, but due to its position as an important transnational geography, this double logic extended to international politics. Here, taming the Rhine created a reliable economic highway for European commerce while eliminating the fractious 'Teutonic insanity' that had hindered Rhine prosperity for centuries. The chapter also explores the Romantic counterpoint to this framing of the Rhine, and how the river as high Romantic fantasy only amplified the need to tame it as steamboats of tourists flooded the river and the Rhine became a different kind of economic commodity.

Chapter 3 explores how taming the Rhine as an internal European highway translated into the creation of the Central Commission for the Navigation of the Rhine at the 1815 Congress of Vienna. Diplomats at Vienna wished to restore a pre-Napoleonic social order, but they also felt the pull of Enlightenment confidence in civilized European society's ability to control the Rhine and reform centuries of irrational river politics to secure free trade and economic benefits for all European states. To placate the impulse for both reform and restoration, European diplomats struck an awkward compromise between three existing legal interpretations of the transboundary river: the river as the private property of individual sovereigns; the river as shared commons between states; and the river as international commons open to all. While subsequent narratives suggest that the third interpretation won out at the Congress of Vienna, an examination of the contingent politics of the Congress shows that the 1815 Rhine Commission was largely a return to pre-Napoleonic interpretations of the river as private property – but with a liberal twist driven by imaginaries of the Rhine as a trans-European highway. By establishing the Rhine Commission, the Congress of Vienna affirmed freedom of commerce and created a consultative body to implement rational and sensible regulations to maintain the river as an efficient economic highway.

In the mid-nineteenth century, Europeans envisioned the Danube as a commercial highway for a quickly industrializing Europe. However, if the Rhine represented an internal European highway, the Danube signified a connecting river that emanated from the heart of European civilization toward the near periphery. Chapter 4 draws out this distinction between the two rivers and argues that taming the Danube's physical and metaphysical dangers not only reflected legitimate authority along the banks but also signified control over this conduit to the East so that free trade and civilization could flow from Europe outward. Controlling the connecting Danube also signified control over temporal dynamics and guarded against reversing the river, and therefore reversing the progressive flow of history and European civilization and allowing instability to flow from the East back upriver.

Most famously, Bram Stoker's Count Dracula represents this haunting possibility of invasion from the East and civilizational norms upended. If taming the Danube signified legitimate political authority, then Russian unwillingness or inability to control the Danube's mouth in the mid-nineteenth century threw Russia's civilizational status into question and set the stage for the establishment of the 1856 European Commission of the Danube.

The Danube as a connecting river represented the flow of European power and civilization outward to command the eastern periphery, but the river as conduit can flow both ways, and in the 1850s instability at the far reaches of the Danube delta threatened to destabilize European politics. Chapter 5 examines the Paris Conference to end the Crimean War and the creation of the European Commission of the Danube to ensure that a civilized and rational authority controlled the mouth of the Danube. At Paris, competing interpretations of the transboundary river as private property versus international commons again took the diplomatic stage, but imaginaries of the Danube delta as an untamed space at the fringe of European civilization moved diplomats, particularly the French and British, to reject the Rhine Commission model as too weak a body to control this untamed geography. Instead, diplomats at Paris created a strong commission with independent authority not only to conduct engineering works to clear shipping channels, but with policing and judiciary powers to maintain order and fiscal powers to borrow money on the international market. By the 1930s, the commission had become such an extraordinary international actor that historian Glen Blackburn described it as being 'at the twilight of statehood' (1930: 1154).

If the Rhine represented an internal European highway to be tamed for European civilization, and the Danube represented a liminal space between the civilized European self and the semi-familiar other to the east, then in the late nineteenth century, the Congo represented an abstract and empty colonial geography waiting to be filled with European ideas, practices, and institutions. Chapter 6 examines the construction of the Congo – by European legal experts, cartographers, and explorers – as a colonial highway that would impose commercial rationality and European civilization onto a conceptually empty space. This imaginary of the river collapses time and terrestrial space into the same civilizational and developmental continuum that elevates western Europe as the model of progress. However, I contend that exporting civilization to the Congo basin not only erased indigenous histories and political agency but contorted Europe's own messy experience with state-building and economic development into a generalizable model applicable across time and space. At the same time as the Congo represented endless possibilities for ambitious colonizers, it also represented a disconnected geography separate from the normal politics of civilized European society and a foreignness that threatened to reverse rationality and uncivilized

Europeans who traveled upriver – a fear made vivid in Joseph Conrad's *Heart of Darkness*. In doing so, I highlight how European imaginaries of the Congo looked inward at European superiority and anxieties about their own geopolitical and civilizational position in the late nineteenth century.

If the Rhine and Danube commissions could be considered accomplishments in global governance, then the abortive International Commission of the Congo proposed in the text of the 1885 General Acts of the Berlin Conference was an international disaster. Chapter 7 examines diplomatic efforts to bring European normative and institutional models to the conceptual emptiness of the Congo basin. At first glance, it seemed that diplomats at Berlin faced the same dilemma as their predecessors at Paris in 1856 – whether to tame the river through private sovereign control or as international commons. However, the Congo represented a particular colonial geography in the European imagination – first, as a blank canvas waiting to be filled with European models, and second, in the Congo's primary importance as a token in European balance of power politics. Combined, these framings led to the imposition of ill-fitting models taken from Europe's own historical development onto the morally and politically 'empty' spaces of the colonial periphery. Hence, European diplomats' inability to transform the Congo into a peaceful, non-sovereign, and neutral space for the benefit of international commerce reflected failings in the western European geographical imaginary – both of the conceptually empty Congo as well as its understanding of Europe as a geography of universal and generalizable political possibilities.

Chapter 8 examines international society's efforts to construct the ideal river in the twentieth century. I begin with World War I and the 1919 Paris Peace Conference which finally seemed to affirm that Europe's transboundary rivers were unequivocally international commons. Standing at 1919, it would seem that a century of international cooperation had finally culminated in victory for liberalism, free trade, and progress. However, I challenge this narrative by showing how 1919 could be understood otherwise and argue that narratives of institutional success and failure depend very much on where in history we stand and the thickness and orientation of our analytical blinders. This chapter then traces the continuation of Enlightenment confidence in science's ability to tame the river for economic and moral progress. Controlling the river continued to inform a state's legitimacy, first as a tool of imperial control, and then, after the mid-twentieth century, as a mantra adopted by newly independent states to showcase their rising status and self-sufficiency. I focus on megadams as a monumental symbol that illustrates how our efforts to create the ideal river continued throughout the twentieth and into the twenty-first century.

Finally, in the conclusion, I reflect on how the history of transboundary river cooperation and the creation of the first IOs is largely absent from IR literature and theorizing, but how, despite this absence, the river and its sociopolitical importance permeates IR in the way we privilege the sovereign territorial state, the way we are bound by global hierarchies, and the way we trust in IOs to resolve the collective action dilemmas of the twenty-first century. I conclude by contemplating the challenges of the Anthropocene, and in particular, how perpetual economic growth continues to be the modern benchmark for moral and political progress. This standard leads us, as Amitav Ghosh eloquently warns, to a 'great derangement'. It is my hope that in understanding how the standards and desires of modern life emerged from a global history of entanglement between international society and the natural world, we will recognize the power and politics behind modern standards of progress – but also, in looking to the future, challenge the myth that these standards are somehow natural and immovable.

Notes

1 Wittfogel argued that scarce and concentrated water resources led to what he called 'oriental hydraulic despotism' in societies such as China and Egypt. These societies developed 'hydro-bureaucracies' to organize large-scale hydraulic projects. Non-hydraulic civilizations, such as Greece, Japan, and early Europe, had plentiful rainfall or widely available water sources and therefore developed decentralized and fragmented governing structures of feudal or aristocratic rule.

2 Rittberger et al. (2019: 2) follow Pevehouse et al. (2004) in defining international organizations as bodies that have 'three or more states as members, a plenary meeting at least every ten years, and a permanent secretariat and correspondence address'.

3 Some would consider the 1865 International Telecommunications Union as the first IO due to its global membership. However, given the less restrictive definition I adopt of IOs, both the Rhine and Danube commissions would qualify. I distinguish between the Rhine and Danube commissions in that the Rhine Commission included only riparian states (hence, interstate or intergovernmental), while the Danube Commission included non-riparian powers (Britain and France) exercising power over a geography on the other side of the European continent. The Danube Commission also exercised surprising independent powers – it had its own flag, its own policing and courts, employees who swore an oath of allegiance to the commission, and the independent ability to borrow money internationally.

4 For examples of this, see Michael Barnett and Martha Finnemore (2004), Paul Diehl (2005), and Margaret Karns and Karen Mingst (2010). There are some very notable exceptions in IR scholarship that do address the historical foundations of global governance structures beyond the post-World War II moment, particularly scholarship by Jennifer Mitzen (2013), Charlotte Epstein (2008), and Bentley Allan (2018) that underscore the influence of eighteenth- and nineteenth-century institutions, discourses, and ideas on current structures of international order.

5 A periodization popularized by historian Eric Hobsbawm that frames the period between the French Revolution and World War I (1789 and 1914) as a historical era.

6 Here, I build on the scholarship of Antony Anghie (2005), Andrew Fitzmaurice (2012), Lauren Benton and Lisa Ford (2018), and Jennifer Pitts (2018). This body of scholarship highlights the importance of empire and imperialism in the foundation of international law. I also draw inspiration from Mark Mazower (2009) and Adom Getachew (2019) who stress empire and imperialism in the foundation of the United Nations system.

7 This develops Max Weber's famous proposition that ideas create 'world images' that act as switchmen to 'determine the tracks along which action has been pushed by the dynamics of interest' (1946: 280). Goldstein and Keohane translate this into a thin understanding of ideas in international politics where ideas only determine the path at one point in time, and afterward, interests take over. For them, 'ideas put blinders on people, reducing the number of conceivable alternatives ... not only by turning action into certain tracks rather than others ... but also obscuring the other tracks' (1993: 12). However, I follow scholarship that emphasizes the first aspect of Weber's quote in which ideas constitute worlds by creating meaning and making certain sets of interests possible (for example, Eastwood 2005). Hence, ideas are not simply blinders obscuring certain paths, but create political possibilities.

8 As a methodological choice, focusing on three European diplomatic conferences and cultural elites constrains the analysis by centering the ideas and practices of elites (and specifically western European elites) at the expense of subjugated people and their agency in constituting global structures. This is a limitation of my focus on official international diplomacy and the creation of IOs. However, one of my aims is to amplify the silences where subjugated peoples and knowledges are absent from official deliberations and to highlight the negative consequences of these silences.

1

The taming of nature, legitimate authority, and international order

In *Scientific Man vs. Power Politics*, Hans Morgenthau begins with a puzzle of twentieth-century intellectual life: 'We think in terms of the outgoing eighteenth century and live in terms of the mid-twentieth century' (1946: 11–12). This intellectual bent upholds two principles based on rationalist assumptions – first, that the social and physical world can be understood through the same rational processes, and second, that understanding these processes will allow us to exercise rational control over the social and physical worlds in order to improve them. This faith in science and progress 'sets our age apart from preceding periods of history' (1946: 11). However, this faith is problematic because it 'perverts the natural sciences into an instrument of social salvation for which neither their own nature nor the nature of the social world fits them' (1946: 12). Despite this weakness, our abiding faith in science to solve all problems, a relic of the late eighteenth century, has continued to shape our political outlook even when 'conditions of life … have undergone the most profound changes in recorded history' (1946: 5). Since the mid-twentieth century, continued faith in rationality and social progress in mainstream IR theory and practice seems to confirm and extend Morgenthau's assessment into the twenty-first century.

Although situated in a different intellectual tradition, Timothy Mitchell interestingly begins his book on techno-politics in Egypt in a similar manner: 'We have entered the twenty-first century still divided by a way of thinking inherited from the nineteenth' (2002: 1). In this era, the progressive forces of human reason supplanted notions of divine will and natural balance to become the driving forces behind historical development. Mitchell argues that this mindset had several effects:

> This moment of history could be ascribed to the growing technical control that reason acquired over the natural and social world, to the power of reason to expand the scope of human freedom, or to the economic forms that were said to flow from the spread of rational calculations and freedom. (2002: 1)

One outcome of this intellectual transformation is the division of the world – the social from nature, the economic and technical from politics, reason from the real world, and ideas from their objects. The same rational, technocratic logic, then, is applied across these divisions, allowing the first to dominate the second. Despite increasing evidence of deviation from these modernist assumptions, we continue to make abstract rationalist arguments about the interconnected social and natural world. Even as we advance into the twenty-first century, Mitchell echoes Morgenthau in maintaining that we remain 'captives' of late eighteenth- and nineteenth-century thought (2002: 2).

The following chapter takes Morgenthau's and Mitchell's insights on the staying power of a certain way of thinking inherited from the late eighteenth and nineteenth centuries as the starting point for exploring how this prevailing confidence in society's ability to tame nature and usher forth social progress informed the development of the modern international order. Rooted in the European Enlightenment, this way of thinking sees the messy natural and social world around us as a barrier to human progress and places trust in scientific and technocratic governance to transform this natural messiness into rational sites of social improvement. Taming nature, then, legitimizes the people and institutions in power by securing increased economic growth as well as moral progress for the community. The immense staying power of this ideational frame in the international order, I contend, derives from its embeddedness in key international norms, hierarchies, and institutions, which gained global prominence in the nineteenth century and continues to hold sway over international politics. By examining how society's ambition to control nature shaped three core IR concepts – the territorial sovereign state, imperial and global hierarchy, and international organizations – this chapter outlines the key theoretical contributions that frame the historical narrative to follow.

The taming of nature and the sovereign territorial state

One central argument running through this book focuses on the quest to tame nature and its influence on the development of the modern territorial state. In the late eighteenth and nineteenth centuries, various intellectual, social, and material forces contributed to the consolidation of the modern state system – a system that 'differentiated its subject collectively into territorially defined, fixed, and mutually exclusive enclaves of legitimate dominion' (Ruggie 1993: 151). One major force that contributed to this transformation was the onset of the Industrial Revolution, which, with its accompanying technological innovations in transportation and communication, allowed the state to concentrate and centralize its workings. This centralization created what Andreas Osiander called 'integrated economic circuits' (2001: 281) and what Barry Buzan and George Lawson describe as administrative functions that were 'accumulated and "caged" within national territories' (2015: 6). In this process, Jordan Branch stresses cartography as a key technology that helped reshape legitimate authority from non-territorial and overlapping forms prior to the nineteenth century to the linear, cartographically bounded states we know today (2011; 2014). Justin Rosenberg's (1994) and Benno Teschke's (2003) historical-materialist arguments foreground capitalist structure and state–society relations as central to the development of the modern state. In addition, emergent ideologies such as nationalism unleashed in the aftermath of the French Revolution enabled and legitimized the consolidation of territorial states as exclusive and exclusionary realms of domestic political order (Rejai and Enloe 1969; Gellner 1983; Mayall 1990; Breuilly 1993).

My focus on controlling natural resources such as rivers adds to these arguments by investigating how confidence in society's ability to tame nature and therefore control and improve a bounded territory helped constitute what it meant to be a legitimate modern state. Here, I contend that legitimate territorial authority did not rest solely in the state's capacity to control populations and police social behavior, but implied a hierarchical relationship with nature where the state bends nature to its will for moral and economic progress. The ability to control nature contributes to a well-functioning state by improving the productivity of the land and people, hence reinforcing the state's legitimacy over a fixed territory. Chandra Mukerji's work (2010) frames this control of nature as 'logistical power' that displaced traditional patrimonial networks and contributed to impersonal rule as a hallmark of the modern territorial state. In the nineteenth century, the taming of nature as a marker of a civilized state authority gained political traction among European states and enabled the creation of national and transnational projects to tame the river. In this section, I first outline the Enlightenment ethos that informed the state's mission to tame nature and its double economic and moral logics. Then I examine a central analytical blind spot inherent in this Enlightenment ethos and how reconceptualizing that blind spot challenges longstanding hierarchies between nature and society.

High modernism, science, and the double logics of taming nature

In *Seeing Like a State*, James C. Scott argues that the central objective of the modern bureaucratic state is to impose what he calls legibility on illogical nature and society. For the modern state that aims to maximize efficiency, the complexity and variations in local social practices present a major barrier to the state's consolidation of its bureaucratic capacity. To make these practices legible, the state imposes administrative standardization and simplification to transform idiosyncratic local practices into uniform and standardized information that the state can then process. Once these practices are made legible, the state can more easily control, govern, and profit from its domains and subjects. What I wish to highlight here is not so much Scott's emphasis on the all-seeing authoritarian state that can impose such legibility on its territories – a vision of the state that has taken much criticism (Bayly 2004; Mukerji 2007; Benton 2010). Instead, I wish to focus on the Enlightenment ethos that legitimated the state's desire to seek legibility as a standard of effective governance.

Here, Scott highlights high modernism as the driving ideological force. He defines high modernism as a 'strong ... version of the beliefs in scientific and technical progress that were associated with industrialization' in the Western world in the nineteenth century. It was, as Scott contends, a 'sweeping vision of how the benefit of technical and scientific progress might be applied' to rationalize and control nature and all human activities (1998: 89–90). In other words, high modernism was the animating ideology of nineteenth-century European politics where Enlightenment confidence in science's ability to improve nature became entwined with notions of societal progress and state legitimacy.

Enlightenment ideas about individual and societal progress have long shaped western European political thought.[1] In particular, Enlightenment ideas contributed to a shift away from the divine as the primary source of a state's legitimacy and toward rational administration (Reus-Smit 1999; Bukovansky 2002; Hurd 2004; Kubalkova 2006). However, in the nineteenth century, these ideas combined with new scientific and technological advances to transform the ordering of domestic and international society. Historian Richard Holmes describes Europe in the early nineteenth century as experiencing what he describes as a 'second scientific revolution', in which scientific progress combined with Romanticism to create a vision of nature as infinite and mysterious but also open to human intervention (2008: xviii; also see Bellone 1980; Watson 2010). This allowed society, through science, not only to observe and study nature, but to play an activist role in improving nature for the benefit of humankind.

In this, we have what Ian Hacking (2002) termed the laboratory style of reasoning. Here, science was no longer just important for its own sake, but, as sociologist Zygmunt Bauman argued, it became a social tool with political purpose as 'first and foremost, an instrument of awesome power allowing its holder to improve reality' (1989: 70). To understand the natural world through science, then, was an act of political mastery. As German scientist Hermann von Helmholtz would declare in the 1860s, science has the ability to 'make the reasonless forces of nature subservient to the moral purpose of humanity' (quoted in Blackbourn 2006: 164). This vision of political purpose centers on the use of scientific tools to bring about social progress. These tools of control help the state expand economic production, generate social order, and satisfy human needs. In doing so, human society rises above chaotic nature by making nature rational and useful to human society.

Confidence in science's progressive political potential highlights a double logic behind the state's drive to tame nature. First, the economic logic highlights how taming nature produces economic benefits for the state. Scott uses the example of scientific forestry in Prussia and Saxony in the late eighteenth century to show how state officials replaced the untamed forests with monocultures to maximize the economic yield from these lands (Scott 1998: 14–16). Rivers have particular economic value for the state as natural highways that facilitate the movement of goods and people to markets. Taming the river allows the state to establish a reliable and efficient transport artery within its territory and to secure economic links to neighboring states. Hence, taming the river creates economic wealth.

Second, entwined with this economic logic, taming nature also achieves a moral purpose in that it fulfills the state's duty to bring rationality and civilization to ungoverned wildernesses within its domain. In other words, the state usurps the divine's role as the moral architect of the earth, and in doing so, the state imposes its moral order on untamed spaces and the untamed peoples who inhabit them. As the Dutch like to boast, 'God created the world but the Dutch created the Netherlands', suggesting that by draining the marshes and engineering a system of channels, Dutch authorities are analogous to God in that they not only created economic prosperity but a fixed moral and political order within their territory. The double economic and moral logic behind the taming of nature is a recurring motif in this book and underpins not only state-level projects to tame the river, but also international efforts to govern the transboundary river.

Rule by experts and technocratic hubris

In investigating how the high modernist ethos informed nineteenth-century national and international projects to tame the transboundary river, another recurring theme of this book concerns the blind spots created by our over-reliance on technical expertise from engineering to international law to 'solve' the problem of the inconsistent river. Across the stories of all three rivers, technical experts labored to fix the river – both physically, to limit the river to a single riverbed of a consistent depth, and ideationally, to attach a single meaning to the river as an open economic highway. These endeavors consistently backfire as the complexity and dynamism of the river and riverain communities across time and space overpowers simple technical solutions. In highlighting the ways in which each river confronts and confounds society's technical expertise, I draw attention to how the river pushes back and challenges international society's high modernist hubris.

One of the features of high modernist ideology is the creation of a hierarchy between nature and culture (or civilization) by privileging rational and scientific human culture (or civilization) over nature as the passive canvas on which society acts (Latour 1993; Bowden 2009). Timothy Mitchell's powerful opening to *The Rule of Experts* (2002) overturns this dichotomy by charting how a combination of interacting human and nonhuman forces gave rise to the 1942 malaria outbreak in Egypt. His lucid prose weaves between the mosquito, the sugar cane, the Aswan Dam, World War II, the chemical industry, and international capitalism – from the small and material to the large and structural – to explain what made the malaria outbreak politically possible. And yet social science research has largely failed to understand the interactions of heterogeneous human and nonhuman agencies. Mitchell argues that this analytical blind spot arises from our overreliance on technical expertise, which tends to reduce the world to simple stories of causes and effects. Therefore, in our quest to distill parsimonious social scientific theories about the world, we abstract outward from the local to the universal. This reinforces the nature–society dichotomy since, as Mitchell explains, 'it is the intentionality or rationality of human agents that gives the explanation its logics and enables particular cases to fit as instances of something general' (2002: 32). In relying on technical expertise, the state is able to streamline the complexity of human and nonhuman interactions into simple causes and oppositions and govern based on those assumptions. Like Scott's high modernist projects, Mitchell's political rule based on technical expertise enables state authorities to rationalize, centralize, and reorganize complex local interactions into an abstract and uniform world ripe for intervention. Throughout this book, national and international authorities rely on technical expertise to transform specific rivers into the ideal river as an efficient economic highway for global trade.

The problem with high modernist projects based on technical expertise, as both Mitchell and Scott highlight, is that these projects invariably run into practical difficulties when the abstract, theoretical world fails to map onto local realities. Nineteenth-century efforts to straighten the upper Rhine and reduce flooding actually produced more intense floods downriver (Cioc 2013: 35). Prussian efforts to seed monocultures in their forests resulted in biological – and hence commercial – decline as the project destroyed the complex biological systems in the soil and undergrowth that sustained forest health. What technocrats had coded as 'useless' turned out to be essential (Scott 1998: 20). However, rather than forcing technocrats to re-evaluate their underlying assumptions, Mitchell argues that these failures only led to future projects that covered up past failures. This series of failures and adjustments are the hallmarks of techno-scientific governance where 'fundamental difficulties [are] presented as minor issues of the implementation of the plans, unexpected complications, bureaucratic delays, or the need to follow up' (Mitchell 2002: 42). Increased flooding downriver along the Rhine demonstrated that the irrational river still needed to be controlled, and this became the rationale for even grander river-rectification projects. Hence, the history of technical progress becomes one of covering up past mistakes and smoothing out the historical record into a story of linear scientific achievement. From this perspective, successive technocratic responses seem a rational and neutral response to external problems often attributed to 'nature'[2] and ignore our own complicity in constituting these 'problems' in the first place. In this way, high modernist projects to tame nature legitimize the modern state through both their successes and their failures – indeed, it is precisely these failures that perpetuate the need for more governance.

However, rather than framing these consequences as technocratic failures, we can equally understand them as evidence that nonhuman characters have importance for human histories, and that the complexity of these nonhuman characters as they interact with human agents disrupts the simplicity of technocratic models. Following David Blackbourn, my narrative of international society's efforts to create the ideal river shows that 'all of history is the history of unintended consequences' (2006: 12). But here, perhaps the notion of 'unintended consequences' is too laden with human-centric assumptions about the agents that matter. Perhaps a better question might be to interrogate who or what has intended a consequence and whether our analytical framing of some institutional outcomes as 'unintended' privileges certain actors' intentionality over others. Hence, by focusing on the 'unintended' consequences of high modernist projects, I not only question the universal applicability of global governance's technocratic models, but also challenge the hierarchical separation of the human and natural worlds that enables and sustains these models.

The taming of nature as global hierarchy

In the nineteenth century, the consolidation of the sovereign territorial state occurred alongside processes that transformed the European political order into a global one based on core–peripheral relations (Buzan and Lawson 2015; Dunne and Reus-Smit 2017). What Buzan and Lawson call 'ideologies of progress', and in particular the notion that scientific progress can 'control nature and improve not only the human condition but the human stock'

(2015: 36), played an important role in this transformation and became a foundational principle of the modern international order. Prior to the nineteenth century, the 'discovery' and subsequent subjugation of the Americas had helped to solidify Europeans' view that civilized societies are able to exercise control over nature – and societies that fail to do so are less advanced (Quijano 2000; Drayton 2000). Indeed, during encounters with native populations, Europeans' use of scientific and technological advancements to measure and control the material world reinforced their sense of civilizational superiority (Adas 1989). Furthermore, it was the confrontation between Europeans and Amerindians of the Americas that informed European conceptions of 'human nature', race, and the legitimate ownership of property (Jahn 1999; 2000). In the nineteenth century, as the European political order became a global one, controlling and exploiting nature as a marker of a legitimate territorial state also became embedded in global standards of legitimate authority that separated civilized polities from uncivilized ones.

The classical Standards of Civilization are rooted in nineteenth-century legal benchmarks that separated states afforded full rights and recognition under international law – or 'civilized' states – from uncivilized polities denied this recognition (Suzuki 2009; Bowden 2009; Yao 2019). These standards traditionally included basic institutions of government and of self-defense, domestic rule of law based on formalized legal codes, and recognition of international law. By examining international efforts to govern three transboundary rivers in the nineteenth century, I emphasize two ways in which the taming of nature operated through these civilizational standards to create and reinforce developing global hierarchies between civilized and uncivilized polities. First, as noted previously, the use of science and technology to control the river brought economic wealth as well as moral progress to a society, thus legitimizing a state's authority over a given territory. Second, taming the river also upheld free trade as a reciprocal practice between civilized polities and under the protection of international law. As classical liberal writers such as Adam Smith argued, commerce does not only lead to wealth but 'order and good government, and with them, the liberty and security of individuals' (Smith 1904 [1776]: 376). Richard Cobden took these principles further and maintained that free trade brings peace as trade acts 'on the moral world as the principle of gravitation in the universe – drawing men together, thrusting aside the antagonisms of race and creed and language' (Cobden 1908 [1846]: 187). Hence, taming the transboundary river reflected a state's ability to maintain civilized relations with other states. The ideal river as an economic highway and conduit of free trade carries with it the trappings of Western civilization, from individual liberty and good government to international peace. A state's ability to tame nature and construct the ideal river signified its civilized status; a state's inability to do so delegitimized its territorial authority before international society.

While the Standards of Civilization as legal benchmarks no longer operate in twenty-first-century international society, scholars have traced the ideological links between the racialized and imperial civilizational standards of the nineteenth century and current international discourses about 'failed states', 'human rights', and the war on terror (Anghie 1999; Gruffydd Jones 2013; Bowden 2014). My argument likewise highlights the ideational legacies of nineteenth-century civilizational standards for twenty-first-century international society, in particular in the ways that the taming of nature informs enduring European geographical imaginaries about its own place in the global. In other words, I stress not only that the taming of nature became part of the civilizational standards against which European and non-European societies were measured, but that it informed the way Europeans collapsed time and space into the same linear developmental continuum. Under the Standards of Civilization, a polity's position in international society depended on its civilizational status, but a polity could advance from barbarism to civilization by achieving certain benchmarks (Bowden 2014: 617). Hence, this understanding of social progress subsumes all societies under the same historical developmental trajectory, and, following Friedrich von Schiller, envisions the civilized European as merely 'a more advanced brother of the Red Indian and the Celt' (1972 [1789]: 328). Taming the river as a metaphor for controlling time, then, helped Europeans envision a material manifestation of their quest to control human progress – and the nineteenth-century engineer's mission to confine the river to a single, rational riverbed took on importance beyond the physical task at hand.

This aim to control and accelerate social progress along a single universal path continues to inform twenty-first-century international society's focus on accelerated economic growth and development – a fixation that has come to threaten the future of the planet. The rest of this section will explore the role that taming nature plays in constructing European geographical imaginaries of a single civilizational continuum and the development of a particular aesthetic shorthand that signified progress along that continuum.

The European geographical imagination

My argument about the ideal river and its variations along the Rhine, Danube, and Congo rests on the notion of the European geographical imagination. In the 1950s, sociologist C. Wright Mills developed the notion of the 'sociological imagination' by which 'the individual can understand his own experience and gauge his own fate only by locating himself within his period ... [it] enables us to grasp history and biography and the relations between the two in society" (Wright Mills 1959). Two decades later, geographer David Harvey developed the contrasting idea of the 'geographical imagination' which

> enables the individual to recognize the role of space and place in his own biography, to relate to the spaces he sees around him, and to recognize how transactions between individuals and between organizations are affected by the space the separates them. (quoted in Harvey 2006: 212)

A host of scholars have elaborated on this notion (for example, Said 1978; Agnew 1982; Daniels 1992; 2011; Norton 2007). In particular, they have investigated the 'geographical imagination' of individuals (examples include Cosgrove 1979; Hunt 2010; Hawkins 2010) as well as specific groups and regions (examples include Gruffudd 1995; Pred 1997; Stock 2019). From the general 'geographical imagination', we can identify certain geographical imaginaries that, as Paul Stock notes, frame the 'way humans view, represent, and interpret spaces both actual and imagined' (2019: 4). Edward Said, whose scholarship emphasizes the interplay between power and knowledge in constructing these imaginaries, observes that 'space acquires emotional and even rational sense by a kind of poetic process, whereby the vacant or anonymous reaches of distance are converted into meaning for us here' (1978: 55). Hence, geographical imaginaries as ideational frames help us make sense of geographical space and our place in it as individuals and collectives.

In this book, I draw on the notion of geographical imaginaries in contending that Europeans imagined the ideal river as a straight, consistent, and frictionless highway that transports people and goods for the benefit of global commerce and social progress. Furthermore, Europeans held specific imaginaries of the Rhine, the Danube, and the Congo – the Rhine as the internal highway of European commerce, the Danube as the connecting highway between Europe and the near periphery, and the Congo as a colonial highway that brought European civilization and institutions to an abstract and conceptually empty place. These imaginaries are drawn from the way Europeans viewed, represented, and interpreted each river to give meaning to each geography, which in turn enabled Europeans' understanding of their own place in the global. Hence, European geographical imaginaries of the ideal river were not only important for the creation of the first international bodies to govern them, but also central in consolidating Europeans' own sense of place in global politics and history. Efforts to transform the messy realities of each river into the ideal river emerged from European civilizational discourses and the construction of a singular developmental continuum, with Europe as its most advanced point. But at the same time, the poetry and politics generated when these imaginaries met with the material river reinforced and reconstituted these imaginaries and gave material expression to the narrative of Europe's civilizational superiority.

In particular, taming the river as a metaphor for time and space had a totalizing effect on how Europeans conflated time and space in their conception of civilizational progress. Critical geographer John Agnew posits this conflation of time with geographical space as a 'fundamental characteristic of European geopolitical discourse' (1996: 28). The temporal continuum between past and present is created by the use of terms such as 'backward' or 'advanced' to characterize political groups, hence ordering all societies along a linear and progressive temporality. Then, Agnew contends, this temporal vision is projected onto terrestrial space so that societies at the periphery are removed spatially as well as historically from the European center. Hence, for nineteenth-century Europeans, sub-Saharan Africa, which Georg Wilhelm Friedrich Hegel famously described as the 'land of childhood ... lying beyond the day of self-conscious history' (2007 [1899]: 91), is distant from the European core in time and space. Hegel continues to characterize 'the Negro' as 'natural man in his completely wild and untamed state' (2007 [1899]: 93) with the implication that these societies are untouched by rationality and civilization. European efforts to tame the Congo as a colonial river, then, were also efforts to lead 'natural man' out of the 'land of childhood' and into the light of European civilization.

Postcolonial scholars have also noted this conflation of time and space, particularly as justification for colonial and postcolonial subjugation and violence (Jabri 2007; Chakrabarty 2008; Holmqvist 2016; Rao 2020). In anthropology, Johannes Fabian identifies what he calls 'temporal distancing' as a longstanding disciplinary move that results in a 'denial of coevalness', or a sense that the researcher and the object of study do not share the same temporal present (1983: 31). In the late nineteenth century, Europeans who attended anthropological exhibitions at the ever-popular World Fairs or read explorers' travelogues to the exotic periphery engaged in precisely this type of distancing. However, not only did the European observer and the observed colonial places and peoples not share the same temporal present, but the observer imagined the observed as analogs to its own past. Hence, for the travelers from the European core, as Anne McClintock vividly writes, 'the movement forward in space is backward in time: from erect, verbal consciousness and hybrid freedoms ... down through the historic stages of decreasing stature to the shambling, tongueless zone of the precolonial, from speech to silence, light to dark' (1995: 10). Paradoxically, nature's role in this imaginary is both as foil and as guide. While nature had to be conquered to enable progress, it was precisely naturalistic metaphors such as those borrowed from biological development or fluid hydraulics that naturalized this way of envisioning the global.

The civilized landscapes: aesthetics and the dreamwork of imperialism

If civilizational standards are central to our imaginaries of distant geographies and peoples, then what differentiates between the civilized and uncivilized landscape is a particular aesthetic. In his 1836 essay on civilization, John Stuart Mill illustrates the core of this aesthetic. Mill describes the savage tribe as 'a handful of individuals ... scattered over a vast tract of country' without fixed habitation, commerce, manufacturing, agriculture, or a legal system. In contrast, a civilized landscape is filled with these and other practices and institutions that showcase the 'systemic employment of the collective strength of society'. Hence, we can identify a civilized society just by looking at the landscape – as Mill notes, 'a country rich in the fruits of agriculture, commerce, and manufacturers, we call civilized' (Mill 1836: n.p.). This suggests an aesthetic shorthand for civilized spaces and societies – a productive and industrious 'look' where nature has been pacified and human society cooperates to create economic value from the landscape. In contrast, in particular along the Danube and Congo rivers, the uncivilized landscape takes on a certain ugliness or unsettled quality, often described by European viewers as without anything on which to rest one's gaze. Hence, to tame the river is also to transform the aesthetic of the riverscape from forsaken wilderness into an ordered and curated landscape that sings the praises of human civilization. This imaginary of the civilized landscape, however, begins closer to home in the European garden.

The impulse to domesticate the wilderness and weed out unruly elements of both the natural and social landscape is central to discourses on civilization – and this impulse did not stop at state borders. Rather, this vision of landscapes naturalized a certain way of envisioning and ordering nature that totalized space across cartographic boundaries and hence expressed an imperial logic. In the opening essay of *Landscape and Power*, art historian W. J. T. Mitchell highlights this darker side of landscape, which he defines as a 'natural scene mediated by culture ... a medium of exchange between human and nature ... both the represented and presented space' (1994: 5). The curation of landscapes as a medium has been widely critiqued for its ease in naturalizing social inequality (Barrell 1980; Cosgrove 2006), but Mitchell takes the association further and argues that landscapes revealed a 'dreamwork of imperialism' that exposed both 'utopian fantasies of the perfected imperial prospect' and unresolved ambivalences within those fantasies (1994: 10). Or, as Ann Bermingham puts it in her essay in the volume, 'landscape gardening and drawing were not ideologically neutral ... they actively inscribed or became the sites of specific ideological attitudes and ambivalences' (Bermingham 1994: 78). Landscapes in the eighteenth and nineteenth centuries, then, sought to naturalize European modernity as 'an inevitable, progressive development in history, an expansion of "culture" and "civilization" into a "natural" space in a process that is itself narrated as "natural"' (Mitchell 1994: 17). Hence, landscapes naturalized the idea of rational progress and envisioned the global spread of European modernity as natural. We see these ideas at work in the stylized and manicured French gardens as much as in the naturalistic English gardens, where a highly curated landscape is presented as a morally and universally desirable improvement on nature.

The careful curation of natural spaces and the systematic classification of nature within these spaces animated the totalizing ideology behind European imperialism. As Richard Drayton's meticulously researched work shows, the improvement of nature conferred political legitimacy on those in power – first, through religious motifs of Adam the gardener and the improvement of land bringing earthly rulers closer to a return to Eden. Then, as political legitimacy shifted from divine will to service to the population, a 'good' king had to demonstrate his suitability to rule by ordering 'land and water in the public interest' (Drayton 2000: 44). The discovery of natural diversity beyond Europe led to the realization that the European garden could not possibly contain the world but could only aim to represent the world, and the European garden represented the world with Europe at its center unfolding outward. Through empire, 'the Edenic miraculous view of Europe's place as a corner of Creation ... gave way to the ideal of a Nature governed by rational mechanism, with Europe as the mistress of its laws' (Drayton 2000: 45). This new way of seeing framed the world as a whole system subject to the same moral and scientific laws. European empires legitimated their rule as the keeper of these laws and improver of these gardens.

The connection between gardening and imperialism went beyond mere symbolism and extended to the political economy of empire. In discussing the political nature of gardens, novelist Leslie Marmon Silko remarked to historian Ellen Arnold that 'you have the conquistadors, the missionaries, and right with them were the plant collectors' (Arnold 2000: 164). Indeed, Silko reminds us that European gardens required not only the dreamwork of imperialism but also its physical infrastructure to collect exotic seeds for the empire's increasingly elaborate botanical desires. Silko focuses on the trade in orchids, a flower that inspired a national craze in Victorian England, but other sought-after flowers included chrysanthemums and hydrangeas from East Asia, and rhododendrons and dahlias from central America. Lucile Brockway (1979) details the vast colonial networks necessary for the curation of botanical gardens at London's Kew Garden and also at scientific and botanical institutions in Holland, Belgium, Portugal, and France. Her pioneering scholarship establishes how colonial botanical institutions not only beautified European gardens but also cultivated useful plants to fuel the colonial economy. By focusing on the cultivation of rubber, cinchona, and sisal, Brockway traces how colonial extraction from Latin America led to development and mass production in colonial plantations in Asia and Africa. She shows how empires engaged in competition and collaboration, but ultimately united in the way they profited from commodities and labor extracted from the colonial periphery. Hence, in this very material sense, gardens perpetuated and legitimized European empires.

The dark side of landscapes can be taken even further. Zygmunt Bauman's provocative work on European modernity argues that the impulse to rationalize and weed the metaphorical social garden – which he terms the gardening impulse – is closely associated with the darkest moments of the late nineteenth and twentieth centuries, including European imperialism, scientific racism, and the Holocaust (Bauman 1989; 1991). He describes a shift in modern thought that transformed social management from the role of the gamekeeper to the gardener. The gamekeeper leaves society largely to its own devices for it to 'reproduce itself year by year', but the gardener is more active, 'armed with a detailed design of the lawn, of the borders and of the furrow dividing the lawn from the borders' (Bauman 1989: 57). As in medicine, gardening actively separates useful elements from harmful ones, allowing the former to live by killing off the latter. Hence, the gardener distrusts chaotic nature and must constantly wage battle against the spontaneous and uninvited weeds that threaten the planned order. Inspired by Bentham's and Foucault's panopticon, which sought to impose rational order over society, the gardening impulse treats human society as a messy natural canvas on which the gardener can design an arrangement of artificial order and imminent rationality. The gardener wields power and mastery over life and death, not out of malice or for vengeance, but in the execution of a preconceived plan that would impose order and rationality on the natural world.

For Bauman, the gardening impulse is a legacy of the European Enlightenment, which welcomed 'the enthronement of the new deity, that of Nature' – and science became the only legitimate way to worship Nature (1989: 68). However, if Nature as the new deity spoke moral truths, then physical characteristics became an outward sign of inward morality. Through the new science of phrenology, which gave rise to racial sciences, science could be used to categorize, separate, and eliminate undesirable traits as a gardener weeds the garden. As Herbert Spencer noted, nature 'exterminates' the parts of society that hinder human progress 'with the same sternness that they exterminate beasts of prey and herds of useless ruminants' (1868: 455).[3] Here, the gardening metaphor is extended to human beings, and the irrational and uncivilized in nature becomes synonymous with the uncivilized in society. Hence, through science, the government as gardener works with a rational plan in mind and labors to perfect both irrational nature and uncivilized human nature.

Many have criticized Bauman for essentializing modernity into a simplified gardening parable and for obscuring agency in the Nazi Holocaust by attributing antisemitism to a Western intellectual impulse (see, for example, Crozier 1996: 72; Jay 2007: 49). As Michael Crozier charges, Bauman engages 'in a bit of trimming and pruning on his garden metaphor in order to topiarize a complete picture of modernity', and excludes the empirical messiness surrounding different forms of gardens and the ideological complexities that animate our desire to cultivate them (1996: 72–3). However, Bauman's gardening impulse is a powerful idea that undercuts the prevailing narrative of the garden as an innocent Eden and an inward, domestic concern. It alerts us to the totalizing scope and violence inherent in any scheme to control and reorder the natural world – the fighting of a 'war' against irrational nature. If imperial ideology justifies one polity's rule over the globe, then ideas of progress and improvement embedded in the metaphor of gardening served this purpose. Hence, Candide's final desire to cultivate his garden was not as introspective and innocent as at first glance. The curated shrubbery of the European garden conceals both optimistic faith in science to improve the world as well as an imperial darkness. This vision of the ideal landscape shaped the European imaginaries of all three riverscapes discussed in this book and informed the first international organizations created to tame these wild spaces.

The taming of nature and the first international organizations

Taming nature as a standard of rational governance that informed both the development of the modern territorial state and global hierarchies came together in the nineteenth century in the creation of the first IOs to tame transboundary rivers. IR's engagement with the history of IOs rarely extends beyond the early twentieth century and the creation of the League of Nations that then gave rise to the United Nations.[4] However, IOs as an international political phenomenon did not begin with early twentieth-century Wilsonian optimism or efforts to establish the League of Nations. Rather, the creation of the first IOs was situated in nineteenth-century global interactions and processes which drove early efforts to amass the transnational political will and bureaucratic capacity to manage an increasingly interconnected globe (Murphy 1994; Charnovitz 1997; Mitzen 2013; Buzan and Lawson 2015). By the mid-twentieth century, IOs and IGOs (intergovernmental organizations) were already recognized as legitimate bureaucratic tools in the management of international order.

This historical recognition challenges implicit narratives that IOs emerged in the aftermath of the world wars to address the problem of interstate conflict. Instead, situating the development of the first IOs in the nineteenth century stresses the ways in which these bodies codify and institutionalize existing global hierarchies into international legal frameworks for global governance. Mark Mazower's scholarship (2009), which examines the ideological origins of the United Nations, recognizes the preservation of late nineteenth-century European empires and imperial hierarchies as an important driving force behind the organization's creation. Craig Murphy (1994) highlights how early IOs and IGOs in the late nineteenth century served the growth of global industries and capitalist structures. Ellen Ravndal's research (2020) on two nineteenth-century IGOs – the International Telegraph Union (ITU) and the Universal Postal Union (UPU) – shows how these bodies reflected existing global hierarchies of the late nineteenth century. Additionally, scholars in the history of international law have traced the development of international legal frameworks for organized interstate cooperation to nineteenth-century inter-imperial politics (Anghie 2007; Pitts 2018; Benton and Ford 2018). Situated in this scholarship, my focus on the creation of nineteenth-century international river commissions examines the first international bodies as tools for structuring, reinforcing, and managing a core–periphery European international order.

Imagining the international

Jeremy Bentham first coined the term 'international' in his 1789 *Introduction to the Principles of Morals and Legislation* in his discussion of international law as jurisprudence governing the relations between sovereigns (Suganami 1978). This use of the term presupposes the existence of sovereign states and envisions the international as the relationships between legitimate state actors. However, outside law, the term 'international' took on other meanings to describe political possibilities beyond the state, from cosmopolitan internationalism to anarchist and communist internationalist projects. By the end of the nineteenth century, as Mark Mazower notes, 'the international had become the terrain upon which widely differing political groups and ideologies mapped their dreams and nightmares' (2012: xv). Yet these dreams and nightmares were primarily grounded on a European imaginary of itself as the site of universal possibilities, and the notion of an 'international' order, as Jennifer Pitts reminds us, 'has long been commingled with that of European consolidation and informed by European exceptionalism' (2018: 10). In other words, while the concept of the international emerged from the specific historical development of the European state system, it embodied universal aspirations that strongly reflected European imperialism. This book argues that by applying the adjective 'international' to organizations or institutions, IOs also draw from the concept's roots in the development of a European state system and its universalist and imperial implications.

If the concept of the international emerged from a specific imaginary of Europe as the site of universal possibilities, then what role does the periphery play? By investigating the three riverain geographies in this book and the international bodies designed to govern them, I contend that peripheral geographies played an essential constituting role in nineteenth-century conceptualizations of the international. In particular, envisioning peripheral geographies as untamed spaces devoid of civilization and rational institutions enabled the consolidation of European confidence in its own ideas and political practices as universally applicable and, therefore, international. Hence, a key animating question of this book is what it means for a geography – such as a river delta or basin – to be an international space and subject to the authority of an international organization. As the remainder of this book will detail, the first international spaces subject to international governance were peripheral geographies envisioned by Europeans to be without civilized territorial authority, and hence in need of international intercession.

In particular, I draw a distinction between the 1815 Rhine Commission as an intergovernmental body that envisioned the transboundary river as a shared geography between legitimate sovereign states, and the 1856 Danube Commission as an international body designed to establish a civilized authority over an untamed geography at the European periphery. In other words, the Danube delta where the river meets the Black Sea was designated as an 'international' space due to the absence of civilized authority to maintain control over an important international trade link. Hence, while the Rhine Commission was created to preserve the existing European order, the Danube Commission expanded the civilized European order eastward to prevent instability at the margins from destabilizing the European center.

Here, it is particularly fruitful to note the shades of meaning attributed to early intergovernmental as opposed to international organizations in existing scholarship on IOs. Paul S. Reinsch's 1911 compilation of public international unions, F. S. Lyons's 1963 history of European integration, and Robert Reinalda's 2009 extensive catalog of international organizations all name the 1815 Rhine Commission as the first intergovernmental organization. However, as Lyons stresses, while the Rhine Commission included riparian states, 'it was not international in the wider connotation of the term' (1963: 58). Hence, despite its earlier formation, Reinsch and Lyons barely mention the Rhine Commission and instead focus on the 1856 Danube

Commission as the truly groundbreaking innovation, since it held 'quasi-sovereign power' (Lyons 1963: 62) and 'guaranteed complete independence from undue interference on the part of any riparian state' (Reinsch 1911: 74). This focus on the Danube Commission as a radical achievement and the first truly international body, with not just riparian states but Britain and France holding authority over territory a continent away, portrays the 'international' organization as a political force beyond the sovereign state that steps in to provide civilized governance when local authorities fail.

While the Congo basin was also envisioned as a space without existing legitimate authority, and some actors at the 1884–85 Berlin Conference did work to frame the river as an international geography, late nineteenth-century colonial ambitions won out and disrupted efforts to create an International Congo Commission. This early and understudied failure in the development of IOs is instructive, particularly in the way it exposes the flaws and contradictions in the European geographical imagination between the universality of European experiences and the conceptual emptiness of the colonial periphery. In examining these early institutional bodies, I highlight the confrontation between the European core and peripheral geographies in constructing our understanding of the international and how it developed alongside the territorial state and European imperialism, and through the globalization[5] of the European international order. Indeed, the Danube delta as an 'international' space emerged precisely from this interaction between a European order and the lands and societies that lay beyond.

Conclusion

The Congo basin as an 'international' geography has continued to trouble international society into the twenty-first century. Repeatedly, the United Nations Security Council has passed resolutions expressing concern about the humanitarian situation, condemning violence, and authorizing the deployment of military personnel and observers to the river basin (particularly in UNSCR 1234 and 1291). Despite the requisite nods to state sovereignty as a cornerstone of the UN, these resolutions reinforce longstanding understandings of the Congo basin as a geography absent of civilized and legitimate authority and hence in need of international intercession. Indeed, it is precisely because the river basin does not have a 'democratic and stable' (Holbrooke 1999) territorial state authority that the UN as the main IO of international peace and security must step in to assist in the name of the international community. Into the twenty-first century, a primary mission of IOs such as the UN continues to be the taming of irrational forces in the human and natural world in the service of a stable international order.

I began this chapter with astute observations from Morgenthau and Mitchell on how a certain way of thinking from the early eighteenth and nineteenth centuries continues to frame our understanding of political purpose. The drive to tame nature embodies this way of thinking in its faith in science and rationality to conquer the messiness of entwined social and natural worlds and to maintain a hierarchical divide between civilized society and nature. I contend that this ethos, as a bedrock of modernity, has such staying power over our international political imagination because of the ways in which it has become embedded in key IR concepts and institutions. Specifically, this chapter has detailed three theoretical threads that run throughout this book – first, Enlightenment confidence in society's ability to tame nature shaped our understanding of legitimate state authority; second, this vision of legitimate authority informed global imperial hierarchies as European international society transformed into a global core–periphery order; and third, these ideational frames came together in the establishment of the first IOs to control untamed spaces, politics, and peoples. Although my empirical focus centers mainly on efforts to create three nineteenth-century international river commissions, the argument has wider implications for the way in which the taming of nature has stayed with us and continues to inform international society's troubled relationship with nature.

Notes

1 As with all intellectual movements, it would be wrong to view Enlightenment thinking as a single homogeneous strand – differences include national variations, views of the divine, and a split between moderate and radical strains, which eventually culminated in the intellectual dissonance of the French Revolution (Israel 2010). Here, I attempt to describe an Enlightenment ethos that makes a specific argument about society's relationship with nature.

2 Egon Kunz would later write that these first Rhine rectification projects had 'awoken' the river spirits, which caused the river to become more turbulent and flood-prone (Blackbourn 2006: 111). Such narratives frame the problem as a transhistorical contest between society and nature that reinforce the separation between the two.

3 Spencer was an influential proponent of Social Darwinism, and his works would go on to inspire racist and eugenic policies.

4 Mainstream global governance scholarship places much analytical weight on the role of IOs in forging cooperation based on common economic interests and the commitment to maintaining international peace and security (Barnett and Finnemore 2004; Diehl 2005; Karns and Mingst 2010), with the United Nations system garnering the most empirical attention (for example, see Rosenau 1992;

Weiss and Thakur 2010). For notable exceptions to this focus on the twentieth century and the UN, see Murphy 1994; Murphy and Yates 2019; Ravndal 2020.

5 Dunne and Reus-Smit (2017) prefer the term 'globalization' rather than 'expansion' of European international society to highlight the complex and co-constitutive processes at play rather than a unidirectional and unilateral expansion of European ideas and political institutions globally. This process stressed the uneven, power-laden, and often violent processes of interaction and entanglement that brought new global hierarchies and institutions into being in the nineteenth century.

2

Taming the international highway: constructing the Rhine

Here I have conquered a province peacefully.

Frederick the Great, eighteenth century

Il est difficile, à nous autres Français, de comprendre quelle vénération profonde les Allemands ont pour le Rhin … Pour eux le Rhin est l'emblême universel; le Rhin c'est la force; le Rhin c'est l'indépendance; le Rhin c'est la liberté … c'est un objet de crainte ou d'espérance; symbole de haine ou d'amour, principe de vie et de mort. Pour tous c'est une source de poésie.[1]

Alexandre Dumas, 1842

With the Final Act of the 1815 Congress of Vienna, the most powerful states in Europe created a series of commissions to carry out the settlement which they hoped would maintain peace and security after the intense upheavals of the Napoleonic Wars. These commissions were tasked with fixing borders, building roads, mediating claims, establishing justice, regulating commerce, and adjudicating wartime indemnities. Late in the treaty, Article CVIII called for the establishment of commissions comprised of all states separated or crossed by a navigable river to be created within six months of the Congress. Based on this and the following articles, the Central Commission for the Navigation of the Rhine was established to regulate commerce on the river. Of the creation of the Rhine Commission, Mark Cioc writes in the introduction to his eco-biography of the river, 'None of the Vienna delegates had any inkling as to the significance of what they had just created. All they meant to do was foster trade among the riparian states after twenty-five years of war and bloodshed' (2002: 3). The following two chapters explore the establishment of the Rhine Commission and show that Cioc's statement only skims the surface of the intellectual and political forces at play behind the diplomatic negotiations that led to the oldest continuous interstate institution and the precursor of today's international organizations.

The 1815 Congress of Vienna *did* wish to foster trade among riparian states, but its aims reached beyond the simple functionalist wish to increase commerce on the river. Rather, as this chapter contends, the early nineteenth-century political project to create an ideal river as a frictionless commercial highway revealed the double moral and economic logics that underpinned the relationship between legitimate state authority in Europe and control over nature. To tame the river and transform its unruly flow into a disciplined and useful highway was to make both economic and moral improvements. A straightened and disciplined river decreased economic loss from flooding, reclaimed swampy land for agricultural production, and created the ideal infrastructure for trade, but it also represented a moral conquest from the barbarism of disuse. The Rhine, however, flowed through multiple states, and taming the river as a transboundary geography brought these moral and economic logics to international politics. At the Congress of Vienna, taming the Rhine was an economic project to create a reliable highway for European commerce but also a moral one to tame the fractious 'Teutonic insanity' that had for centuries prevented the Rhine from being an efficient conduit of European trade. The first section of this chapter traces these arguments and shows how the double moral and economic logics of taming the Rhine ran through both domestic and international politics in the eighteenth and early nineteenth century.

Geographical imaginaries are rarely monolithic, and the European conception of the tamed Rhine as an efficient economic highway was not the only longstanding imaginary of this river. The second half of this chapter explores the Romantic counterpoint of the Rhine as an emblem of the German nation and a universal poetic symbol. This framing of the Rhine exposes the relationship between controlling an idealized vision of the pure and untouched Rhine and the building of a modern nation-state. Ironically, these Romantic sensibilities inspired an upsurge of tourism which sped up the commercialization of the Rhine, as the idealized river became a profitable commercial commodity in its own right. Hence, the Rhine as high Romantic fantasy only reinforced the practical need to tame the river and make it safe for steamboats full of tourists. To explore these differing conceptions of the Rhine, I rely on the accounts of engineers, merchants, writers, and artists whose words, paintings, and maps reveal the social and intellectual undercurrents that framed international diplomacy at the 1815 Congress of Vienna.

The Rhine as a high modernist project

In *Seeing Like a State*, James C. Scott identities the ideology of 'high modernism' as a driving force behind large-scale political projects to rationalize nature. High modernism borrows 'the legitimacy of science and technology' and is built on Enlightenment faith in humanity's ability to master nature and create rational and scientific social orders (Scott 1998: 4). In this section,

I show that eighteenth- and nineteenth-century European projects to tame
the river were high modernist projects that aimed both to increase state
wealth and to combat the moral barbarism of swampy disuse. Such river
rectification projects legitimated state power by demonstrating absolute
economic and moral control over a bounded territory. In particular, I detail
how these logics informed Johann Tulla's ambitious project to tame and
straighten the Rhine and how Tulla's scientific aspirations helped build
legitimate state authority in the German state of Baden.

Control over nature, particularly water, as a metaphor for state authority
over the body politic has been a repeated theme in European politics. Roman
emperors built monumental fountains and public water utilities to display
both their power over nature and their authority over the people who
depended on these amenities (Wilson 2012: 1; Salzman 2012: 68). Roman
popes followed in the emperors' footsteps and used fountains to demonstrate
their control over earthly kingdoms, past and future (Bell 2012: 76–7).
Another example of mastery over water as a display of political authority
was Louis XIV's elaborate garden at Versailles, which, Chandra Mukerji
argues, 'was a model of material domination of nature that fairly shouted
its excessive claims about the strength of France' (1997: 2). At Versailles,
national strength was everywhere on display, from the terraced landscaping
reminiscent of military earthworks to the elaborate fountain complexes
suggesting the infrastructure required to support a strong state. Even the
beginning of Versailles was an assertion of royal authority – after seeing
and lusting after Nicolas Fouquet's gardens at Vaux, Louis threw Fouquet
in jail and stole his gardeners (Thacker 1979: 147–8; Schama 2004). However,
under the progressive scientific ethos of the Second Scientific Revolution,
the impetus to rationalize nature took on grander scales and new moral
undertones.

The river has repeatedly been used in European thought as a metaphor
for history, and society's ability to tame the river has consistently been a
metaphor for controlling its own fortunes. From Marcus Aurelius's declaration
that 'time is a violent torrent' to Machiavelli's comparison of history to a
violent river that floods and destroys to Georg Wilhelm Friedrich Hegel's
and Leopold von Ranke's comparisons of history to the flow of rivers, the
metaphor is omnipresent. Machiavelli's actual battle against nature as he
attempted to divert the Arno at Pisa translated into his political advice for
rulers to contrive dams and dikes so the floods of fortune could be managed
(Blackbourn 2006: 11). The struggle was not merely a technical one; it was
imbued with moral implications, as untamed and irrational spaces were
tainted with negative normative connotation. The European Enlightenment
ushered in a new era of scientific confidence in society's ability to tame the
irrational. To overcome the turbulent and unpredictable forces of history

and become the true masters of our fate, society must first tame the river with the new scientific instruments at our disposal. As historian George L. Mosse observes, 'it is impossible to separate the inquiries of the Enlightenment philosophies into nature from their examination of morality and human character' (1978: 2). The two concerns were inextricably linked in the Enlightenment imagination.

Two strands of logic drove society's quest to tame the river. Following the first logic, stagnant water was associated with illness in the human body and in the body politic. Transforming the Rhine from a meandering, uncertain river into a fast and consistent highway was a war against ignorance and barbarism as real as any fought against invading armies. In the mid-eighteenth century, the young Frederick the Great oversaw the construction of a twelve-mile channel on the Oder to drain the swamps and increase agricultural acreage (Blackbourn 2006: 10). Frederick wrote to Voltaire of the project that 'whoever improves the soil, cultivates land lying waste and drains swamps is making conquests from barbarism'. By barbarism, Frederick was referring to the marshes as well as the people, whom he characterized as 'sunk in ignorance and stupidity' as if the swamps had corrupted the character of the populations that inhabited them (Mauch 2004: 13). Here, his language is an Enlightenment argument of ordered rationality against the barbarism of chaos and decay. To fight this war, Frederick brought in cartographers, surveyors, engineers, and statisticians to establish control over the wild world of reeds and marshes. Engineers along the Oder and later the Rhine turned to Renaissance treatises such as Benedetto Castelli's *Della misura dell'acque correnti* (1628) and Domenico Guglielmini's *Della natura de'fiumi* (1719) that proposed scientific ways of calculating, analyzing, and correcting rivers (Cioc 2002: 37). Engineers and political leaders also looked to the experience of Jan Leeghwater in Holland and Cornelius Vermuyden in southern England as models of water management (Bell 2012: 82). Taming the river, then, became a heroic conquest that legitimated the modern state – a battle between the logical human mind and the irrational and unknown forces of nature, as water is harnessed and domesticated for the needs of society. Indeed, Frederick boasted that his scheme on the Oder allowed him to literally conquer provinces and add them to his domain. It would be centuries before swamps and yearly floods would be seen in a more salubrious light.

Second was the logic of cameralism[2] as a state-building project to maximize economic utility. Unruly rivers detracted from a state's economic prosperity as seasonal floods transformed land into swamps unusable for homesteads and agriculture. In his account of Prussia's scheme to rationalize its forests, Scott discusses the state's need to render natural objects simple and legible in order to achieve the most rational economic outcome. In the eighteenth century, under Frederick the Great's guidance, the state reduced trees to simple units of timber or firewood and left out 'everything touching on human interaction with the forest' (Scott 1998: 13). Economic man stood at the center of this reconceptualization of the natural world – everything considered valuable became 'crops' or 'timber' while everything without clear economic value became 'weeds' and 'underbrush' to be eliminated to make room for more useful foliage. Hence, the project not only categorized and calculated the value of all vegetation but also proactively seeded valuable trees while removing foliage considered useless. The result was a grid-like monoculture that maximized economic worth above all else, and 'the German forest became the archetype for imposing on disorderly nature the neatly arranged constructs of science' (Scott 1998: 15). Together, these economic and moral logics also informed early nineteenth-century projects to tame the Rhine.

Johann Tulla: the man who tamed the Rhine

The man credited with bringing scientific discipline to the disorderly Rhine was an engineer from Baden. His ambitious project to streamline the Rhine sought to tame the river as both a moral crusade against the barbarism of irrational nature and an economic and political one to render the river conducive to human exploitation. Even the terminology used to describe the project to 'domesticate', 'tame' and 'harness' the river reinforced these two goals.

An inscription near his birthplace in Karlsruhe on the right bank of the river reads: 'To Johann Gottfried Tulla: The Man Who Tamed the Rhine.' Tulla was born in 1770 and his formative years coincided with turbulence in Europe, as many German states first embraced and then rejected and resisted the political and intellectual tides of the French Revolution. As war and social unrest swept across the Rhine, rather than engage in the political battles around him, Tulla focused on a grander war. He learned the latest Italian and French ideas on river management, traveled through the Netherlands and lower Rhine, and formulated his own battle plans against the river (Blackbourn 2006: 79). When the Holy Roman Empire dissolved, Baden benefitted politically from close relations with Napoleon, and Tulla was able to travel to France to tour projects and converse with French hydraulic engineers about river management. He was a man on a mission and even declined a professorship in mathematics at Heidelberg University to work as Baden's chief water engineer (Blackbourn 2006: 81–2). 'In agrarian regions,' Tulla wrote, 'brooks, streams, and rivers should, as a rule, be canalized, and their flow harnessed to the needs of people who live along their banks' (Cioc 2002: 38). In 1809, Tulla first wrote down his ambitious plans to 'rectify' the entire upper Rhine. These plans were published three years later in *The Principles According to Which Future Work on the Rhine Should be Conducted.*

Tulla, however, was not a one-person intellectual movement. For two generations before him, engineers such as Daniel Bernoulli and Leonhard Euler had been at work straightening and redirecting rivers including the Oder, Warthe, Ruhr, and Niers across northern Germany. At the turn of the nineteenth century, engineers wrote treatises on the subject, including the *Handbook of Hydraulics* published in 1795 by Tulla's mentor Karl Christian von Langsdorf. German states such as Baden saw the importance of advancements in natural sciences and engineering and spent state funds cultivating promising talent like Tulla. A cohort of German river engineers emerged, including Reinhard Woltmann, who worked on the Elbe, and Claus Kröncke and Karl Friedrich Ritter von Wiebeking, who also worked on the Rhine (Blackbourn 2006: 83). These men were already applying rational hydraulic designs to rivers across Germany. Hence, Tulla's proposal to straighten and deepen the Rhine was not an innovation in river engineering, since it reflected the dominant theories of the times. However, it was the scale of Tulla's ambitions that was groundbreaking.

The Rhine was an inconsistent river – it twisted and looped its way roughly 1,250 kilometers from Lake Constance on the Swiss–German–Austria border to the North Sea port of Rotterdam. The upper Rhine between Basel and Bingen was particularly troublesome as islands, sandbars, and wetlands constricted the flow of water. The Rhine Falls below Schaffhausen, Switzerland, is a 30-meter drop and required travelers to use special flat-bottomed boats to descend – in fact, an early nineteenth-century guidebook recommended that travelers cross to Strasbourg by land rather than risk the dangers of the river (Schreiber 1825: 38, 49). Further, a series of underwater reefs near Bingen produced whirlpools that complicated navigation, including the 'dreaded' *Bingerloch* whirlpool immediately below Bingen. To navigate this section, 'a sufficient number of horses should be attached to the vessel by strong ropes ... to drag against the current'. Another whirlpool called *Wildes Gefahrt* below Bacharach presented yet more barriers to navigation (Schreiber 1825: 145–7). In addition, along this stretch, seasonal floods caused damage to villages and agricultural land. The shifting river changed beds, leaving some villages on the French side in the spring and on the German side by winter. The Rhine rectification project promised to tame these dangers and deficiencies.

Tulla's plan for Rhine rectification involved 354 kilometers of the river and was based on insights from Castelli and Guglielmini: to straighten the river so the faster moving water could be restricted to one bed and could cut a deeper river to prevent flooding. The project proceeded in two phases

– first to straighten the river's many oxbows and second to eliminate islands and sandbars that impeded flow. Between Basel and Mannheim, the project would shorten the river by 82 kilometers and impose a uniform width of 200–230 meters (Cioc 2002: 51). Once deepened and straightened, the river would be consistent in all seasons. This would minimize flooding and eliminate navigational difficulties caused by sandbars and reefs. It would also stabilize the riverbanks to create new economic opportunities for factories and businesses that would benefit from proximity to the river.

Rhine rectification was not merely an engineering project. It was also a fight against ignorance and barbarism, and Tulla proselytized the benefit of his plan like a true zealot. Confidently, he asserted, 'Everything along this stream will improve once we undertake the rectification work', including the attitude and productivity of the people and even the climate (Cioc 2002: 38). He saw the project as a battle against nature, and victory would bring many advantages: reduce floods and illness, maximize agricultural production, and stabilize international borders. Framing the project as a military campaign, Tulla referred to his vision for the Rhine as a 'general operational plan' against the river. Even the term 'rectification' implied that the river's natural course was somehow deficient and had to be corrected by science (Cioc 2013: 30). Those who stood in his way were painted as ignorant or malicious. In a letter to Kröncke in 1825, Tulla wrote:

> The difficulties and obstacles that stand in the way of rectification of the Rhine do not lie in the task itself … but make themselves felt for the most part according to the degree to which individual interests or the interests of whole communities come into play, and whether the active agents are more or less enlightened and moral. (quoted in Blackbourn 2006: 95)

Here, riverside communities that resisted Tulla's operations not only stood in the way of economic gain but also became the 'backward' and 'unenlightened' who obstructed moral progress. The hallmark of an enlightened modern state, then, was to eliminate these backward elements in both human society and the river that blocked the path of economic and moral progress.

Tulla's river rectification plan illustrated the double logic of scientific engagement with nature – the moral logic of a battle against barbarism and the state-building logic of transforming nature into a useful economic good. The Enlightenment urge to transform nature's curves into straight lines is perhaps best appreciated through the engineering maps of the time. Figure 2.1 shows a portion of Tulla's plans to correct an inefficient oxbow. Once the narrow channel is cut, the river will do the rest of the labor, abandoning its meandering circular path and taking on a rational riverbed. The oxbows were naturally created by the hydrology of the meandering

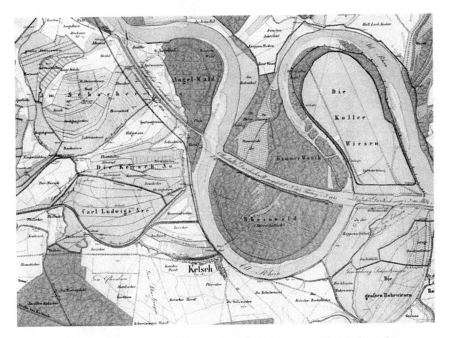

Figure 2.1 Map of the straightening of the Rhine near Ketsch by Johann Gottfried Tulla, 1833

river, in which the outer edge of the curve would speed up and wash away sediment while flow along the inner bend would slow and deposit sediment. This process of deposition and erosion created sharper bends over time, slowing the river down.

However, despite the narrative opposition between rational engineers and the wayward natural river, the river Tulla encountered was not completely 'natural'. Pollen analysis shows that the oldest manmade channels along the river date back to 8000 BCE. Roman historian Tacitus wrote of efforts to *coercendo Rheno* ('bully the Rhine'), and the first cut to remove a bend dated from at least 1391 (Cioc 2002: 47; Blackbourn 2006: 75–6). Throughout, the Rhine pushed back, at times humoring and at times surprising those who wished to control its flow. This everyday mutual engagement between the river and society shaped the cultural and political identity of the region. In Tulla's map, however, the nonlinear and intertwined relationship between the human and natural worlds is simplified into a mathematical schematic of straightened lines and flattened perspectives. The complex dance of co-constitution between society's efforts to control the river and the river's hydrological proclivities is flattened into a one-dimensional story that unambiguously charts a unidirectional relationship of conquest. Through scientific ingenuity, this story tells us, society corrects the blemishes of nature and emerges triumphant.

Taming the river as state-building

For Tulla and the Badenese authorities, the double economic and moral logics of taming the river were central in legitimating a larger state-building project. Rhine rectification not only increased the state's economic and moral authority, but in implementing Tulla's plans, Baden also consolidated borders and promoted economic and administrative integration. In essence, the project not only rationalized the river's flow, but also constructed a more rational state to manage the physical and metaphysical floods of fortune, as Machiavelli had counseled. This reverses Scott's account in which a strong authoritarian state bureaucracy is a necessary precondition for implementing high modernist projects. Instead, the scheme to rationalize the Rhine contributed to the consolidation of state competencies and legitimate state authority over a defined territory.

In 1771, the territory of Baden doubled when Karl Friedrich of Baden-Durlach inherited Baden-Baden. Then, between 1803 and 1806, Baden almost quadrupled as it swallowed formerly independent cities, ecclesiastical estates, and principalities. In the wake of rapid expansion, bureaucrats in the capital Karlsruhe had to find a way to integrate its new lands into a coherent political entity. At the same time, Baden faced internal social and religious tensions in its efforts to centralize and blend traditional aristocratic institutions with Napoleonic reforms (Schmitt 1983: 20, 27–9).[3] By 1848, however, Baden had established a sense of identity with a favorable reputation among democrats and liberals across Europe. In addition, it boasted one of Germany's most centralized administrations and politically dominant bureaucracies (Lee 1991: 248). Tulla and the Rhine played a role in this transformation.

First, rectifying the Rhine solidified political borders. The Rhine as a border has been contested since the Roman Empire. According to Julius Caesar's records of his Gaul campaigns, German tribes settled on the right bank and Gauls on the left, but evidence suggests that Caesar may have exaggerated this difference to gain political support for his military campaigns (Bispham 2008: 29). In spite of the questionable historical veracity of Caesar's statement, the Rhine as a natural and historic border between the Germans and French became part of the French national myth. Cardinal Richelieu's sixteenth-century *Political Testament* argued that the Rhine was France's natural border, and Louis XIV reinforced this notion when his army captured Strasbourg in 1681 to extend France to its natural borders 'jusqu'au Rhin' (Sahlins 1990: 1424; Cioc 2002: 9). Since then, Alsace and Lorraine, located on the Rhine's left bank – the 'naturally' French side – have become flashpoints in Franco-German politics. In the late eighteenth century, treaties fixed France's border along natural boundaries. However, using the river as a frontier presented problems since the river's course and its width are not constant throughout the year. A military engineer in Strasbourg described the issue in 1814:

> Everyone agrees that all boundaries should be as fixed and as invariable as possible; yet what is more variable than the middle of the Rhine, that is to say, the navigable part of the river? The Rhine changes its course every year, sometimes two or three times. With the floods, an island or a commune, which in the spring was French, is German the following winter, then becomes French again in two or three years, and by dams or dikes, the riverfront inhabitants and sometimes the contiguous states bring back an island to their respective banks. These islands, without stable and recognized masters, facilitate disorder of every kind. (quoted in Sahlins 1990: 1442)

Tulla's plan to rectify the Rhine and confine the river to a single riverbed would solve this problem by creating a reliable and consistent geographical border to ensure political order and rationality as opposed to chaos and uncertainty.

Second, the Rhine rectification project was one of many devised to centralize, rationalize, and integrate Baden's new territories into a coherent unity. These reformations involved new maps, legal codes, tax systems, and standard weights and measures. As Blackbourn highlights, 'Rhine rectification held up a mirror to these changes. Dive into the sprawling archival record, look at any one stage of the project, and it is like drawing a cross-section through the life of the state' (2006: 88). Questions of who would provide the labor, funding, and material for the engineering projects involved many organs of the state's bureaucracy – and questions of coordination with other Rhine states consolidated Baden's foreign affairs apparatus. In answering these questions in everyday practice, Baden's bureaucrats built their state through the logic of scientific rationalization, shaping a national identity with tools to control and tame nature for the benefit of society. The end product, a rationalized river, would benefit the state as a commercial highway as well as minimize the cost of flood damage and reclaim agricultural lands from flood-prone swamps.[4] Through the project, the theory of scientific conquest of nature met the practices of state-building and left indelible marks upon the human and physical geography of the river.

Rationalizing the international highway

For James C. Scott, the project to rationalize Prussia's forests depended on a consolidated bureaucratic state controlled by a powerful autocrat who could impose his will on society and nature. However, this logic is less persuasive in explaining the project to tame transboundary rivers that cross the territories of multiple states. Indeed, a strong autocrat jealous of his territorial authority is more likely to impede rather than facilitate interstate cooperation. Instead, I suggest that rather than a strong state, it was high modernist ideology that enabled diplomats at the Congress of Vienna to propose an interstate project to tame the Rhine as a transboundary geography. Informed by confidence in society's ability to roll back irrationality and barbarism, this project aimed to transform the Rhine into an efficient and reliable highway for the benefit of European trade. Rhine rectification as a transboundary scheme also followed the double logics of Tulla's rectification project – to make conquests from barbarism by overcoming the irrational system of tolls and monopolies that hindered commerce along the river, and to render the river profitable for all states with commercial interests along the Rhine.

Although navigation was never Tulla's main concern (Blackbourn 2006: 111), river rectification projects that followed in Tulla's wake focused on the Rhine's economic usefulness as a commercial road. The international project to rationalize the Rhine was very much an economic mission, with free navigation as its central motif. Prior to the French Revolution, almost a hundred local German princes competed for power along the Rhine, fighting over control of small islands and fishing rights (Cioc 2013: 27). As an economic highway, the river bestowed power and wealth to local authorities through three main practices: toll collection, *Stapelrecht* (the right of unloading), and *Umschlagsrecht* (the right of transfer). However, these practices discouraged commercial activity along the river and were painted by observers as regressive and medieval.

Levying tolls on river traffic was at first an imperial prerogative reserved for the Holy Roman Emperor, but toll collection devolved to local secular and religious authorities by the end of the Middle Ages (Chamberlain 1923: 147; Heckscher 1994 [1931]: 61). Legally, toll rates could not be raised and new tolls could not be levied without the emperor's consent, but in practice, local lords competed with one another to establish extralegal tolls.[5] By the late twelfth century as many as sixy stations dotted the Rhine (Mellor 1983: 70). In the sixteenth century, the Archbishop of Mainz and Archbishop of Cologne instituted a toll every 15 kilometers, only to be surpassed in the seventeenth century by the Duke of Cleves who charged a Rhine toll every 12 kilometers (Heckscher 1994 [1931]: 57). In the eighteenth century, tolls equivalent to a third of a boat's cargo were levied over just 64 kilometers of the middle Rhine between Bingen and Coblenz. By the French Revolution, boats encountered roughly thirty toll stations between Strasbourg and the Dutch border (Clapp 1911: 6; Spaulding 2007: 8).[6] To make matters worse, the toll rates were not always advertised and depended not only on the amount of cargo, but 'the capacity of the boat, the judgment and corruptibility of the officials, or according to all four standards together' (Clapp 1911: 7). A popular boatman's song describes the burden of tolls (translated in Clapp 1911: 6):

> The Rhine can count more tolls than miles
> And knight and priestling grind us down.
> The toll-man's heavy hand falls first,
> Behind him stands the greedy line: –
> Master of tolls, assayer, scribe, –
> Four man deep they tap the wine.

Indeed, this proliferation of tolls became synonymous with insanity – *furiosa Teutonicorum insania*, wrote English chronicler Thomas Wykes in 1269 as he described the local lords who were 'not deterred by fear of God or king' and 'extorted from each and every one new and intolerable payments' (quoted in Heckscher 1994 [1931]: 56). However, it was a rational form of insanity, as no lord wanted to be outdone in profiting from river traffic.

Five hundred years later, the situation remained unchanged as a late eighteenth-century writer noted:

> One sees rivers and very beautiful rivers become almost useless for navigation by the tyranny of tolls. The Moselle, the Rhine, the Elbe Rivers and many others groan under this extravagant despotism, a remainder of traditions of barbarism and ignorance as much as greed. Their banks are infested with insolent pirates, under the name of officials, charged to ransom, in the name of the princes whose domains the waters fertilize, the unfortunate merchants who expose themselves to these ruinous excursions. (Engelhardt 1879: 22)

Another traveler in the 1790s, Thomas Cogan, echoed these sentiments by describing how these illiberal tolls checked Rhine commerce: 'the value of Rhenish wines is greatly increased to the consumer by the number of tolls exacted by every distinct potentate, and in every distinct jurisdiction'. In addition, Cogan complained about the manner in which tolls were collected as 'humiliating to the passenger'. Further, he describes the origins of the tolls as a way to raise money for local princes to reward their followers, as the strongmen only knew war and 'they envied the wealth which began to follow commerce' (1794: 101, 343–5). Revealing his bias against the medieval system and in favor of free trade that would benefit merchants like him, Cogan depicts the Rhine's tolls as medieval, thuggish, and specifically anti-commerce. Here, he fumed against not only the economic burden but the moral injustice of Teutonic insanity.

The problem was widespread not just on the Rhine, but, as the previous quote from Engelhardt suggests, on many European rivers. In exchange for tolls, local authorities had the implicit obligation to maintain towpaths and protect travelers. As another local song maintained, 'tolls and protection come in the first place from necessity and not from greed', but this was not always the case, as towpaths were often left in unusable condition (Clapp 1911: 7; Chamberlain 1923: 147). Lords often did not follow through on their public duty. Indeed, as highlighted by petitions from lords who wished the emperor to grant them the legal right to extract tolls, lords often levied tolls for their private financial gain rather than public need. In the sixteenth century, Count Hans Georg of the Palatinate at Veldenz wrote of the possibility of an imperial rejection: 'God have mercy and help us and our six poor uneducated children and our wife with her heavy belly big with child' (Heckscher 1994 [1931]: 64). Nowhere does he mention upkeep of the towpaths and protection of merchants. A number of Holy Roman Emperors, including Frederick Barbarossa in the twelfth century, sought to control the proliferation of tolls, but the imperial framework operated against them and thwarted their efforts to rein in the feudal lords.

In addition to toll stations, authorities along the Rhine clung to two other practices: *Stapelrecht* and *Umschlagsrecht*. *Stapelrecht* required goods traveling along the river to be unloaded for a certain amount of time – typically three days – so local merchants could be the first to purchase the goods. This likely goes back to 1259 when Archbishop Konrad von Hochstaden of Cologne claimed the right, which was later confirmed by Holy Roman Emperor Charles IV in 1355 (Spaulding 2011: 204). During the Middle Ages, five towns along the Rhine – Strasbourg, Speyer, Mainz, Cologne, and Dordrecht – held *Stapelrecht* and prospered from this right, which conferred upon these towns an economic advantage and transformed them into wealthy market centers. By the eighteenth century, *Stapelrecht* was limited to Strasbourg, Cologne, and Mainz, and as a practical measure, it was reduced to a tax. In addition, exceptions were made for coal, foodstuffs, and timber (Clapp 1911: 8; Chamberlain 1923: 149; Mellor 1983: 72).

Umschlagsrecht or the right of compulsory transfer (also known as transhipping) required merchants to transfer their goods to local boats – operated by each city's boatmen's guild – for each section of the river. The Dutch controlled the river's mouth, Cologne's boatmen monopolized the lower Rhine, Mainz boatmen controlled the middle, and Strasbourg and Basel shared the upper Rhine. The practice was tightly controlled as boatmen's guilds colluded with city authorities to determine rates and regulations. Boatmen operated according to strict guidelines, with each boat only moving out once filled (Clapp 1911: 9; Chamberlain 1923: 150). These rights were negotiated in the first instance, but were quickly institutionalized and became difficult to overturn. For example, in 1681, the Archbishop of Mainz and the city of Strasbourg signed a compact that, with the exception of the spring and autumn Frankfurt festivals, only Mainz ships could carry goods upriver. In 1751, after France conquered Strasbourg, the French disputed this arrangement, but the institutionalized practice held (Chamberlain 1923: 149).

There was a strong practical argument behind the practice of mandatory transfer to local boats: the same boat could not safely transport goods the entire length of the Rhine from Basel to the North Sea. Roy Mellor's 1983 study meticulously catalogs the different water transports along the Rhine. The fast and steady trapezoidal Oberlander navigated the lower Rhine but were not allowed past Cologne, and the Lauertanne, derived from a dugout canoe, was better suited for the shallower and faster currents of the upper Rhine (Mellor 1983: 75). Given the navigational limitations of some boats, transferring goods to the right boat, guilds maintained, was cheaper and safer for commerce, and local boatmen had the knowledge necessary to safely navigate their stretch of the river. However, while this argument makes sense for why goods should be transferred, it does not account for why certain towns and guides monopolized the right of transfer at the expense of others. To understand these practices is to understand centuries of contingent societal interaction with the river.

The practices outlined above were not neutral; they enriched certain cities rather than others and exposed underlying networks of power that ran through the Rhine community. Cologne, an important commercial center since Roman times, held its monopolies as a result of and as a way to further its wealth and power. Existing institutions perpetuated Cologne's privileges. It is no surprise then that Cologne was known as the 'mother of German towns' and led the way in developing early modern urban institutions in northwest Germany (Dollinger 1964: 14). Newer urban centers such as Rotterdam, Mannheim, and Frankfurt, which became important economic centers in the late Middle Ages, challenged the disproportionate power held by Cologne and Mainz. However, institutionalized practices were difficult to alter. But for advocates of free trade, these practices hindered civilizational progress and tilted incentives against efforts to transform the river into a more efficient economic highway.

As it expanded eastward in the late eighteenth century, the French Republic undertook to reform the Teutonic insanity of the Rhine's system of tolls and monopolies in the name of Enlightenment reason and equality. In place of arbitrary tolls, the French sought to establish a more rational economic system. In opening the Scheldt to traffic of all nations on 16 November 1792, the French Republic decreed:

> no nation can without injustice claim the right exclusively to occupy the channel of a river and to prevent the neighboring upper riparian States from enjoying the same advantages; that such a right is a remnant of feudal servitude, or at any rate, an odious monopoly which must have been imposed by force and yielded by impotence; that it is therefore revocable at any moment and

in spite of any convention, because nature does not recognize privileged nations any more than privileged individuals, and the rights of man are forever imprescriptible. (Kaeckenbeck 1918: 32)

Here, the French Republic linked free navigation of international waterways to the rational, egalitarian spirit of the age. This decree aimed to sweep away the 'feudal servitude' embedded in ancient rights and monopolies in favor of Enlightenment confidence in the laws of nature, which made nations equal and overrode the dense layering of ancient privileges that hindered trade along Europe's rivers. In essence, this argument elevated freedom of navigation and trade along international rivers to a natural right and eschewed any opposition as backward, immoral, and unnatural. It supports the idea that history is a progressive flow from the irrational conflict of the Middle Ages to a rational and cooperative future.

The French Republic's decrees and later those of Napoleon paved the way for the creation of the 1815 Rhine Commission. The two logics that drove Tulla's engineering projects also shaped the rationale behind the Rhine Commission – that it would first battle the untamed chaos of fractious Hobbesian competition between local lords, and secondly, promote the economic logic of a trans-European governance project to transform a contested geography into a rational highway for international commerce. Indeed, as the next chapter will discuss, the underlying narrative of the river as an economic highway permeated the discussions in the International Rivers Committee as it permeated the treaty articles that emerged from the Congress of Vienna. As French diplomat Charles Maurice de Talleyrand wrote to King Louis XVIII of France from Vienna on 15 February 1815, 'the arrangements relating to the free navigation of rivers are as yet barely sketched in; but the principles have been decided on, and they will secure to commerce all the advantages that European industry could ask for...' (Talleyrand 1881: 19–20). Even those who argued in favor of traditional monopolies did so in the language of economic gain – for example, indigenous knowledge allowed local boatmen to provide safer and less costly transport of merchants' goods. The aim of the Rhine Commission, then, was to use rational methods to end divisive interstate competition and transform the river into an economic highway that would not only generate economic benefits for all European states but also advance European civilization. These logics gave legitimacy to the creation of an interstate governance body that would inspire others in its wake.

Counterpoint: the Romantic Rhine

As a counterpoint to the scientific project to tame the river, the turn of the nineteenth century also saw the blossoming of a Romantic conceptualization of the Rhine. At first glance, the Romantic Rhine might seem like a contradiction to the ideal river as a tamed and reliable economic highway that legitimated state authority. However, in the Romantics' use of the image of an idealized Rhine to strengthen claims to German and European identities, the Rhine also served to legitimate national state-building and international institution-building projects. Indeed, the Romantic Rhine even had its own economic logics – as the transcendental beauty of the Rhine attracted more and more artistic attention, the river had to be straightened and controlled for the safety of the ever-growing numbers of tourists who came on steamboats to witness this Romantic wonder for themselves.

According to historian Isaiah Berlin, the Romanticism that developed in late eighteenth-century Germany represented a major turning point in Western thought 'through the destruction of the notion of truth and validity in ethics and politics' (1996: 168). The movement bloomed with a wealth of literary and intellectual talent from the emotive *Sturm and Drang* artists to the Jena circle to Immanuel Kant's revolutionary philosophy. The Romantics celebrated the Rhine as a river full of heightened beauty and deep nostalgia inspired by personal emotional connections to the landscape. However, the Romantic German river was a human narrative subject to the same anthropocentricism as the narrative of scientific and enlightened progress detailed above (Taylor 1998). For the Romantics, natural landscapes were reflections of the human soul. As such, the Romantic project imperfectly mirrored the twin logics of Tulla's rectification project – as a moral crusade to recover the wild, beating soul of unspoiled nature and a nation-building enterprise that coded the Rhenish landscape as German.

Legends about the Rhine represent the river as a beautiful but magical and menacing force, a reflection of dark, ominous, and brooding elements in the human soul. In Joseph Snowe's 1839 collection, legends and traditions from the Rhine show the dangerous aura surrounding the mysterious river. One tale recounts the story of a dying boy on a boat who hears the water-wolf howl. 'To hear the water-wolf howl, was, in the superstition of the age, and of the people, to hear the voice of the angel of death', and subsequently a storm followed by floods ravages the boat and kills almost everyone onboard (Snowe 1839: 138–9). The most popular Rhine myth is that of the Lorelei, a tale first popularized by Clemens Brentano in 1801, retold by Heinrich Heine in an 1824 poem, and featured in an unfinished opera by Felix Mendelssohn in 1846. The Lorelei is a rock formation located in the narrowest section of the Rhine between the Swiss border and the North Sea. Though there are many variations to the story, Lorelei is most famously remembered in her role as a siren, luring sailors to a watery death with her beauty. Of an unfortunate victim, Wilhelm Ruland's version of the tale recounts, 'His eyes were fixed on the features of this celestial being where he read the sweet story of love … Rocks, stream, glorious night, all melted into a mist before his eyes, he

saw nothing but the figure above, nothing but her radiant eyes' (1908: 100).
It was death bathed in beauty. Echoes of this legend can be seen in Wagner's
beautiful maidens who guard the precious Rhine gold.

This vision of the Rhine as a distinctly German emblem can be traced
to the early nineteenth century, as the Romantic movement and Napoleon's
eastward expansion inspired Ernst Moritz Arndt to write his 1815 essay
The Rhine – Germany's River, but not Germany's Border, arguing that
German culture dominated both sides of the Rhine (Cioc 2002: 9). A journey
down the Rhine in 1802 inspired German Romantic poets Achim von Arnim
and Clemens Brentano (assisted by his sister Bettina) to compile a collection
of folk songs according to Johann Gottfried Herder's notion of *Volk* and
Volkspoesie (Plonien 2000: 81–2). German writers Karl Simrock and Joseph
von Eichendorff also published collections of Rhine legends in the early
nineteenth century (Taylor 1998: 59). In these works, Romantic inclinations
commingled with nationalism – if the German people did not have a mythology, one must be invented; and if the Germans did not remember their
mythology, their memories must be reawakened.

Lyric poet Friedrich Hölderlin composed *Der Rhein* in 1801–02, a poem
that Martin Heidegger featured in a 1942 lecture along with another poem
titled *Germania*. In this poem, Hölderlin celebrates the Rhine's picturesque
Alpine origins and the river's journey through Germany:

> And it is beautiful
> Leaving the mountain behind
> That he should slip through Germany's landscapes
> In silent delight, stilling his longing
> With useful labor working the land
> As Father Rhine, and nourishing children
> In towns that he has founded. (Hölderlin 1801–02: n.p.)

The Rhine spreads civilization and industry as it journeys across the countryside – a hardworking paternal figure creating a nation of German cities
and people. Similarly, an 1847 volume of *Lays and Legends of the Rhine*
begins with a poem titled *The Rhine* that twists and blends a description
of the Rhine's natural landscape with an idealized Germany identity: 'Around
his diadem rich flowers did twine, / Of Song and Poesy; – this father Rhine
/ shall be for evermore the pulse of German story!' (Grattan 1847: 3). The
notion that the Rhine is a German river was adopted not only by local
poets and musicians but by foreign writers. For example, Henry Wadsworth
Longfellow wrote in *Hyperion: A Romance* in 1839:

> O, the pride of the German heart is this noble
> river! And right it is; for of all the rivers of this
> beautiful earth there is none so beautiful as this. (Longfellow 1857: n.p.)

Through these works, the river's beauty and even its physical dangers were being 'recoded' as German (Plonien 2000: 84). This distillation of aesthetic beauty into political truth can also be seen in the nearly 400 songs about the Rhine published in the 1840s that spoke of a growing German national consciousness (Porter 1996).

However, the Germans did not have a monopoly on rapturous visions of the Rhine. Dutch poet Joost van den Vondel wrote in 1629, 'Your Highness Rhine, my sweet dreams / How can I sing your praise?', reminding readers that the river meets the sea not in Germany but in Holland (quoted in Cioc 2002: 8). As van den Vondel's poetry suggests, in contrast to the Rhine as a distinctively German river, the early nineteenth century also saw the emergence of an international and commercial construction of the Romantic Rhine that reinforced imaginaries of the river as a trans-European geography that connected as much as it separated.

Internationalizing the Romantic Rhine

As the fame of the scenic Rhine spread, international visitors appropriated the river as their own. In the early nineteenth century, artists and writers traveling along the river on the European Grand Tour transformed the Rhine into a universal Romantic symbol and must-see tourist destination. J. M. W. Turner's paintings and the words of Victor Hugo, Lord Byron, Ann Radcliffe, and Henry David Thoreau attest to the river's international appeal. These artists and subsequent multitudes celebrated the wild twisting beauty of the upper middle river between Bingen and Koblenz, dotted with crumbling medieval castles and tollbooths. Lord Byron famously describes the river in *Childe Harold's Pilgrimage* (1812–18):

> A blending of all beauties; streams and dells,
> Fruit, foliage, crag, wood, cornfield, mountain, vine,
> And chiefless castles breathing stern farewells
> From gray but leafy walls, where Ruin greenly dwells.

Unlike their counterparts, international luminaries coded the Rhine's dark beauty as more than merely German. Victor Hugo's literary travelogue on the Rhine combined three trips he made with Juliette Drouet in 1838, 1839, and 1840. Woven into his vivid descriptions of the river is his political visions of a borderless Europe (Thompson 2012: 145). Disguised as letters to his wife, Hugo's prose celebrates the Rhine's pan-European character:

> Yes, my friend, the Rhine is a noble river—feudal, republican, imperial—worthy, at the same time, of France and of Germany. The whole history of Europe is combined within its two great aspects—in this flood of the warrior and of the thinker—in this proud stream, which causes France to bound, and by whose profound murmurings Germany is bewildered in dreams. (Hugo 1843: 111)

For Scottish philosopher Thomas Carlyle, the Rhine represented something even grander than the dream of a united Europe. On an 1853 trip, Carlyle first encountered the Rhine and described the noble river as 'the most magnificent image of silent power I have seen; and in fact, one's first idea of a world-river' (quoted in Kaplan 2013: 593). In a letter to Ralph Waldo Emerson about his journey, Carlyle describes how this world-river 'rolls along, mirror-smooth ... voiceless, swift, with trim banks, through the heart of Europe, and of the Middle Ages wedded to the Present Age' (Carlyle and Emerson 1888: 13 May 1853). For Carlyle, who was unimpressed with Germany otherwise, the Rhine connected spaces and epochs as he felt swept away by this pure nature – it was an ideal river that transcended nationalities and momentary philosophies of the day to unite the world. It is important to note that Carlyle's smooth river with trim banks was the creation of multiple rectification projects. But poetry transformed the combined work of science and nature into an idealized 'natural' state.

With the first steamships to travel up the Rhine in 1816, tourism boomed and the river became crowded. An 1825 travel guide suggests that the visitor 'should procure as many letters of recommendation as he can, since they are often the only means of obtaining a view of curious objects' (Schreiber 1825: 1) – a testament to the intense public interest in the Romantic Rhine. The Netherlands Steamboat Company began regular services between Rotterdam and Cologne in 1825, and a Prussian company followed suit two years later. Published in 1828, J. A Klein's guidebook *A trip on the Rhine from Mainz to Cologne* became a bestseller (Cioc 2002: 145–6). In fact, descriptions of the picturesque river became so clichéd that writers did not even need to see the Rhine to wax poetic about its scenic shores. In 1862, from the other side of the Atlantic, Henry David Thoreau wrote after only glimpsing a painting of the river: 'It was like a dream of the Middle Ages. I floated down its historic streams in nothing more than imagination, under bridges built by the Romans...' (quoted in Cioc 2002: 8). Here, Thoreau's words reflect the constructed Romantic aura surrounding the river rather than the river itself. The goal here is not to know the river but to capture poetic truth.

Amid Romantic enthusiasm for the Rhine's magnificent scenery, glimpses of dissatisfaction with the river's lack of navigational efficiency shine through, particularly before the combined force of steamboats and river rationalization transformed travel along the river. Gothic novelist Ann Radcliffe's account of her journey down the Rhine in the summer of 1794 highlighted the sublime cliffs, wild and romantic landscape, melancholic castle ruins, and bucolic countryside. But the account also described the difficult river passage between Cologne and Mainz, where the river was so rapid and narrow that 'a loaded vessel can seldom be drawn faster than at the rate of six English miles a day, against the stream', requiring a fortnight to make the journey (Radcliffe 2009 [1794]: 153).

In Mary Shelley's *Frankenstein*, published in 1818, Dr. Frankenstein attempts to journey by boat from Switzerland to Rotterdam along the Rhine and then back to England. As expected, Frankenstein describes the ruined castles, tremendous precipices, and meandering river being so captivating that 'even I, depressed in mind, and my spirits continually agitated by gloomy feelings, even I was pleased' (1818: 188). However, his progress was painfully slow and required five days' sailing between Strasbourg and Mainz. At Cologne, he was forced to abandon the river and continue overland. In fact, as we later discover, his journey was so slow that the monster was able to track him on foot: 'I crept along the shores of the Rhine, among its willow islands, and over the summits of its hills' (1818: 205). In addition to satisfyingly Gothic images of a dark monster creeping through the Rhine's stormy ruins, the story reminds us of the practical consequences of inefficient river travel. Steamboats simplified navigation, but also required additional engineering works to further transform the river into a suitable steam highway.

One of the glaring paradoxes of the 'wild' Romantic Rhine is that the tourist destination required a controlled and predictable river that could handle the increasing number of tourist boats steaming up its currents. Hence, perpetuation of the Rhine's Romantic image meant that the river needed to be made into a safe and efficient highway for a different type of commerce as the Rhine itself became a lucrative commodity. The vistas these visitors saw were far from being untouched by humans; any notion that the river ran untamed arose from high Romantic fantasy. In addition to the castles, tollbooths, and majestic ruins on every bend, extensive dredging and blasting were required to make the river safe for the tourists who flooded onto it (Blackbourn 2008: 18).

However, the narrative of the Rhine as a picturesque natural wonder gained a permanent place in the European imagination, and once established this idea would flower into the early murmurs of a nascent environmental consciousness. As Samuel Taylor Coleridge wrote in his poem 'Cologne' as early as 1828:

> The river Rhine, it is well known,
> Doth wash your city of Cologne;
> But tell me, Nymphs, what power divine
> Shall henceforth wash the river Rhine?

Coleridge's question would not be answered until the mid-twentieth century, when pollution as an imminent threat to the river entered political discourse. By then, hydroelectric dams would also chock the river. Martin Heidegger described a hydroelectric plant built on the Rhine as a 'monstrousness' that fundamentally altered the essence of the river, transforming it from the Rhine of Romantic art into merely 'a water power supplier – that derives from the essence of the power station' (quoted in Cioc 2002: 46). However, these critical themes in Coleridge's and Heidegger's writings did not reach the chambers of the Rhine Commission which, throughout the nineteenth century, continued to view the river solely as an inter-European commercial highway, and its own role as one of facilitating smoother navigation and trade. The commission was successful in pursuing this goal. As Cioc observes, 'this single-mindedness of purpose – the promotion of trade through improved navigation – allowed the Rhine commissioners to achieve their goals effectively and efficiently; in less than a century, they transformed the Rhine into a world-class commercial waterway' (2013: 26). At the start of the twenty-first century, the Rhine remains the second busiest commercial artery in the world.

Afterward: the consequences of Tulla's conquest from barbarism

Tulla's rectification project officially began in 1817 and lasted until the 1870s. Tulla's project was followed by similar schemes in Prussia, the Netherland's Rhine delta, and the Swiss Alpine stretch, which focused on navigation as well as flood control. Through these projects, the Rhine was measured and disciplined despite local resistance and even violence between villagers and the implementing authorities. At first, Tulla's project successfully created a stable river and turned riverside swamps into arable land, prime real estate, and ideal plots for new factories. However, unintended consequences soon surfaced. Tulla's plan had only intended to deepen the river by one meter, but riverbed erosion deepened it by up to six or seven meters in some locations, creating dangerous rapids and other navigational difficulties that had to be corrected with further projects (Cioc 2002: 54). Following his trip along the Rhine in the late eighteenth century, Johann Goethe had lyrically described the forty-five species of fish that made the upper Rhine their home, including salmon, shad, and sturgeon. Rhine rectification projects combined with factories and steamboats disrupted quiet resting pools and breeding grounds necessary to replenish fish stocks, altering the fishing industry along the river. The Rhine's faster currents also put an end to the gold deposits that once washed up on the river's gravel banks (Blackbourn 2006: 98–101). Addressing these environmental consequences, however, would require policymakers to reimagine the Rhine as a different type of geographical space – an understanding that diverged from their vision of the ideal river as a straight and rational economic highway.

Not only did Tulla's ambitious rectification project destroy wetland habitats, adversely affect breeding grounds for migratory fish, and end gold extraction; the project ironically did not achieve its intended goal of flood control. After damaging floods struck the middle and lower Rhine in 1824, Prussia submitted a request to the German Confederation to examine Tulla's rectification project. The nascent Rhine Commission was still stymied by political impasse and working to establish its formal apparatus, so the German Confederation established an ad hoc committee that included the united Netherlands to discuss Tulla's plan. This ad hoc committee met a dozen times in 1832 (Cioc 2013: 36). By then, Tulla had died in Paris and was buried in Montmartre Cemetery in 1828 with a schematic representation of Rhine rectification on his tombstone (Figure 2.2) – an eternal celebration of the German engineer's determined battle to tame the unruly forces of nature.

At the ad hoc commission, engineers and bureaucrats argued for and against Tulla's plans. As critic Fritz André contended in a treatise published in 1828, Tulla and his engineers should have known that without allowing the floodplain in the upper Rhine to absorb the Alpine spring melt, floods downstream would become more intense. André wrote: 'If the Upper Rhine is rectified as completely as envisaged by the Tulla Project, it will create a shorter and swifter current that will cause all of Germany's rivers to reach their peak discharge at or about the same time' (quoted in Cioc 2013: 35). Flooding along the upper Rhine had acted as a delay that syncopated the rush of spring melt; without it, the melt along the Rhine's tributaries all peaked at once and hit downstream locations with increased force (Cioc 2002: 69–70). Deliberations raged on and the ad hoc commission failed to reach a scientific consensus on whether society or nature was responsible for the floods – and Tulla's rectification plan proceeded as before. Thus, as Timothy Mitchell observed, technocratic hubris has a self-reinforcing logic where failures results in adjustments that reinforce rather than rethink the existing models responsible for the failures in the first place (2002: 41–2). The only way to correct the unintended consequences of the first project was through additional rectification projects that sought to marshal even more sweeping scientific plans to make the river an even more rational highway.

In the final act of Goethe's *Faust, Part II* (1832), the protagonist is given a piece of coastal land deemed useless. Faust cleverly drains the 'noisome bog' and creates an earthly paradise where 'man and beast, in green and fertile fields, will know the joys that new-won region yields'. However, the 'fierce devouring flood' eats away at his conquest and forces Faust to continue his labors and 'daily conquer it anew' (Act V). Here, Goethe pinpoints the Faustian bargain that underpinned nineteenth-century river-rectification projects to tame the river and make conquests from barbarism. The river

Figure 2.2 Johann Tulla's tombstone in Montmartre cemetery, Paris

has its own logic that often eludes technological conquest, and the myth of society's absolute ability to command nature needs to be perpetually reasserted at every turn.

Conclusion

The conceptualization of the Rhine as an economic highway that ought to be tamed for the moral and fiscal benefits of European international society formed the intellectual backdrop to the 1815 Congress of Vienna's International Rivers Committee as a crucial moment in international politics. This imaginary of the ideal river drew on high modernism and its confidence in science's ability to transform nature into economically productive and morally progressive objects of governance. Indeed, in the eighteenth and early nineteenth centuries, the ability to tame the river for the benefit of society became a hallmark of the legitimate modern state that could not only control but improve territories within its domain. The double moral and economic logics that informed projects to master the Rhine contributed both to local state-building as well as the creation of the oldest continuous interstate institution and the early development of global governance.

A 24-year-old Johann Tulla wrote in his diary: 'Most hydro-technicians have studied the effects of engineering works on a river only on the surface' (quoted in Blackbourn 2006: 81). Tulla intended to also study river hydraulics beneath the surface, and his Rhine rectification plan exemplified his commitment to view the river as a holistic engineering system. By beginning my analysis of the 1815 Rhine Commission with an exploration into the sociological undercurrents that informed and enabled its creation, I follow Tulla in an effort to look beyond the formal diplomatic negotiations in the halls of Vienna. Underneath the surface of a seemingly perfunctory and technocratic discussion flowed the social and intellectual undercurrents of the Enlightenment and Second Scientific Revolution, which framed society's understanding of its relationship with the natural world. This relationship conceived of the untamed river as a danger to both the moral and political health of surrounding populations and necessitated a rational political solution to correct and tame the unruly river for society's benefit. By centering the Rhine and the co-constitution between the river and society in this analysis, the river becomes more than just a backdrop to international politics and becomes instead an important animating force in the story of early global governance.

Notes

1 'It is difficult for us the French to understand the deep reverence Germans have for the Rhine ... for them, the Rhine is a universal emblem; the Rhine is might; the Rhine is independence; the Rhine is freedom ... it is an object of fear or hope; symbol of hate or love, principle of life and death. For it is a source of poetry' (Dumas 1842: 101).

2 German cameralism, or the science of administration, had a French equivalent in the seventeenth-century economic policies of Jean-Baptiste Colbert, who sought to rationalize all economic activities and focused these activities on improving the fiscal standing of the French state.

3 At first, Frederick II of Baden sided against Napoleon from 1792 to 1805. In 1805, Baden switched sides and fought with Napoleon, gaining territory after the Peace of Pressburg (1805) and the Peace of Vienna (1809) and joined Napoleon's Confederation of the Rhine. In 1813, after the Battle of Leipzig, Baden switched sides again, landing on the victorious side at the Congress of Vienna. As Talleyrand famously quipped at the Congress, 'Treason is a matter of dates.'

4 This point should not be overstated. Not all of Baden's actions led to cooperation over Rhine rectification – in the mid-nineteenth century, Baden fought to delay works on the Mannheim to Strasbourg section of the river in an effort to protect

Mannheim's status as the start of the navigable river (Clapp 1911: 18). However, for the most part, the rationalization of the Rhine into a tame and predictable highway coincided with Baden's interests.

5 These illegal tolls were often granted legal status by the emperor after they were created.

6 Clapp (1911) claims that 29 stations operated between Strasbourg and the Dutch border. Spaulding argues that while Prussian reports at the Peace of Luneville (9 February 1801) recorded 29 stations, 16 on the right and 13 on the left bank, Eberhard Gothein's number of 32 is the more accepted figure (Spaulding 2007).

3

The 1815 Congress of Vienna and the oldest continuous interstate institution

The 1815 Congress of Vienna is often seen by historians and political scientists alike as a turning point in European politics, with lasting consequences for international security and order. In this chapter, I examine one of the Congress's lesser-known outcomes – the creation of the Central Commission for the Navigation of the Rhine – to interrogate the extent to which the Congress and the Rhine Commission represented a new direction for European politics. Two opposing forces framed the Congress of Vienna and its stance toward cooperation over transboundary rivers. First, diplomats conservatively aimed to restore a pre-Napoleonic social order that had been overturned by French Revolutionary politics. But at the same time, diplomats wished to improve Europe's political order to maintain balance and forestall future political chaos – and in the case of the Rhine, they felt the pull of Enlightenment confidence in European civilized society's ability to control the river as well as centuries of irrational river politics. Controlling the Rhine would guarantee free trade to the economic benefit of all, but it would also transform European politics into a more orderly and rational arena of diplomatic engagement.

To satisfy the impulse for restoration and reform, an awkward compromise had to be struck between three existing legal interpretations of the transboundary river: the river as the private property of the sovereign state; the river as shared commons between riparian states; and the river as international commons that ought to be open to all on the basis of equality. Medieval Rhenish politics had assumed the first interpretation while Napoleon forced the adoption of the second, as the Rhine became the shared property of France and the Holy Roman Empire. At Vienna, liberal forces led by British diplomats pushed for the third interpretation. For subsequent commentators who look back on the Treaty of Vienna as the moment when freedom of navigation and trade along the transboundary river entered into international law, and consider the Rhine Commission to be the first international organization, it would be easy to conclude that the third liberal interpretation of the river clearly won out. However, a detailed examination of the contingent politics of the Congress's deliberations shows that the 1815 Rhine Commission was largely a return to the pre-Revolution interpretation of the river as private property. But there was a liberal twist – the Congress also adopted good neighborly principles and created a consultative body to implement rational and sensible regulations based on the understanding of the Rhine as a European commercial artery. This twist speaks to the importance of imaginaries of the Rhine as an internal European highway that ought to be open to commerce. But the incomplete adoption of liberal principles cautions us not to overestimate social forces for change and underestimate political resistance that made the construction of the ideal river far from certain or irreversible.

This story of the creation of the 1815 Rhine Commission questions two simplistic narratives sometimes told about it. The first is that the commission represented a clean break from the irrational competition of the medieval past and ushered in the modern era of international cooperation. Instead, the complex history of cooperation and conflict along the Rhine and the ways in which the 1815 commission represents a return to medieval politics challenges this teleological view. The second, and relatedly, is that the commission was a straightforward victory for technocratic cooperation that went beyond longstanding political rivalries to secure benefits for all. Instead, debates in the committee were highly political and contested. The political context of the post-Napoleonic moment complicated the progress of liberal economic norms and led to a hybrid solution rather than an outright victory for the river as a rational international highway. The aim here is not to argue that the Congress of Vienna's International Rivers Committee and the creation of the Rhine Commission were not important moments, but rather to challenge the ways in which historical narratives often tell too clean a story of progress, and obscure the messy, contingent politics behind even a powerful idea such as the ideal river.

Cooperation, Napoleon, and the institutional origins of the Rhine Commission

Despite its status as the first intergovernmental organization (Reinalda 2009), the Central Commission for the Navigation of the Rhine has received surprisingly limited attention from IR scholars. Much of the existing scholarship has an underlying liberal narrative that celebrates the Rhine's transformation from the playground of fractious medieval lords who stood in the way of free trade into a rational commercial highway with the removal of these barriers to trade. Economist Edwin Clapp praised early nineteenth-century changes on the Rhine as liberation so that 'the real development of the river traffic' could begin (1911: 10). Joseph P. Chamberlain,[1] whose scholarship on the legal details of the Rhine and Danube commissions are referenced heavily in this book, reveals in the preface of his volume on the Rhine and Danube that his work was commissioned by the United States to study the question of peace and the harmonization of interests between states (1923: 50). Robert Spaulding (1999) characterizes the events that led to the creation of the 1815 Rhine Commission as an example of the evolution from international anarchy to hegemony to cooperation. However, a closer examination of the history behind the creation of the Rhine Commission shows that these accounts overemphasize the commission as a historical break. Cooperation along the river did not begin with 1815.

While no overarching organization united the Germanic peoples during the Roman era, these groups were able to come together to ambush and decisively defeat a Roman army under Publius Quinctilius Varus in 9 CE in the Teutoburg forest. This defeat stopped the Romans at the Rhine and prompted Emperor Augustus to strengthen his forts along the river at Cologne, Mainz, and Strasbourg (Wells 2003: 15) – cities that would dominate Rhine politics in the following centuries. In the ninth century, under Charlemagne, the western part of the Roman Empire was renamed the Holy Roman Empire, a limited political framework that oversaw principalities numbering in the hundreds by the eighteenth century. The Empire was a complex entity that differed from other European monarchies in the early modern period in that individual 'princes and other subordinate corporations and individuals retained a far greater degree of autonomy from the monarch', with limited power to levy taxes, raise armies, and regulate society (Whaley 2012: 2). However, local princes lacked absolute sovereignty and were subject to the Empire's overarching policies and laws.

In the mid-thirteenth century, political turmoil following the death of Frederick II and the collapse of the Hohenstaufen authority allowed local strongmen to foment chaos and extract illegal taxes along the river. In 1254, cities starting with Mainz and Worms, and growing to 70 members to include all the major Rhine river towns, united in the League of Rhenish Cities to establish order and maintain safe passage. While the League also claimed the protection of church property as part of its mission, its primary purpose was the protection of merchant interests. King William of Holland recognized the League, which boasted an army and a river fleet reportedly numbering a hundred boats (Engelhardt 1879: 24). The League dissolved after a number of years and its military forces were disbanded, but informal cooperation remained an important practice along the Rhine.[2] Another decline in the Holy Roman Empire's authority in the fourteenth century created the political space for the four electors along the Rhine – the archbishops of Cologne, Mainz, and Treves (Trier), who had also been a part of the League a century before, and the elector of Palatine – to conclude an agreement in 1354 to regulate tolls and maintain towpaths along the Rhine. The agreement was formalized through a treaty in 1506 with the objective of standardizing toll collection and guaranteeing the safety of merchants, provided they paid the toll. A council met regularly to discuss navigation problems, and the four electors made an effort to jointly maintain infrastructure and police the river (Engelhard 1879: 26–7; Chamberlain 1923: 152–3). They went so far as to sue Cologne and Mainz in the Empire's court to end the two cities' monopolies on the Rhine – a suit that went undecided for 92 years until Napoleon dissolved the Holy Roman Empire in 1806 (Spaulding 2007: 12). Hence, while the river that revolutionary France occupied in the late eighteenth century was very much the world of Teutonic insanity, with excessive tolls and competing authorities as described in the previous chapter, the Rhine was also a fertile political space for testing and refining cooperative frameworks. Both laid the groundwork for the establishment of the Rhine Commission.

As its revolutionary armies swept east, France's attention turned toward dismantling the longstanding aristocratic power structures of central Europe and establishing liberal regimes in their place. One area for liberalization was along international rivers such as the Rhine and Scheldt. In fact, in 1648, Holy Roman Emperor Joseph II had tried to liberalize the Scheldt by forcing the Dutch to open the river to freedom of navigation and trade. He failed (Kaeckenbeeck 1918: 31). Following Joseph II, when the French Republic invaded the Netherlands in 1792, the executive council issued a decree opening the Scheldt and the Meuse to freedom of navigation. It stated that 'the stream of a river is the common, inalienable property of all the countries which it bounds or traverses'. The 1795 Treaty of The Hague between Holland and France confirmed this principle and applied it to the Rhine, and the principle was then reinforced by the treaties of Munster, Ryswick, and Baden (Kaeckenbeeck 1918: 32–3; Chamberlain 1923: 158–9). This principle of common ownership between riparian states, while a departure from past views of the river as an individual state's property, was not quite the later norm that an international river should be a shared geographical space open to all of humankind – that interpretation would remain debated and contested throughout the nineteenth century. And yet this principle of common ownership was revolutionary in that it threatened the individual rights of local authorities to tax and regulate river traffic based on their individual whims and needs.

As expected, local Rhenish authorities resisted efforts to standardize tolls and break the monopolies that boatmen's guilds had held for centuries. With the Congress of Rastadt in 1798, France gained control of the river's left bank and aimed to abolish tolls on goods and open up free navigation to foreign vessels – the other Rhine states objected to this as an encroachment on their sovereignty and the congress ended in stalemate. After Napoleon Bonaparte took over the French state in November 1799, he championed the same principles, which were again proposed at the 1802 Conference of Ratisbon. Finally, in Paris on 15 August 1804, Napoleon and the arch-chancellor of the Holy Roman Empire, Karl Theodor von Dalberg, signed an agreement known as the Octroi Convention. This convention standardized regulations along the Rhine and created a joint France–German body, the Magistracy of the Rhine, to enforce the new regulations and supervise engineering projects (Chamberlain 1923: 164–5; Spaulding 2007; Cioc 2013: 29). The convention abolished monopolies and excessive tolls. It also declared the river the common property of both empires and that 'its navigation shall be subject to common regulations' (Kaeckenbeeck 1918: 34). Hence, perhaps it was Napoleon's Magistracy rather than the 1815 Congress of Vienna that marked the beginning of the world's oldest intergovernmental organization.

In the progressive Enlightenment spirit of the French Revolution, the Magistracy sought to govern the Rhine based on rational principles. This shifted the legitimate political authority to tax and regulate river traffic to a cooperative interstate body. The Magistracy was an independent administrative organization headed by a director-general jointly appointed by France and the Holy Roman Empire to supervise toll collection, maintain towpaths, and police navigation from Switzerland to the Dutch border. The director-general was aided by four assistants – two to represent France on the west bank and two to represent the German states on the east. Any disagreements would be discussed at an annual meeting in Mainz.

The Magistracy went to work immediately. It established three classes of goods and reduced toll stations to twelve – six on each bank. The 1804 agreement required authorities to use the toll revenue to maintain infrastructure rather than to fill state coffers as had been the practice previously (Chamberlain 1923; Van Eysinga 1935: 10; Spaulding 2007). The French sent Charles Coquebert-Montbret to oversee the creation of the Magistracy; he not only set up the body as defined by the agreement but also established procedures for legal appeals, dispute settlement, and trials to enforce the newly standardized regulations (Spaulding 2007: 17). The Magistracy set up administration centers at Cologne and Mainz – cities which, ironically, had historically been centers of resistance to the Rhine's liberalization.

The Octroi Convention's attempt to liberalize and rationalize the Rhine based on a new definition of the transboundary river as the shared property of riparian states was pioneering. However, as this brief outline of Rhine history demonstrates, the Magistracy was not the first attempt to build a cooperative framework along the river. It would be inaccurate to mark the

Magistracy as the first wave of liberal rationality that swept away the archaic practices of a medieval past. Rather, the Magistracy was at the same time a liberal system aimed at regulating the river as a European economic highway and an imperial system imposed by a hegemonic French power to control the river. The new body was as much a result of liberal principles as the French Empire's interest in standardized tolls and efficient navigation, both a product France's need to work with and compete against German rulers along the Rhine.

The Magistracy was very short-lived. In 1806, the Holy Roman Empire dissolved, effectively ending the Octroi Convention. With Napoleon's forced abdication in 1814 and the dismantling of the French Empire, Napoleon's reforms along the Rhine were also in danger of disappearing. At the 1815 Congress of Vienna, the major underlying question for diplomats was how to rebalance Europe to forge a more stable European order. The question before the International Rivers Committee, then, was which French reforms to keep and how much to walk back from French innovations on the Rhine in order to maintain European peace and security.

Of interests and zeitgeist: forces shaping the Congress

The creation of the Rhine Commission was shaped by three political objectives at the Congress of Vienna: first, the notion of balance or equilibrium in central Europe to limit French and Russian power; second, Prussia's ambition for territorial gains to become the foremost German state; and lastly, an emerging notion that European states should collectively work for the common good (see Mitzen 2013), particularly when it came to security and economic gain. Negotiating between the first two pushed for a return to political arrangements as they were before Napoleon, while the last, shaped by social and intellectual forces outlined in Chapter 2, suggested a new way of conceptualizing the transboundary Rhine and a new type of interstate body to govern it.

The four Great Powers at the Congress of Vienna – Britain, Austria, Russia, and Prussia – arrived with their own security agendas and desired territorial settlements, along with a general concern for restoring some form of equilibrium to Europe's geopolitical landscape. Of these players, Russia had the largest population, territory, and standing army, but diplomatic ineptitude and the combined interests of other powers barred it from achieving its main objective of annexing Poland (Chapman 1998: 23–4). Prussia aimed to increase and consolidate its territories to establish control over northern Germany (Jarrett 2013). However, Prussia lacked leverage as it had been sidelined from the war since its 1806 defeat by Napoleon at Jena. Prior to the conference and without the other powers, Russia and Prussia had agreed to the 1813 Treaty of Kalisch by which Russia would annex Poland and Prussia would gain Saxony. Disagreement over this treaty almost triggered war between the powers in January 1815 as Britain, Austria, and France signed a secret agreement to oppose Russia's and Prussia's territorial ambitions with force if necessary (Nicolson 1946: 176–9). Territorial gains and particularly the status of Saxony dominated Prussian efforts at the Congress, as is evidenced in Prussian diplomat Wilhelm von Humboldt's lengthy letters to his wife.

The wish for a balance in central Europe united Austria and Great Britain. Austria entered the war against Napoleon late – not until 1813 – and therefore lacked diplomatic leverage, despite being ably represented by the incomparable Klemens von Metternich. Napoleon's liberal political ideas threatened the precarious internal unity of the multiethnic Austrian Empire just as a strong France and Russia loomed threateningly for Austrian foreign policy. Metternich couched his call for a strong central Europe in what he termed a 'just equilibrium' – a concept that squared well with Britain's aim for a balance of power in Europe (Chapman 1998: 17). With a diplomatic team headed by Lord Castlereagh, Britain wanted a balance in central Europe to prevent any possible French invasion of England. To achieve this, Castlereagh worked to establish a united Low Countries of the Netherlands and Belgium as a single state closely allied to Britain under the House of Orange (Nicolson 1946: 206–8). This combined state would have unforeseen consequences for the Rhine Commission. From 1815 until Belgium declared independence in 1831, the United Netherlands' refusal to accept free navigation on the Rhine would slow liberalization along the river. In addition, in compensation for not allowing Prussia to swallow all of Saxony, the Congress granted Prussia half of the east bank of the Rhine and a large part of Westphalia as part of a buffer zone (known as the *cordon sanitaire*) against future French aggression. This territorial concession made Cologne a Prussian city and Prussia the largest state along the Rhine. From that moment onward, Prussian attitudes toward the river would be inseparable from its ambition to lead a unified Germany. These historically contingent factors would shape the cast and contours of the political contest that played out over the Rhine Commission.

In addition to a balance on continental Europe, Great Britain aimed to promote political and particularly economic liberalism to include the abolition of the slave trade, freedom of the seas, and free trade along international rivers (Chapman 1998: 20). Britain was victorious at sea against Napoleon, a fact that allowed it to maintain lucrative international trade routes, contest Napoleon's Continental System, and capture most of France's overseas colonies. Stability in Europe would allow Britain to freely pursue political and economic gains internationally. Liberalizing European rivers and transforming them into efficient economic highways would allow Britain to expand its markets within continental Europe as well.

France arrived at Vienna defeated, and the restored Bourbon monarchy viewed damage control as its first priority. Throughout the proceedings, the French diplomatic team headed by Charles Talleyrand – an experienced diplomat who had worked for the French Republic, Napoleon, and now the reestablished Louis XVIII – cleverly argued that the restored Bourbon monarchy would lose legitimacy if the Great Powers punished France too harshly, as the Prussian general staff wished. Talleyrand's appeal spoke convincingly to diplomats' desire to restore a pre-Napoleonic political order and doubled as a veiled threat hinting at the revolutionary forces that still simmered in French politics (Jarrett 2013: 64). Further, squabbles between the Great Powers over territorial settlements gave France an opportunity to reassert itself, and it emerged from Vienna having made relatively light territorial concessions, and therefore maintaining its riparian status on the banks of the Rhine. As part of its strategy to maintain its influence, the French would push to keep Napoleon's reforms along the Rhine as a cooperative framework.

The particular geopolitical fears and interests of the Great Powers shaped how they viewed the peace conference. However, diplomats at the Congress did not deliberate in a vacuum, with only political interests driving their actions. Recent historiography has highlighted the importance of the Congress's intense social obligations in shaping interactions and fomenting interpersonal rivalries between key diplomats (Jarrett 2014; Sluga 2015). In addition, as the top echelon of educated European society, diplomats at Vienna were also inevitably products of wider social and intellectual milieus that influenced their thinking, particularly the intellectual undercurrent that shaped their understanding of the natural world. As historian Paul Johnson eloquently wrote:

> And here we must pause to note that statesmen, however much they may think they are guided by the unalterable laws of realpolitik and national self-interests, are in fact as much influenced by cultural trends and fashions as everyone else. Castlereagh, Metternich, Talleyrand and Alexander lived in the same world as Beethoven and Byron, Turner and Victor Hugo, and felt the same intellectual breezes on their cheeks. (1991: 111)

Hence, while diplomats at Vienna were concerned about territorial gains and containing France, their thinking was also shaped by the intellectual forces of the Second Scientific Revolution that combined Romantic sensibilities with a driving faith in rationality and scientific progress. Diplomats' attitude toward freedom of navigation and commerce on the Rhine partially hinged on their geopolitical fears and interests, but was also informed by one of the prevailing ideas of the age: that taming the river would bring moral and economic benefits to European society.

One prominent example of how the intellectual trends of the age entered the committee rooms of Vienna was in the person of the Prussian representative Wilhelm von Humboldt. He was the most active member of the Congress of Vienna's International Rivers Committee which established the Rhine Commission. He was also the brother of naturalist and explorer Alexander von Humboldt, who journeyed up the Rhine in 1789 and wrote a treatise on the mineralogy of basalts along the river before heading further afield to Russia and the Americas. Both grew up tutored in Enlightenment ideas; in fact, with the onset of the French Revolution, their first tutor, Joachim Heinrich Campe, ran off to France to witness 'the funeral of French despotism' (Bauer 2012: 27; Wulf 2015: 96). Pursuing politics rather than the natural sciences, Wilhelm became a noted humanist who corresponded with luminaries including Goethe and Schiller. Later, he would be credited with the reform of the German educational system and the establishment of the modern research university, in which 'the institutionalization of discovery was integrated with teaching for the first time' (Watson 2010: 226). This new system represented an understanding of the role that knowledge plays in society that embodied the spirit of the Second Scientific Revolution. At Vienna, Humboldt was admired for his powers of reasoning, which, one newspaper article stated, was as 'cold and clear as a December sun' (Bauer 2012: 347). Humboldt's views of how the Congress should approach transboundary rivers, then, cannot be sealed off from these broader intellectual commitments to scientific rationality and its role in bettering society. Rather, the scientific and Romantic spirit of the times seeped into the formal conference chambers.

The Congress of Vienna and the International Rivers Committee

By all accounts, the Congress of Vienna was an impressive affair, with more than 200 delegations in attendance, and except for the final plenary meeting, negotiations took place in smaller committees and during the Congress's never-ending array of social functions (Reinalda 2009: 18). As one of the smaller committees, the International Rivers Committee met 12 times between 2 February and 27 March 1815. The committee included the four Great Powers with interests on the Rhine – France, Britain, Austria, and Prussian – and all the riparian states (Nicolson 1946: 217).[3] Commentators looking back on the International Rivers Committee marked it as a critical juncture for the evolution of norms governing freedom of navigation and commerce along international rivers. At the 1856 Paris Conference, the Austrian representative Count Karl Ferdinand von Buol would reflect on the Congress of Vienna as a decisive moment when the European community adopted two moral ideas – the abolition of the slave trade and the free navigation of rivers (Thayer 1917: 39). In C. K. Webster's 1919 account of the Congress written for the British Foreign Office, amid a scathing paragraph on the statesmen's limited outlook and lack of faith and courage, Webster identifies 'regulation of International Rivers' as one of the minor points on which the statesmen 'did much for the future government of Europe' (1919: 148). In their work on European rulemaking, Wolfram Kaiser and Johan Schot describe the Congress's general principle regarding international rivers as a revolutionary idea that 'signaled a new interest in stimulating trade for the sake of progress and peace' (2014: 113). According to these diverse accounts, then, the committee's work represented a turning point when actors adopted the norm of freedom of navigation and commerce on international rivers and established the first international river regime on the Rhine.

A closer look at the diplomatic discussions in the International Rivers Committee, however, suggests a less straightforward story of normative innovation. Rather than a clear-cut moment of progress toward a liberal global governance regime, what emerged was actually a step backward from the liberal reforms begun by the French. The committee did not adopt an institutional body with the independent authority to rise above fractious river politics – a point that will be driven home later in this chapter by the United Netherlands' recalcitrance in following through on any reforms. The committee also rejected the notion that the transboundary river is not the private property of individual sovereign states but joint property or international commons. As Humboldt noted, under the agreement, 'no riparian State should be disturbed in the exercise of the rights of sovereignty' (Kaeckenbeeck 1918: 44). Discussions in the committee and afterward show that, far from being a unanimous agreement on liberal norms to govern all international rivers, the outcome was ambiguous and open to interpretation and manipulation.

However, the committee was not a complete rejection of French reforms either. Diplomats debated how best to engage with Napoleon's sensible liberal reforms on the Rhine – what Humboldt described as 'a very good piece of work, the utility of which has been proved by experience' (Kaeckenbeeck 1918: 43) – without the unsavory baggage of French revolutionary ideology. They agreed that some standardized regulations should govern navigation on the Rhine in an effort to make the river a more efficient highway, and they tried to end the system of tolls and monopolies that had hindered free navigation of the river. These reforms rested on the vision of an improved Rhine as a road to European peace and prosperity.[4] Hence, in order to achieve both aims, the committee reached an awkward hybrid compromise to adopt some liberal economic reforms and establish a weak consultative institution in the Rhine Commission, while returning to a pre-Napoleonic understanding of the transboundary river informed by balance of power politics. But in establishing an institutional framework on the Rhine, the committee did make it possible for the body to evolve and gain competencies in the late nineteenth and early twentieth centuries and become an inspiration for other transboundary rivers.

The forgotten politics of technocrats

The International Rivers Committee barely warrants a mention in most histories of the Congress of Vienna, perhaps because aside from a handful of international lawyers, commentators have overlooked the salience of its deliberations. After all, more explosive political stakes occupied the Congress during the early months of 1815, including intense negotiations over territorial gains and losses and Napoleon's escape from Elba on 26 February. Compared to this high drama, technocrats debating navigation regulations along the Rhine seemed quotidian and dull – a subject only for those interested in bureaucratic minutiae rather than politics that mattered. Mark Jarrett's 400-page book on the Congress barely dedicates a sentence to the committee. He combines international rivers and a uniform system of ranks between diplomats as 'an instructive demonstration of what could be achieved through conference diplomacy, honest negotiation and a willingness to compromise' (2013: 146). Harold Nicolson's classic analysis of the Congress of Vienna only offers a paragraph and a less sanguine account of the political machinations that played out in the committee. Nevertheless, he characterizes the International Rivers Committee's accomplishments as 'definite and effective' (1946: 216). How could a committee be both too insignificant to describe in historical detail but at the same time a definitive accomplishment and an example of what could be achieved by good diplomacy?

Similarly, IR scholarship on the Congress of Vienna focuses on the balance of power, collective action, the Concert system, security commitments, and hegemonic interests, but largely leaves out freedom of navigation and the creation of the first international body to govern the Rhine (Holsti 1992; Schroeder 1994; Ikenberry 2001; Mitzen 2013). John Ikenberry argues that Britain's hegemonic leadership forged the post-war order by locking actors into subsequent collective security institutions (2001: 80–116). Jennifer Mitzen contends that the Congress innovatively persuaded its members that European public interests could only be preserved through the collective intentionality of public power channeled through consultative forums – 'these states committed themselves to replacing the individualistic norms of the eighteenth-century balance of power system, where European order was produced by an invisible hand, with self-conscious, collective management, that is, with a more visible hand' (2013: 101). The creation of the Rhine

Commission might have been a good example of either, but aside from a footnote or as a line item on a list of the Congress's accomplishments (see Schroeder 1994: 573; Mitzen 2013: 88), the International Rivers Committee is invisible in these accounts.

This lack of commentary reflects the few words diplomats themselves wrote on the committee. In Wilhelm von Humboldt's letters to his wife Caroline – letters that were almost certainly monitored by Metternich's spies – he mentions the committee only at the end of a letter dated 23 February couched in complaints about the heaviness of his workload (Humboldt 1910: 486). The British representative Lord Clancarty's official correspondence also rarely mentioned the committee, and when he did it was also in connection with his impossible workload (FO 92/17, 1815: no. 743). In Talleyrand's correspondence with King Louis XVIII, only one sentence mentions his satisfaction with the adopted principles on river navigation (Talleyrand 1881: 19–20).

Reading between the lines, it seems that the International Rivers Committee might not have warranted much discussion because of the impression that such a technocratic body was a straightforward example of cooperation without the friction of politics. Mark Jarrett describes two members of the committee – France's Duke of Dalberg and Britain's Lord Clancarty – as the Congress's 'technocrats' who took a 'more consistent and scientific approach' (2013: 116). Both men also served on the Congress's Statistical Committee, which is framed as a technocratic body tasked with dividing the territorial spoils of war based on rational population science. Similarly, the International Rivers Committee's task was to decide on a functional framework for protecting and improving the Rhine as an economic highway. This technocratic designation, however, elides the deeply political nature of both committees' work, which shaped underlying ideas about how international truths might be judged and how international politics should be conducted. Furthermore, this 'technocratic' designation brackets the social forces that pushed for the use of technocratic methods as a rational and generalizable way to approach international affairs. In delving into the politics of the International Rivers Committee and its debates over three legal definitions of the transboundary river, I challenge the assumptions that the committee is an uninteresting subject of political analysis, or that due to its technocratic nature, its success was a foregone conclusion.

Three legal meanings of the international river

In February and March 1815, the International Rivers Committee discussed the nature of the interstate body that would manage the Rhine. It deliberated on the legal language of the preliminary treaty articles concluded at Paris, the status of tolls, boatmen's monopolies and compulsory transfers, and the amount of independent authority the eventual commission ought to have. Scholars have debated whether the Congress of Vienna represented a radical new conceptualization of international politics and cooperation (Jervis 1985; Schroeder 1994; Mitzen 2013) or a deeply conservative return to pre-Napoleonic power politics (Kagan 1998; Slantchev 2005). In the International Rivers Committee, the Congress was a largely conservative force that rolled back liberal reforms and returned Rhine politics to previous patterns of competition, but with a few notable exceptions – an end to tolls and monopolies, an effort to standardize river regulations, and the creation of a standing commission. These exceptions emerged from a collective understanding of the Rhine as an artery that must be kept free for the moral and economic benefit of society. It is an understanding of the river that speaks to the Enlightenment logic of taming and rationalizing nature for the good of society.

Legally, during feudalism, the transboundary river was treated as private property and few limits were placed on what landlords and local sovereigns could do to extract wealth from their river or whom they might bar from using it. This definition of the river, however, was challenged by two legal arguments – Roman law and the law of nature. Under Roman imperial law, rivers were considered *res publicae jure gentium* and 'a thing common to all'. The right to freely navigate, fish, and use the banks for loading and unloading belonged to all citizens (Kaeckenbeeck 1918: 6–7). Similarly, those who saw the law of nature as the legitimate source of international law, as laid out in the writings of Hugo Grotius and Emer de Vattel, also argued that the transboundary river should belong to all rather than to a specific sovereign. Drawing from reason rather than positive law, these natural law proponents argued that no one of any nation could be excluded from the use of inexhaustible things such as the sea and flowing water (Kaeckenbeeck 1918: 6–7). While this seemed like a technical legal dispute, where states stood on questions of international law reflected their geopolitical fears and interests. Throughout the committee's deliberations, diplomats used three subtly different definitions of the transboundary river – as sovereign private property, as joint property between riparian states, and as international commons – to play out political contests over control of the river. Each interpretation of the transboundary river would have different economic and political implications.

Early in the International Rivers Committee's proceedings in February and March 1815, French diplomat the Duke of Dalberg proposed a memo-randum as the basis of discussion that defined the Rhine as the joint property of all riparian states (Klüber 1819–36: 13)[5] – a definition based on Napoleon's Octroi Convention. At the following meeting, Lord Clancarty representing

Britain argued that Dalberg's proposal failed to reflect the principles of free navigation agreed to in the Paris Treaty. Instead, Clancarty suggested that free navigation and commerce on the Rhine should be extended to all nations, not just riparian states, and be forbidden to no one (Klüber 1819–36: 21). This dispute over subtle wording represented a deeper conflict. The British saw the river as a global commons and viewed free navigation and commerce on international rivers as the right of all people – a legal interpretation that stemmed from Britain's position as the only non-riparian state on the committee and from its commitment to liberal economic policies. The riparian states did not favor this view. According to Klüber's account, smaller states along the Rhine rejected both the common property and international right interpretations. Instead, they believed that the Paris Treaty's preliminary articles promising 'free navigation' only aimed to eliminate navigation obstacles such as sandbanks and 'did not give all subjects of non-riparian states an equal navigation right as those of riparian states and for which they cannot reciprocate' (Klüber 1819–36: 171). Riparian states did not wish to give away rights and power over the river with nothing in return. Hence, these states did not interpret the term *free* as an abstract universal principle but as meaning a river absent of physical obstacles.

Another example of this contestation over defining the river was the role of tolls. Clancarty proposed an amendment stating that tolls should not be viewed as a revenue source, and should only be collected to cover maintenance costs along the river (Klüber 1819–36: 171). Accepting this amendment meant that riparian states were custodians and caretakers rather than private owners of the river. Again, the riparian states disagreed – they were reluctant to sacrifice any advantage to the liberal notion of the Rhine as an open international highway. The theory of common ownership, however, fared no better as the committee rejected French attempts to establish a common toll office and maintain towpaths from a common fund. While they agreed that tolls should be standardized, states affirmed the old interpretation of the river as private property and decided that toll revenues would be divided according to the proportion of bank ownership. Towpaths remained the responsibility of each state individually.

Further, although the committee agreed to establish a body to oversee the river, the Rhine Commission itself would have little power. Rather than an independent body with the authority to enforce standard regulations along the entire river, the Rhine Commission would only be a consultative assembly of riparian states meeting every six months to discuss disputes over regulations (Klüber 1819–36: 83). Britain, as a non-riparian state, would not be granted a position on the Rhine Commission until the 1919 Versailles Treaty a century later. The only independent responsibility left to the commission, then, was a judicial one to decide cases, but since it would have no power to enforce outcomes, this power existed in theory rather than practice (Chamberlain 1923: 179–80). Hence, the commission would function as a consultative body that would in no way encroach on state sovereignty. Having agreed to these general principles, the committee left the drafting of regulations to the commission.

However, this was also not a straightforward victory for those who wished to revert to pre-Napoleonic definitions, since the smaller powers along the Rhine protested any permanent central organization. They feared that such a commission would be an infringement on their sovereign rights. In a dispatch from late March 1815, Count Georg Münster representing Nassau wrote to his sovereign regarding the International Rivers Committee: 'It seemed to me that this business was ill-digested, and I do not think myself called on to make sacrifice gratuitously, at your Royal Highness' expense, to favor some vague ideas on the liberty of commerce!' (Münster 2013 [1868]: 233).

In addition, the boatmen's monopolies operating out of Cologne, Mainz, and Strasburg became a point of political contestation. The committee invited representatives from Mainz and Frankfurt as well as M. Mappes, a former director-general of Napoleon's Magistracy, to present their case for and against traditional privileges. Interestingly, arguments for and against boatmen's monopolies were both framed in terms of rational economic interests. Frankfurt maintained that monopolies harmed competition and the free market – after all, 'a merchant knows his own interest'. In response, Mainz argued that the monopolies were good for global trade because they guaranteed speed and security for the transport of goods at a reasonable cost to merchants (Klüber 1819–36: 24). The committee sided with Frankfurt in favor of ending monopolies and traditional privileges. The Rhine might be the private property of sovereign states, but certain good neighbor principles must apply.

In the end, the committee adopted an awkward and ambiguous compromise. Article CIV of the Final Act of the Congress stated that 'the navigation of the rivers ... shall be entirely free, and shall not, in respect to commerce, be prohibited to anyone'. The ambiguity here is that 'shall be entirely free' can be interpreted in different ways – as an abstract principle or as a river free from physical obstructions. In fact, the phrase 'in respect to commerce' was inserted to narrow the scope of freedoms. Ultimately, the definition favored a return to river politics prior to the French Revolution. While riparian states agreed to streamline tolls and end monopolies in favor of more efficient commerce, they did not wish to define the Rhine as an open, international highway. Navigation rights, then, were a prerogative of riparian states, to be conferred on commerce of all nations at their discretion – it was not meant to be a declaration of natural law principles. However, control over private property must also conform to civilized rules to make commerce more rational, and the Rhine Commission was created to establish and oversee these rules. Despite the intentions of diplomats in the International Rivers Committee, the phrase 'entirely free' would take on a life of its own. The idea that rivers ought to be free for all entered into European law and would have lasting consequences, as the 'Vienna model' would be invoked again and again at subsequent diplomatic conferences, particularly by the British. This phrasing would, by the 1856 Paris diplomatic conference to end the Crimean War, be accepted as a declaration of universal principle, not just a description of a physical lack of obstacles.

A detailed study of the discussion and outcomes at Vienna largely shows that the International Rivers Committee did not decisively embrace new liberal norms nor introduce a revolutionary international institution. Instead, like the Congress itself, the committee was conservative and represented a retreat from Napoleonic reforms. Rather than the river as the joint property of riparian states or the common right of all humankind, the committee favored the rights of sovereign states to govern the river as they wished, and it was these sovereigns that allowed others the right of navigation and commerce at their discretion. However, the committee did not revert completely to the pre-Napoleonic status quo. Instead, diplomats decided to eliminate traditional privileges, streamline the tolls system, and create the Rhine Commission to resolve disputes between states. As a result, the committee produced a hybrid solution between the restoration of old practices – as necessitated by the conservative mood of post-Napoleonic European politics – and the adoption of sensible and rational French innovations. These innovations reaffirmed the river as a chaotic force that should be tamed and harnessed for the benefit of society, and they did so by erasing other dimensions of society's engagement with the river.

Legal simplification and the politics of erasure

Hidden in the formal, often opaque language of international law, the diplomatic agreement reached in the International Rivers Committee had important ramifications for European society's relationship with nature. The last chapter highlighted how Johann Tulla's Rhine rectification scheme flattened the river's curves and streamlined its multiple meanings into a one-dimensional economic object for the purpose of increasing a state's wealth as well as its moral and political legitimacy. A similar simplification took place at Vienna, which reduced international society's engagement with the Rhine to one of economics. In the Final Act, diplomats transformed the Rhine's messy history into a few lines that fixed the river as a commercial artery to the exclusion of all other aspects:

The navigation of the rivers, along their whole course, referred to in the preceding Article, from the point where each of them becomes navigable, to its mouth, shall be entirely free, and shall not, in respect to commerce, be prohibited to any one; it being understood that the regulations established with regard to the policing of this navigation, shall be respected; as they will be framed alike for all, and as favorable as possible to the commerce of all nations. (Article CIX)

Further, the Treaty granted the new Rhine Commission the power and responsibility 'to regulate, by common consent, all that regards its [the Rhine's] navigation'. Navigation regulations, duties, and policing along the river all reflected this single purpose: 'in order that no obstacle may be experienced to the navigation' of the river (Articles CVIII–CXVII). This legalistic language may seem mundane and impartial, but behind these taciturn sentences lurks the politics of erasure.

In simplifying the river into an economic object, the Treaty neglects other functions that are essential to international politics – the river as drinking water, as spiritual inspiration, as a habitat for wildlife, and as an essential resource for the health of human and nonhuman communities along its banks. Framing the international river as an economic highway was a political statement that elevated one dimension of the river, and therefore one set of policy tools to 'secure' the river, above everything else. It reduced river management to a question of profit and loss and created collective action impasses that ignored environmental degradation as long as commercial shipping continued unhindered. Beyond the Rhine, Vienna also paved the way for international relations to view other facets of the natural world – from rainforests to animal populations to the climate – through the single and simplified lens of short-term cost-benefit calculation. The consequences were often tragic. In the commission's first decades, the introduction of steamboats in 1816 and the growth of industry quickened the pace of economic extraction from and pollution of the river. By the 1970s, the Romantic Rhine was given another title: 'Europe's most Romantic sewer' (Loucks and Gladwell 1999: 49; Cioc 2002: 3).

In addition, the parsimonious language of the Treaty naturalizes this singular understanding of the river and erases hundreds of years of local conflict, cooperation, and resistance on the Rhine. If we understand freedom of navigation as the fixed norm 'enshrined' in the Final Act of the Congress, we miss the messy history of local politics on the Rhine and ignore the continued disagreements over how to interpret and govern the international river. We obscure the contingent politics of the post-Napoleonic moment that forged consensus and shaped the design of the commission. This simplification allowed later scholars to pinpoint the story of the Rhine as a linear narrative of forging cooperation from conflict. It transformed the

Rhine's particular history into a generalizable model for taming international rivers that could be applied across time and space. The remainder of this book examines this move with respect to two other rivers and exposes the myth of the generalizing model.

Continued resistance to the international river: 1815–31

The International Rivers Committee's hybrid solution did not end disagreement over how to define the transboundary river – and as this final illustration shows, it did not even end disagreement over whether sovereign states had the right to extract arbitrary tolls without international interference. Even as the ink dried on the Final Act of the Congress of Vienna, local actors along the Rhine continued to resist its conclusions. It would be over fifteen years before the 1831 Mainz Convention would give a clearer picture of how to apply the general principles established at Vienna.

Notwithstanding agreement at Vienna for states to cooperate in removing navigation obstacles such as unnecessary tolls and monopolies from the Rhine, it was easier said than done. The commission's first task was to draft new statutes for the river, but states worked to maintain their advantages, and this inaugural task took until 1831 to complete. The Dutch, supported by Baden and France, stood by their right to regulate trade at the Rhine's mouth into the North Sea. First, the Dutch claimed, the principles established at the Congress of Vienna were applicable 'jusqu'à la mer' or 'to the sea', and not *into* the sea. Therefore, the Dutch maintained the right to regulate and tax shipping that passed through their territorial waters between the Rhine proper and the open seas (Chamberlain 1923: 193).

When this first attempt at legal gymnastics failed, the Dutch tried a different tack: once the river entered the Rhine delta, only the branch still called the Rhine would be subject to the principles established at Vienna. Less than 20 kilometers upstream from Nijmegen in Holland, the river splits into three main branches: the Waal, the Lek, and the Ijssel. The Ijssel meanders north and enters the sea north of Amsterdam, while the Lek and the Waal flow west toward Rotterdam. The branch that retains the name Rhine is unnavigable and vanishes into the sand before even reaching the sea. At Vienna, the Dutch agreed that the Waal would be considered the continuation of the Rhine, but now they argued that the Waal ended at Gorinchem, and all else beyond was either the Meuse or part of Dutch territorial waters (Phillimore 1879: 237; Wheaton 1864: 350). By these two technicalities, the Dutch clung onto their right to unilaterally regulate shipping in the Rhine delta.

Austria and Britain protested repeatedly against the Netherlands' legal contortions to circumvent the Vienna agreement. At the 1821 Congress of

Verona, the Duke of Wellington, representing the British and supported by Austria, Prussia, and Russia, requested that the Netherlands abide by the principles agreed to at Vienna. At the 1822 Congress of Laybach, the British representative again protested against the Dutch. Austria wrote another protest in 1826 in strong language:

> It was inconceivable how the Government of the Netherlands could flatter itself with the hope of making a right obscure and doubtful by prolix observations on the main resolution, and to do away with the principle of free navigation of the Rhine, which was proclaimed in the face of the world in the first document of the political restoration of Europe, and on the same day when Holland was given up to the House of Orange. (Phillimore 1879: 239)

Not only did the Netherlands' arguments not pass the common-sense test, but it is portrayed here as being ungrateful and hypocritical. After all, the united Netherlands owed its existence to the Congress of Vienna, and now, after benefitting from the treaty, the Netherlands was turning against the spirit of the concordance. However, beneath the quibble over legal language was a quibble over power. The Dutch wanted to maintain the power to define the river as they wished – as their private territory subject to their regulations rather than as an international object under the administrative purview of the Rhine Commission, or managed for some vague notion of a greater global good.

In response, Prussia, with Cologne within its borders, and Hesse-Darmstadt with Mainz refused to give up their rights and boatmen's monopolies. If the Netherlands would not allow their boats access to the sea, then Cologne and Mainz would not allow free shipping up the river. France and the other German states, however, were more concerned about local trade along the Rhine than international trade into the sea and demanded that Cologne and Mainz end their now illegal privileges as stipulated by the Congress of Vienna. French trade bypassed the Netherlands completely through overland networks that directed traffic to French ports on the English Channel. Frustrated by Mainz, Frankfurt organized an overland service by wagon around the city (Chamberlain 1923: 194–6).

Therefore, a decade into the commission's life, political stalemate paralyzed the fledgling body and negotiations over the river were conducted bilaterally rather than through the commission. In 1820, France and Baden concluded an agreement to regulate the river between Strasburg and Basel, and Baden concluded another bilateral treaty with Bavaria in 1825 (Central Commission for the Navigation of the Rhine 1918: 165, 182). The United Netherlands softened its position as time dragged on, and in 1831 it disintegrated, with Belgium gaining independence. During this period, Prussia and the Netherlands turned to bilateral negotiations to hammer out a deal on how to proced and presented the settlement to the commission in 1829. This agreement became the 1831 Mainz Convention (Chamberlain 1923: 198). The treaty stipulated that the Rhine should be free from the point it became navigable into the sea ('bis in die See') and that the Waal and Lek rivers would both be considered the continuation of the Rhine (Phillimore 1879: 240). The traditional privileges of cities along the Rhine finally came to an end. In fact, all tolls soon disappeared altogether under Prussia's project of establishing a customs union across the German states. The attempt to define the Rhine as a German river, then, began to play its part in German unification.

However, even in this period of political impasse, it would be too simplistic to frame Rhine politics as only a politics of conflict. As Prussia and the Netherlands disagreed over interpretations of the Vienna Treaty and whether the Rhine constituted international or private property, they also cooperated under the understanding of the river as an economic highway. In October 1816, the two states agreed that if a sandbank appeared, they would cooperate on measures to protect shipping (Chamberlain 1923: 199). Hence, despite squabbling over control of the river, local states continued to be influenced by the understanding that the Rhine was a transboundary economic corridor and willingly cooperated to engineer a more efficient European highway.

Conclusion

The Congress of Vienna is rightly understood as an important moment in the evolution of European international society, and it marked the beginning of many important international agreements including freedom of navigation and commerce on international rivers. To address cooperation and conflict on the Rhine and other transboundary rivers, the Congress established the International Rivers Committee to decide whether Europe should continue the liberal reforms initiated by the French Revolution on rivers such as the Rhine and Scheldt, or step back from these reforms and return to the pre-Napoleonic status quo. To accommodate these opposing forces, the committee fashioned a hybrid and ambiguous solution that retained limited Napoleonic reforms to improve navigation while returning to the pre-war definition of the transboundary river as the private property of individual sovereign states. It created a weak interstate organization with the stated objective of standardizing navigation relations on the Rhine, but, as the United Netherlands' post-Congress recalcitrance illustrated, it had little power to enforce decisions. This mixed, and perhaps contradictory, outcome reflected both the conservative orientation of the Congress of Vienna and its intention to restore pre-Napoleonic balance to Europe, and the underlying intellectual ethos of the times which viewed the river as an unruly danger that ought to be tamed and rationalized for the benefit of international society.

While the core discussions in the International Rivers Committee revolved around legal definitions of the transboundary river as the private property of sovereign states, the joint property of riparian states, or an international commons, the outcomes had wider political implications. The Final Act of the Congress of Vienna may have tried to qualify the statement that the navigation of rivers 'shall be entirely free' and 'not be prohibited to anyone', but subsequent international actors would interpret this declaration of principle as the final word on how to understand the transboundary river – the ideal river as an economic highway that must be safeguarded for global commerce. This interpretation simplifies the messy political history along the Rhine and ignores local political contests over the meaning of the Rhine and other transboundary rivers long after the Congress had concluded. It overlooks the fact that this liberal vision of the ideal river did not win outright but only took hold precariously under ongoing resistance. To view the Final Act of Vienna as a radical international normative innovation invites the construction of a linear story of progress from conflict to cooperation.

Furthermore, the Final Act of the Congress of Vienna also frames and fixes the international river as an economic object to the detriment of the river's other roles in human and nonhuman communities. Importantly, this simplification not only harmed the Rhine but paved the way for international society to frame other facets of the natural world as questions of economic efficiency and legitimize cost-benefit analysis as the main arbiter of nature's value.

Notes

1 Joseph Perkins Chamberlain was an American lawyer and law professor at Columbia University from 1923 to 1950. He should not be confused with the prominent nineteenth-century British politician of the same name.
2 The League was not unique. According to historian Tom Scott, regional and temporary self-defense associations such as the League were commonplace across central Europe in the Middle Ages – these groups were usually created to address a threat and lasted only while the danger persisted (Scott 2012: 61).
3 The delegations on the International Rivers Committee were Austria, France, Baden, Bavaria, Hesse-Darmstadt, Nassau, Prussia, the Netherlands, and Britain.
4 For a detailed account of the Rhine Commission as an attempt to secure Europe, see Schenk (2020).
5 Johann Klüber was a law professor who was granted permission to attend the Congress of Vienna and collected information to publish eight volumes on its proceedings. Almost all the secondary sources that discuss the 1815 International Rivers Committee convened as part of the Congress of Vienna rely on Volume III of Klüber's work.

4

Disciplining the connecting river: constructing the Danube

> The Danube is the river along which different peoples meet and mingle and crossbreed, rather than being, as the Rhine is, a mythical custodian of the purity of the race.
>
> Claudio Magris, 1986

> Yet almost this river seems
> To travel backwards and
> I think it must come from the East
>
> Friedrich Hölderlin, 1803

Diplomats gathered at Vienna in 1855 and then in Paris in 1856 to negotiate a peace treaty to end the Crimean War. All parties agreed on four main points that must be addressed to restore order to European international society. The second point centered on establishing freedom of commerce and navigation at the Danube's mouth, based on principles outlined at the 1815 Congress of Vienna. However, taming the Danube was a fundamentally different task than taming the Rhine – not only because the Danube was a different river hydrologically, but also because it held different meanings in the intellectual and political imagination of mid-nineteenth-century Europeans. Like the Rhine, the Danube was seen as a commercial highway to be tamed and rationalized for a quickly industrializing Europe. However, unlike odes to the German or even the pan-European Rhine, depictions of the Danube celebrated the river as a conduit for free trade and civilization to flow from the heart of Europe outward. This chapter draws out this distinction and details the construction of the Danube in the Western geographical imagination.

Under the Roman Empire, the Danube represented the frontier that separated the civilized world from the barbarians, and since those times, no single power has governed the entire Danube valley. As the second longest river in Europe after the Volga, the Danube flows 2,860 kilometers from Germany's Black Forest to the Black Sea through ten current European countries: Germany, Austria, Slovakia, Hungary, Serbia, Croatia, Ukraine, Bulgaria, Moldova, and Romania. The Danube has seen the ebb and flow of many empires including the Roman, Ottoman, and Austro-Hungarian empires, the Third Reich, and the Soviet sphere of influence. The upper and lower Danube are divided by the Iron Gates – imposing rock formations that hindered navigation for centuries and currently form the border between Serbia and Romania. Near its mouth at Cernavodă in Romania, rather than heading straight into the Black Sea, the Danube turns north and slows down. At Galatz (Galați), the river again turns east to form the Danube delta. This hydrological quirk reduces the speed of the river and contributes to sediment buildup in the delta – navigational barriers that became the focus of nineteenth-century Anglo-Russian disputes over control of the river's mouth. If controlling the river was intended to secure and protect free trade and civilization, Russian inability or unwillingness to tame the river threw its civilizational status into question. Hence, the 1856 Paris Conference created an international commission to clear the river's clogged mouth not only to liberate commerce, but also to end political conflict over control of the delta and secure the flow of civilization from Europe outward.

To tame the Danube was also to control natural, chronological time and become the creative agent of one's own moral and political destiny (Hutchings 2008; 2018). In *Meditations*, philosopher and Roman Emperor Marcus Aurelius wrote: 'Time is a river, or violent torrent of things coming into being; each one, as soon as it has appeared, is swept off and disappears, and is succeeded by another, which is swept away in its turn' (1794: 165). All things including 'a rose in spring' or 'diseases, death, calamities, treacheries' came and went in the natural course of things; only fools felt joy or sorrow. Between 171 and 173 CE, Marcus Aurelius fought the German tribes along the Danube at Carnuntum – and perhaps he watched the Danube flow by as he contemplated the futility of his repeated wars against the outside world. However, Enlightenment confidence that science and rationality could tame rivers, create ever-blooming gardens, and stave off death and disease – and ultimately, political calamities and treacheries – challenged Marcus Aurelius's stoic certainty regarding the violent and unstoppable flow of time. As a metaphor, taming the river also disciplined time – both in the sense of overcoming destructive histories and preventing future calamities. Diplomats at Paris in 1856 intended to do both with the establishment of the European Commission of the Danube – to at once end past conflicts and propose a new international body that would ensure the future of peaceful cooperation along the river.

This chapter first highlights the taming of the Danube's physical and metaphysical dangers as a standard of legitimate rule for Ancient Rome as much as for nineteenth-century empires that competed for imperial control over the river. The Danube as a civilizing conduit between Europe and the near periphery relied on liberal understandings of the link between free trade, peace, and civilizational progress. Hence, a ruler's inability or unwillingness to control the river as an efficient highway for trade detracted from their legitimacy as a civilized and modern political authority. The second section details the specific case of the Danube delta and how Russia's failure to tame the delta shaped British perceptions of its civilizational status. However, the highway that connects can also be reversed, threatening to bring instability back upriver. The final section explores these fears, which dramatically express themselves in the dark Gothic tales of the vampire Count Dracula, who comes from the far reaches of the Danube to conquer the West. Here, the Danube links the familiar West with a semi-familiar eastern Europe, a distorted self that threatened to corrupt and destabilize the familiar. Taming the Danube, then, signified the ability to regulate the ideas, people, and monsters that sought to migrate upriver. These imaginaries of the river enabled the establishment of the first truly international organization in 1856.

Taming the dangerous Danube as a civilizational standard

Echoing accounts of the hazardous journey along the Rhine, the untamed Danube has long been framed as a dangerous force that necessitated constant management. The river's perils were expressed in two interrelated ways. First, the Danube presented physical dangers, from the floods that repeatedly devasted communities along its banks to navigational difficulties for those who intended to travel and trade along it. Second, the unruly Danube also represented metaphysical dangers – the chaos that threatened to overwhelm orderly and rational commercial civilization. Taming the river, then, required political authorities along the river's banks to address both the physical and moral dangers of uncontrolled nature – dangers that could only be overcome by human ingenuity and political will. Indeed, since the Roman Empire, leaders able to tame the river had also claimed the legitimacy to rule through their demonstration of mastery over nature to protect the population and harness nature for society's benefit. Conversely, a political authority's inability or unwillingness to transform the Danube into a tame and reliable highway signaled the opposite and threw doubt on its status as a civilized member of international society.

Perhaps the most treacherous section of the Danube for navigators was the Iron Gates, or Kazan gorge, a rocky 120-kilometer stretch of limestone cliffs in the Transylvanian Alps that separates the upper and lower Danube. The name Kazan, Turkish for 'hissing kettle', describes the sound of the rushing water as the river squeezes between the jagged rocks, creating dangerous eddies and whirlpools. Irish writer Michael Joseph Quin describes this treacherous section of river:

These rocks, though so long washed by the torrent are still as rough as when the river first found or forced its way amongst them. They are in large masses, tumbled about in every sort of shape and position, and now that they are completely exposed to view, in consequence of the depression of the river, they looked terrific; the gaping jaws, as it were, of some infernal monster. When the Danube is at its ordinary height, replenished by its usual tributaries, the roar of its waters, in hurrying through the 'Iron Gate,' is borne on the winds for many miles around, like the sound of continued peals of thunder. (1836: 122)

For centuries, the Iron Gates barred large vessels from navigating between the upper and lower rivers. To circumvent this obstacle, the Roman Emperor Trajan built a road to bypass the treacherous rapids and connect the upper and lower rivers. This Roman road was a remarkable engineering feat that combined footpaths hewn into the rock with a wooden road suspended from the cliffs. To commemorate this achievement, Trajan installed a victorious tablet, which read: 'The Emperor Caesar, son of the divine Nerva Trajan Augustus Germanicus, High Priest and for the Fourth Time Tribune, Father of the Country and for the fourth time consul, overcame the hazards of the mountain and the river and opened this road' (Beattie 2010: 208). Carved in stone, this inscription celebrates Trajan's victory over the river as a reflection of his political greatness and authority to rule – the conquest was both physical and moral, showcasing Trajan's power over nature and his ability to control and conquer all that stood in his way.

Indeed, what stood in Trajan's way was not only an uncooperative river but also the barbarian tribes along it who resisted Roman rule and civilization. In a relief at the bottom of Trajan's Column directly above the base (Figure 4.1), the conquest of the river and the Dacians came together. The sculpted tableau depicts the Roman army crossing the Danube on a pontoon bridge, with the river personified as a wild-haired giant passively observing and acquiescing to Rome's power. The scene uses architectural tropes to separate the refined and civilized Roman structures on the right from the rough and barbarian Dacian structures on the left (Thill 2010). The visual language of the column spirals from the river scene upward, and, as archeologist Penelope Davies argues (1997), it relies on the context of Roman funerary monuments to show the journey from darkness into light. Trajan stands at the top of the column in imperial majesty as the ruler who conquered the river and the Dacians for the glory of Rome. The scene portrays the Danube as a liminal space between civilization and barbarism – a space that must be tamed and brought onto the side of Roman civilization.

Seventeen centuries later, Austrian rulers continued to frame the taming of the Danube as a declaration of imperial authority. Upriver from the Iron Gates, narrow gorges created interlaced fluvial channels that threatened

Figure 4.1 Trajan's Column: detail of Roman army departing across the Danube

navigation. Two infamous whirlpools – the *Strudel* and *Wirbel* – gained much notoriety in nineteenth-century travelogues (Coates 2013: 47). In his 1827 account of the descent down the Danube from Ratisbon to Vienna, British writer James Robinson Planché describes the *Wirbel*:

> On the northern side is the celebrated whirlpool, formed most probably by the violence with which the two currents of the Danube are hurled against each other on leaving the Worthinsel, and again checked and divided by the Hausstein [a large 150-meter long rock]. This whirlpool measures sometimes nearly fifty feet in diameter ... in the centre the water forms a perfect funnel, and a large branch of fir was whirling round and round in it, as if some invisible hand were stirring the natural cauldron, making it boil and bubble. (1827: 194–5)

Local legends surrounded both whirlpools, often blaming water spirits that demanded sacrificial victims from passing boats. Both Planché and William Beattie refer to the *Strudel* and *Wirbel* as the Scylla and Charybdis of the Danube, borrowing from Homer's *Odyssey* to confer a mythical grandeur on the journey and a sense of heroic conquest to the successful navigation of the river.[1] The combination of these perils and the wildly sublime landscape, Beattie writes, 'produces a powerful sensation on the minds even of those who had been all their lives familiar with danger' (1843: 100). These depictions of the Danube conjure physical as well as metaphysical dangers by envisioning evil spirits stirring the natural cauldron as innocent victims watch in horror. Another account published in the *Aberdeen Journal* describes navigational difficulties along this stretch of river:

> The excited waters drive on the boat until it flies before them with the rapidity of an arrow ... the boat must cut them rapidly and decisively, like a knife, and the utmost precision, boldness and local knowledge are required in the steersman.[2]

In the eighteenth century, equipped with gunpowder, Austrian Empress Maria Theresa's engineers removed 30 cubic fathoms of rock from the riverbed to tame the *Strudel*. This plan backfired, as the redirected currents created new navigational dangers and required additional treatments of gunpowder.[3] In the nineteenth century, to tame the *Wirbel*, Emperor Franz Josef blasted through the Hausstein rock formation. He then mounted a plaque on the left bank to declare victory against the river: 'Kaiser Franz Josef freed shipping from the dangers of the Donau-Wirbel by blowing up the island of Hausstein 1853–1866' (Coates 2013: 51). Here, Franz Josef declares himself a liberator and reinforces his legitimacy to rule by delivering the Austrian people from the perils of nature. By the mid-nineteenth century, Beattie was assuring travelers that 'rocks in the bed of the river have been blasted, and the former obstructions so greatly diminished, that in the present day the *Strudel* and *Wirbel* present no other danger than what may be caused by the ignorance or negligence of boatmen; so that tourists may contemplate the scene without alarm' (1843: 100). The Austrian Empire's victory against nature provided imperial protection for modern passengers to enjoy the beautiful scenery without fear.

Imperial projects to tame the Danube also sought to end the persistent danger of floods that devastated riverside communities. One curious phenomenon that threatened riverside cities, including Vienna and Budapest, was the *Eisstoss* or ice dam. During the winter, ice would form along the river and block its flow until the spring thaw released a wall of water. In the winter of 1837–38, weather conditions created a massive ice dam a meter thick that shut down the river, and when the ice broke in mid-March, a wall of water rushed onto Budapest at a peak of 29 meters above average river level (Coates 2013: 45).[4] Similar devasting ice floods ravaged Regensburg in 1784, Bratislava in 1809, and Vienna in 1830 (Pišút 2009). To end these floods, the Viennese authorities established the Danube Regulation Commission in the mid-nineteenth century and proceeded with comprehensive engineering works to straighten the river and contain its flow in an artificial riverbed (Hohensinner et al. 2013: 131). By 1875, Vienna's mayor was toasting the taming of the Danube as the sweetest human triumph over nature (Coates 2013: 62).

If taming the river reinforces a ruler's political legitimacy, the inability to tame the Danube suggested a lack of legitimacy. By the nineteenth century, Trajan's road had long since disintegrated and the Iron Gates continued to hinder navigation. Before the mid-nineteenth century, passengers and freight disembarked and bypassed the Iron Gates overland. Starting in the 1830s, various attempts to blast through the Iron Gates met with hydrological and political resistance. In his travelogue, Adolphus Slade describes how Count Istvan Szechenyi, a local notable, attempted to blast through the reef. He was hindered not only by water levels but also by the Ottoman authorities. In response to Szechenyi's request for permission to blast the reef, the Ottomans declared that 'as Allah had placed the rocks there, it would be impious to remove them' (Slade 1840: 165).[5] Szechenyi's projects aimed to overcome both the physical and political barriers to trade on the Danube. Ottoman refusal to assist in controlling the river put the legitimacy of their rule into question, as civilization discourses mixed with river politics to frame the Ottomans as primitive and superstitious, unwilling to support a modern project that would lead to economic gain and progress. The Ottomans were not the only empire to be measured and found wanting against this civilizational standard – the history of the 1856 European Commission of the Danube shows how Russia's inability to tame the Danube delta contributed to its declining status in the eyes of western Europe.

It would take another century of continuous engineering projects to finally control the Iron Gates. The 1878 Treaty of Berlin, which ended Ottoman authority in Europe and therefore its authority over the Danube, authorized a tax on shipping to fund the Hungarian government's ongoing engineering works to ease navigation at the Iron Gates. Throughout the first half of the twentieth century, shipping continued to need assistance to navigate the rapids. In the 1960s and 1970s, the Iron Gates Dam – the largest on the Danube and a showcase for cooperation between socialist Romania and Yugoslavia – finally pacified the dangerous currents and silenced the hissing kettle (Coates 2013: 57).[6]

The civilizing Wasserstrasse: *the Danube as an economic highway*

The Danube has always been an avenue of trade. Goods such as wine, ore, and salt have enriched local populations along the river's banks since Neolithic times.[7] Before the eighteenth century, trade along the river was largely localized and the Mediterranean Sea offered a more attractive and navigable international transport link (East 1932: 337). In the eighteenth century,

Austria consolidated control over the upper Danube and sought to transform the river into a commanding imperial highway. It organized weekly transit for passengers, merchandise, and mail from Vienna to Ulm – roughly 650 kilometers over ten days – on large flat-bottomed rafts known as *Ordinari* powered by either horses or rowers (East 1932: 339; Coates 2013: 47). However, despite Vienna's efforts to control trade along the river as part of its imperial infrastructure, intra-empire politics impeded its development as a large-scale commercial artery.

In the mid-nineteenth century, however, the Danube as a potentially lucrative international highway emerged into the geopolitical limelight. One reason was technology – the introduction of steamboats helped overcome navigational difficulties along the river, making the Danube a viable long-distance transport route. In 1830, the Austrian Danube Steam Navigation Company began operations between Vienna and Pressburg, and travelers celebrated the promise of steam for further economic development of the river (East 1932: 340; Quin 1836). The other reason that Danubian trade was propelled onto the international agenda was the ideological links made, particularly by liberal thinkers and politicians, between trade, peace, and civilizational advancement. Here, the Danube as a liminal space between civilization and barbarism took on international significance as the river became a physical and metaphysical conduit that brought liberal values and Western civilization eastward.

For the British, the 1846 repeal of the Corn Laws pushed commercial interests to search for new sources of raw material abroad, and the fertile Danube valley was a tantalizing source. An article published in the *Dublin University Magazine* in November 1854 extolled the bounty of the Danube, quoting McCulloh's *Commercial Dictionary* which states: 'the capacities of this great river as a commercial highway are certainly unequalled by those of any other European stream; and their full development would be of incalculable advantage not merely to countries on its banks but to all commercial nations'.[8] The lands alongside the river are described as overflowing with resources – metals, rock salt, timber, hides, wool, tallow, sheep, goatskin, grain, hemp, and cotton. McCulloh's description almost salivates with commercial desire in describing 'the enormous resources of the country, its exuberant fertility, the lowness of price, and the laboriousness and parsimony of the people...'[9]

Detailed reports from British vice consul Charles Cunningham, stationed at the port of Galatz (Galați), confirmed the booming international trade transiting through the Danube delta. In a report on shipping setting off from Galatz, Cunningham tallied 133 Austrian, 160 English, 13 French, 447 Greek, 96 Russian, 44 Sardinian, and one Prussian vessel registered to enter Galatz in 1849 (FO 78/977, 1835–53: p. 116). In a different letter prepared for diplomats at the 1855 Vienna negotiations, Cunningham reports that 132 British vessels entered the Danube delta at Galatz and Brăila in 1848, 129 in 1849, 106 in 1850, 304 in 1851, and 339 in 1852. Further, Cunningham charts the dramatic increase in British vessels departing from Galatz and Ibraila on the Danube's mouth from a mere seven vessels in 1843, to 52 in 1846, and 395 in 1847. By 1847, vessels bound for the UK were carrying 577,387 imperial quarters of wheat (FO 78/977, 1835–53: pp. 281–3; see also Chamberlain 1923: 20).[10] The increase of British trade passing through the Danube delta highlighted its increasing importance for British foreign policy.

Increasing trade on the Danube created access to markets and the potential for vast material wealth. However, this is not a simple story of interests driving foreign policy. The promotion of free trade was linked intimately with civilizational discourses. In a speech before the House of Commons in 1842, Lord Palmerston advocated for the repeal of the Corn Laws by laying out this liberal economic vision:

> Why is the earth on which we live divided into zones and climates? Why, I ask, do different countries yield different productions to people experiencing similar wants? Why are they intersected with mighty rivers – the natural highways of nations? Why are lands the most distant from each other, brought almost into contact by the very ocean which seems to divide them? Why, Sir, is it that man may be dependent upon man. It is that the exchange of commodities may be accompanied by the extension and diffusion ... multiplying and confirming friendly relations. It is, that commerce may freely go forth, leading civilization with one hand, and peace with the other, to render mankind happier, wiser and better. (HL Deb, 16 February 1842: vol. 60, col. 618)

Here, Palmerston echoed a litany of prominent European thinkers who stressed the positive links between free trade, peace, and civilizational progress (including Montesquieu, Hume, Kant, and Mill). His evocation of the river as the natural highway of nations not only envisions the river as a functional object of human commerce and progress, but also naturalizes his liberal economic argument. According to Palmerston's logic, the existence of natural geographies such as rivers and oceans can only be explained by their usefulness to human commerce. At the same time, commerce naturally leads not only to interdependence and wealth but wisdom, peace, and ultimately civilization. Palmerston then describes this commercial civilization as the *natural* state of affairs, and charges that restrictive duties 'fetter the inborn energies of man'. Hence, Palmerston embeds the geographical imaginary of the ideal river as an economic highway into the foundations of his liberal and civilizing rhetoric. While Palmerston did not explicitly mention the Danube in his speech, the river figured prominently in mid-nineteenth-century British policy toward Russia and the Ottoman Empire.

This civilizing rhetoric was commonplace. Romanian scholar Constantin Ardeleanu (2014: 136) clearly draws the link between Britain's liberal economic policies and growing anti-Russian sentiment through the polemical works of David Urquhart, whom John Howes Gleason (1950) credits with shaping the character of anti-Russian sentiment in Britain in the nineteenth century.[11] A purported expert on Turkish affairs who was sent by King William IV on a commercial mission down the Danube in 1833, Urquhart's writings painted Russia as a protectionist power with the malicious intention of hampering British access to cheap and abundant goods. Again, this is not a simple argument of economic interest; rather, Urquhart saw commerce as a political and even military tool:

> What more advantageous ally can we find for our diplomatic exertions than commerce itself? Let extensive depots of English wares be established on the Danube and at Trebizonde, and Turkey will find in them better support than in fleets or armies. (Urquhart 1833: 174)

Here, Urquhart describes British commerce as a defense for the Ottomans against Russian aggression and reveals the political impetus behind Danubian trade. In the same account, Urquhart also describes commerce as producing not only economic wealth but also other benefits: 'communications are opened, connections established, desires created, energies raised, and progress commences. Commerce naturally, in every case, has this effect...' (1833: 142–3). Echoing Palmerston, Urquhart also argues that commerce has a naturally civilizing effect beyond pure accumulation of wealth, and a Russian Empire that hinders commerce denies the blessings of civilization to eastern Europe.

Travelogues along the Danube also reflect this imaginary of the ideal river as an economic highway that transported progressive ideas and civilization alongside goods. In the 1836 introduction to his travelogue down the Danube, Michael Joseph Quin described how expanding steam locomotion along the river would increase commercial enterprise. Quin suggests that transforming the Danube into a commercial waterway will be a boon to riverside populations by developing local resources and mobilizing the energies of local populations. There is a decidedly moral dimension to this understanding of commerce. Quin declares that 'commerce, it is well known, brings blessings both physical and intellectual in her train', and that the opening of the Danube to steam travel would inevitably bring 'liberal principles among the strongholds of absolute power, or of aristocratic pride' (1836: 3). For Quin and like-minded liberals, the river carried ideas as well as goods, but unlike the flow of goods, civilizational ideas flowed in only one direction.

The destination of these civilizational ideas was the 'East'. Throughout his narrative, Quin describes the advantages of steam in bringing 'those countries, which have hitherto seemed scarcely to belong to Europe', into the 'pale of civilization'. Again, Quin iterates that commerce will not only multiply the natural riches of the region but also improve laws and institutions, bringing to the people 'new combinations, not only of physical, but also of moral strength', with the potential to catalyze changes for the entire European continent (1836: 107–8). Quin even quoted Prince Milosch of Servia (modern-day Serbia), whose speech to the Servian nation encouraged his people to give up their provincial habits for the 'civilization and enlightenment characterizing the nations of Europe' (1836: 120).

Similarly, R. T. Claridge's 1837 travel guide to the Danube declared that as the most important river that 'runs through the heart of Europe', the Danube brought 'the highest purpose of civilization, commerce and political freedom', which Russia's 'sinister policy' now jeopardized (Claridge 1837: 74–5). When Adolphus Slade reached the delta, he lauded how commerce was transforming Galatz and Sulina into civilized places despite other political forces that wished otherwise (Slade 1840). William Beattie's 1843 descriptions echo other accounts as he proclaims that connecting the Danube by steamboat is 'an event which has led to important consequences, both as it regards the advancement of trade and the general progress of civilization in the East' (Beattie 1843: iv). Later in his account, Beattie portrayed the Turkish towns along the Danube as having an air of 'neglect' and 'decay', but claimed that 'the steam navigation of the Danube is now giving a fresh and unexpected impulse' to them by reviving the native industry of the region (1843: 223–4). Commerce, then, had the ability to civilize and revitalize. Both political and popular discourses presented the Danube not only as a site of economic profit but also as a civilizing tool that naturally brought progress to the East. Civilization and commerce went hand-in-hand down the river.

The lasting effects of this ideational connection between liberal economics, civilizational progress, and control of the river continue to the modern day. At the end of the twentieth century, after the Iron Gates were finally tamed for international shipping, Romanian businessman Iosif Constantin Drăgan commissioned an imposing rock sculpture of Decebalus, the last king of the Dacians, to be hewn onto a cliff face along the gorge. Written into the rock under the statue is the prominent inscription: 'Decebalus Rex / Dragan Fecit' – King Decebalus / Made by Dragan – as much a commemoration of an imagined Romanian past as a celebration of Dragan himself, elevating the millionaire to the status of a king who commands the rocks and the river. The statue is the largest rock sculpture in Europe, and like emperors before him, Dragan used dynamite to etch his mark onto the natural landscape and shape the flow of history. He noted that those traveling toward the statue also voyaged 'towards the origins of European civilization and will discover that a United Europe represents the natural course of history' (Decebalus Rex official website, 2021). Here, the progressive course of history – this time toward a political vision of united Europe – is again naturalized in the confluence of international commerce and civilizational discourses.

The Danube delta and Russian intransigence

In the final stretch before reaching the Black Sea, navigating the Danube was particularly hazardous. The lower Danube has a peculiar hydrological character – unlike rivers that rush into the sea, the Danube turns north at Cernavodă in modern Romania and slows down. At Galatz, the river again turns east to enter the Danube delta. This quirk reduces the speed of the river at this juncture and deposits sediment along the already-narrow channels to obstruct shipping. Many routes twist through the wild and swampy Danube delta, but large merchant vessels were only able to navigate the middle route, known as the Sulina (or Soulina) channel (Chamberlain 1974 [1918]: 20). The delta's navigational challenges often proved fatal for inexperienced pilots in the nineteenth century and many demanded state interventions to ensure that the untamed delta did not impede development of the river as an effective trade route.

With the 1829 Treaty of Adrianople, the Danube delta came under Russian control, and it was now Russia's responsibility as sovereign to maintain the Danube's mouth for commerce (Geffcken 1883: 6). Russia's inability or unwillingness to do so shaped perceptions of it as a civilized and legitimate authority. As the British Vice Consul at Galatz Charles Cunningham wrote of Russian efforts at the Danube delta, 'Notwithstanding the intention of the Imperial government, it is clear that the duties assumed at Sulina have hitherto not been satisfactorily performed' (FO 78/977, 1835–53: p. 189). As early as 1829, the British Foreign Office under the foreign secretary George Hamilton Gordon, 4th Earl of Aberdeen, began voicing objections to Russian control of Danubian trade (Ardeleanu 2014: 133; FO 97/402, 1828–30: p. 259). This and volumes of British Foreign Office and merchant correspondence suggests that Russia did not fulfill its obligation to keep the river's mouth open to commerce in three important areas: first, in maintaining the depth of the river for shipping; second, in ensuring law and order in the delta; and third, in keeping a reasonable quarantine at the Danube's mouth.

First, accounts of navigation in the delta stressed Russia's willful neglect in maintaining the depth of the river. According to merchants and British foreign office reports, when the delta was under Ottoman control, the authorities maintained the channel at a depth of 16 feet. But under the Russians, channel depth reduced to 10 feet or even 8.5 feet during adverse winds (*Newcastle Courant*, 18 June 1841; Chamberlain 1923: 35; FO 78/977, 1835–53: pp. 85–6).[12] To maintain channel depth, the Ottomans reportedly did not use expensive methods. Instead, according to an article in *London's Daily News* on 28 June 1853, they kept the channel at sufficient depth by 'means of heavy iron rakes, which they obliged all vessels to drag after them during their passage out of the Danube'. Lieutenant Colonel Edward St. John Neale, British Counsel at Varna, reported the same story heard from a pilot of the Austrian steamer company (FO 78/977, 1835–53: p. 87). The British pointed to this fact as proof of Russia's antagonism toward free trade on the Danube – Russia could have easily maintained the channel but actively stalled to favor trade from the Russian port of Odessa on the Black Sea.

Correspondence from Charles Cunningham at Galatz and St. Vincent Lloyd, British vice consul in Ismail, related a similar story. Cunningham framed the situation as simple: Russia had neglected to maintain the depth of the Danube channel and therefore had become a barrier to British trade:

> There is little doubt that a small steam-boat of 20 or 30 horse-power passing and repassing over the bar when the weather permitted, drawing a heavy iron rake after her, would keep the water on the Sulina bar at 16, perhaps 18, feet English (at least, it appears that while the Sulina was in possession of the Turks, the depth of 16 feet was kept on the bar by causing each sailing vessel as she went out to drag a similar rake after them); and it is evident this might be done at a very trifling expense. (*Correspondence* 1853: 30 September 1850)[13]

Lloyd concurred with Cunningham's assessment. To help Russia clear the Sulina channel, the British had sent a steam dredging machine. The machine was designed to dig up and deposit sand and silt from the river bottom onto an awaiting barge. Lloyd described the machine's ineffectiveness and questioned whether it was the best means for clearing the bar. 'It appears to me, and my opinion has been confirmed by that of most persons competent to judge, that the only effectual means to be employed is the dragging of a properly constructed harrow in and out of the river, over the bar, by a steam vessel.' All that was needed, Lloyd writes, was to loosen the sand and silt so that the river's natural flow could carry the debris into the Black Sea. This simple solution, Lloyd maintained, did not require complex equipment and saved on fuel and manual labor (*Correspondence* 1853: 13 July 1851). The implication here is that any legitimate authority that wished to maintain its treaty obligations and clear the channel for international trade could easily have done so, and Russian neglect of shipping navigation threw the legitimacy of its control over the Danube delta into question.

Second, the delta under Russian control was portrayed as lawless, uncivilized, and dangerous. The shallow depth of the Sulina channel due to silt build-up meant that merchants had to remove weight from their ships and carry the excess cargo overland or in smaller vessels (a practice called lighterage). Lighterage not only increased transport costs, but also exposed merchants to extortion and piracy. Russian authorities did little to regulate the increasing traffic or impose rules on locals who provided lighterage services for foreign merchants (*Correspondence* 1853; Chamberlain 1923: 35). The anarchic situation was described in a lively account from a merchant in London's *Morning Post* on 21 May 1847:

> No harbour master, no regulations. Greeks, Turks, Austrians, Russians, English, and all nations jumbled together, and might is right … knives and pistols continually in requisition. Thank goodness, we are all right yet, though we have had two or three hair-breadth escapes … But I have not told you our worst predicament; the winding up of which will be that the large vessels cannot tell what their expenses will be, or when they will get over the bar. Half-a-dozen lighters to lighten 700 or 800 sails of ships, some of 400 tons. The whole place is mad.

In addition to lighterage, foreign ships traversing the Danube delta needed to hire experienced pilots to navigate the treacherous sandbars. Charlatans often took advantage of foreign vessels and passed themselves off as experienced pilots; suitable pilots often charged extortionate rates. Lloyd described the situation in a November 1848 report: 'good pilots are difficult to be procured and demanded enormous wages, persons totally incompetent offered themselves as pilots and were accepted as such; many of them having several such engagements at the same time, employing others to fulfil them' (FO 78/977, 1835–53: p. 32). Writing from the British Consulate in Varna in January 1849, Neale amplified Lloyd's account of the dangers to British shipping from 'the ignorance and unskillfulness of the persons who under the present regulations of the Russian authorities, are not prohibited from offering their services as pilots to shipping at the mouth of the river' (FO 78/977, 1835–53: pp. 29–30). These practices led to wrecks that contributed to the already hazardous obstructions to navigation, and commercial vessels were often left disabled in the channel as their cargo spoiled.

Here, the delta's dangers were pointedly twofold: first, the hydrological challenges of the river; but second, and more frustrating, the anarchic lawlessness that compounded the river's physical dangers. E. L. Butte, British Consul at Bucharest, reported as early as 1830 on the lawless conditions at the Danube delta: 'great obstacles thrown into the way of commerce by the irregular and arbitrary conduct of the Russian authorities', who searched some vessels more than eight times as they transited through the shipping channels (FO 97/402, 1828–30: p. 259). Almost two decades later, Neale characterized Sulina as a 'little California' – a boom town where people flocked to get rich quickly (FO 78/977, 1835–53: p. 60). Lloyd described Russian control of the delta as chaotic and uncivilized, with characters of ill-repute, likely under the protection of the authorities, waiting to prey on merchant ships entering Sulina (*Correspondence* 1853: 14 November 1848). Cunningham described one incident in which an Austrian commander was arrested without reason as 'a dangerous precedent' that prompted Austrians to complain through diplomatic channels (FO 78/977, 1835–53: p. 190; Hajnal 1920: 64).

Thirdly, in addition to its responsibility to maintain shipping routes, the 1829 Treaty of Adrianople gave Russia the right to establish a quarantine station at the Danube's mouth. Russian authorities argued that the quarantine station protected Russian territory from criminals and the spread of epidemics such as cholera and plague (Hajnal 1920: 63; Chamberlain 1923: 31–2). The British, however, cried foul play and spun a different narrative. Goods were subject to quarantine for up to forty days (Baumgart 1981: 125) – an outrageous barrier to free trade. Butte wrote that at the quarantine station, Russians arbitrarily discriminated against foreigners, as 'loaves of sugar, etc. are spoiled or damaged through their exposures to the rain in the open air. Other goods insusceptible to contagion such as truncheons of rum are equally placed under a quarantine of many days' (FO 97/402, 1828–30: pp. 259–60). In addition, Butte reported that the Russians arbitrarily arrested foreigners, breaking down doors and forcing foreigners to house Russian soldiers at their own expense (FO 97/403, 1830–32: p. 329). A British merchant's account in the *Manchester Guardian* in December 1853 described the dangerous conditions brought about by the unnecessary quarantines, and even invasive searches, as the 'barbarism of the Russian system'. The language of civilizational standards permeated the narrative at all levels as merchants and officials alike questioned the legitimacy of Russian control over the delta.

Navigational difficulties in the delta highlighted the river's two dangers – first, the physical perils caused by natural hydrological forces, but second, the moral dangers posed by anarchy and lawlessness that allowed the first set of perils to persist and triumph. Russian neglect permitted nature to gain the upper hand in hindering free trade; and in doing so, Russian policy also impeded the trappings of civilization that naturally accompanied free commerce. In failing to control the river, Russia was viewed as derelict in its duty as a sovereign power and a member of the civilized nations, and – in the eyes of European Great Powers – forfeited authority over the river. At Vienna in 1855 and Paris in 1856, Russia's inability to discipline the Danube precipitated discussions among European diplomats that led to the creation of a new international commission. This new body would not only be a strong authority capable of keeping nature's physical forces at bay, but also a moral and political commitment to banish the chaos that prevented civilizing forces from taking root on the eastern edge of Europe.

'Desolation of desolation': internationalizing the ugly delta

The aesthetics of the Danube delta revealed much about western European imaginaries of the far reaches of the river and the need for a civilizing force to flow eastward. While travelogues waxed poetic about the splendors of the upper Danube, travelers depicted the lower Danube and particularly the Danube delta in less than bucolic terms. In 1836, Englishman Edmund Spencer journeyed down the Danube by steamboat, and his portrayal of the landscape changed from sublime beauty, to loveliness, to miserable desolation. Upon reaching Wallachia on the approach to the Danube delta, he lamented that one settlement was 'miserable to the extreme' and described the marshy banks of the broad river as infested with mosquitoes and sandflies, making sleep impossible. Julia Pardoe's (1837), J. J. Best's (1842), and William Beattie's (1843) accounts also echoed this perennial complaint. Spencer goes on to write dismissively that 'throughout the whole of that immense district, notwithstanding it has the advantages of a fine climate and fertile soil adapted to every production, there was not a single object to delight the eye and gladden the heart' (1837: 81). As he enters the Danube delta, Spencer continues to depict the landscape negatively: 'as to cultivation there is none, being literally a desolation of desolation' (1837: 89). This language juxtaposed the 'emptiness' of the lower Danube with the splendor of the history-laden upper Danube, and coded the untamed natural landscape as something repulsive and undesirable.

Other travelers described the lower Danube and delta with surprisingly similar vocabulary. In his 1837 travel guide, R. T. Claridge compares the beauty around Kazan to the beauty of the Rhine valley. In Adolphus Slade's 1840 account, he maintains that the same scenery surpasses the best along the Rhine.[14] However, Claridge describes the delta as 'a monotonous extent of flat, muddy, marshy, and dreary country, as far as the eye can reach, without anything to relieve it' (1837: 172). He goes on to describe the town of Galatz as 'a miserable place, though said to be of considerable commercial importance' (1837: 173). Similarly, Beattie describes Galatz and Brăila as practical but terrible cities full of mosquitoes and noxious fumes without comfort. He depicts the Danube delta in particularly unflattering terms:

> A dreary monotonous track of flat swamps covered with reeds, and inhabited by gulls, pelicans, and water fowls, and presenting hardly a feature, during seventy or eighty miles, to refresh the eye or awaken historical association. (Beattie 1843: 23)

Likewise, other authors either chose to say very little about the landscape of the lower Danube and delta or used similarly dismissive language. Poet Robert Snow describes the lower river as 'endless forests and wild ugly swamps' (1842: 27). Scottish writer Felicia Skene dismisses the 'unhealthy' mists and the 'flat, uninteresting stretch of lowlands' of the lower Danube (1847: 297–9). English traveler and writer Julia Pardoe's account describes entering the Danube's mouth from the tempestuous Black Sea and characterizes the landscape as 'low, marshy, and treeless, presenting as desolate an appearance as can well be conceived' (1854 [1837]: 316).[15]

In their narratives, authors offered two reasons for the lower Danube's aesthetic ugliness. First, the deserted and 'semi-barbaric' countryside is attributed to Ottoman despotism (Spencer 1837: 80–1) or Russian repression (Slade 1840: 200). Second, the very uninhabited and wild state of the lower river and delta is said to lie at the heart of its unattractiveness. Spencer relates the countryside's lack of cultivation to its desolation. In his anti-Russian tract on the Danube, David Urquhart writes that the Danube 'loses itself' in swamps as it turns north, and 'its useless wanderings extends a hundred and fifty miles, carrying it away from the direction of its usefulness' (1853: 107). The uninhabited islands of the marshes, Urquhart writes, are 'in themselves utterly valueless' (1853: 17). When Julia Pardoe landed in a 'wretched' little hamlet on the Silistrian river bank, she was surprised that 'not the slightest attempt at a garden was visible, though the village stood upon the verge of an extensive wild' (1854 [1837]: 317). Given the fertility of the land, she could not understand why the inhabitants had not sought to improve upon nature through the medium of the garden. Here, Pardoe's offhand remark not only reveals her English prejudices but speaks to a wider sentiment about how the delta might be improved – through human industriousness and the transformation of an ugly useless swamp into a useful, rational, and habitable transport hub.

The two logics outlined above are interrelated. Uncivilized Ottoman and Russian rule had failed to tame the river and squandered the delta's potential as a fertile and useful land, unjustly leaving it a desolate wasteland. However, a civilized authority would transform the delta into a rational and useful landscape that facilitated, rather than restricted, the forces of free trade. The Danube delta, unfortunately, lacked such a civilized authority. At the 1855 Vienna and 1856 Paris conferences, British and French insistence on being part of an independent international commission to manage the delta can be read as a desire to establish a civilized authority not only as an economic necessity but also a moral one. Hence, the 1856 Danube Commission was a civilizing project to bring rationality and progressive rule to the furthest reaches of Europe. The argument that legitimate political authority arose from the proper use of and improvements made to the land echoes justifications for colonialism, particularly as laid out by James Dunbar in his call to wage war against the elements rather than other societies. The same logic would also resound in subsequent projects to tame the river and transform useless land into a useful resource for modern society.

The river that flows backward

The Danube as an economic highway flows from west to east, connecting western Europe to the near periphery. However, in a metaphorical sense, the Danube could also be conceived as flowing backward from east to west, connecting Europe with its ancient past in Greece and reversing the natural flow of time and geography. Unlike most rivers, which measure distance from source to mouth, mile markers on the Danube begin with zero at the river's mouth and increase upriver. Apart from a brief period in the mid-eighteenth century when German Swabians headed downriver to settle, goods, ideas, and conquering armies have almost always flowed upriver from the east (Thorpe 2013: xv). In this sense, the Danube as a human highway may be said to flow in the opposite direction to its natural course. However, if a river that ran from west to east brought civilization and commerce, a river that flowed from the periphery backward threatened to bring the opposite and overturn Europe's civilized order.

In the early nineteenth century, noted German Romantic poet Friedrich Hölderlin wrote a series of river poems. In addition to works about the Rhine and the Necker, he wrote an untitled poem about the Danube, which his editor posthumously entitled the *Ister* from the ancient Greek name for the lower Danube. The poem draws on a longstanding analogy between the river and time – and Hölderlin's vision is of the Danube flowing backward bringing intellectual gifts from Ancient Greek civilization through time to nineteenth-century Germany:

> Yet almost this river seems
> To travel backwards and
> I think it must come from the East (quoted in Coates 2013: 80)

Hölderlin left the work unfinished. Almost a century later, Martin Heidegger focused on the poem in a series of lectures. For Heidegger, Hölderlin's hymn of praise for the Ister highlighted the fundamental tension between the foreign and the native – the foreign East as ever-present even at the river's source in Germany (Coates 2013: 80). Throughout history, the Danube often did seem to flow backward, bringing the Romans, the Mongols, the Slavs, the Turks, and finally British and French commercial vessels upstream with all their newfangled ideas about trade, civilization, and legitimate authority. At the same time, reminders of ancient battles and sagas seem embedded into the Danube's riverscape, transporting those who traveled down the river backward in time. Taming the Danube and in particular the Danube delta – the source of the foreign East – offered nineteenth-century Europeans the chance to tame their own bloody histories and stem the dangerous passions that threatened to flow back upriver.

Hence, taming the Danube reflected what theorist Kimberly Hutchings conceptualizes as Kairos or 'creative time-making', which relies on Baconian science to impose order on Chronos, or 'natural, chronological time' (2018: 256). This creative act endows the time-makers with ethical and political agency while making natural time, and by metaphorical extension the natural river, the passive object of human intervention. Indeed, Hölderlin's Romantic conception of nature did not mean he believed the river should be left alone – in fact, civilization depended on human action to improve nature. If time is a torrent that flows in one direction, as Marcus Aurelius proposed in his *Meditations*, then reversing the river to bring back ancient Greek civilization is a deliberate act of human will upon time, changing its natural flow for our purpose. In addition, central to Hölderlin's poem is the sense that human agency can and should shape nature to render it conducive to civilization:

> But the rock needs incisions
> And the earth needs furrows,
> Would be desolate else, unabiding (quoted in Coates 2013: 81)

This passage could almost have been written for the 1856 European Commission of the Danube and its mission to create furrows and incisions in order to tame the river and transform a desolate landscape into a civilized one. Flowing backward, however, posed certain dangers – if the West failed to control Heidegger's foreign that penetrated into the heart of Europe, it would threaten not only free trade but also challenge deeply held ideas and identities that underpinned a stable European international order.

Taming the red Danube

Despite Johann Strauss's indelible imprint on the European imagination as to the color of the Danube, nowhere along its length could the river genuinely be considered blue. Instead, as Hungarian author Emil Lengyel's 1940 book suggests, the river flows brown, green, and bloody red. Of the metaphorical red Danube, Lengyel writes, 'it has seen more wars than any other river' (1940: 3), from its position on the Roman frontier as the last defense against barbarian tribes to multiple setpiece battles during the Napoleonic Wars.[16]

Despite his overwrought prose and utopian political agenda,[17] Lengyel's color for the lower Danube makes metaphorical sense. By the mid-nineteenth century, travelers' narratives of trips down the Danube often evoked its bloody past, allowing the flowing river to lead them across time as much as space. As Henry Fromby declared after describing the Danube's intimate links to European history, 'the lambent gliding movement of the so mighty and ancient a stream, could not fail irresistibly to float the memory of the past before the voyager' (1843: 14).

The ruins of Carnuntum, one of the most important Roman fortifications on the *limes* where Marcus Aurelius wrote his *Meditations* and fought the Marcomanni tribe, can be seen on the river bank halfway between Vienna and Budapest (Beattie 2010: 109). The remains of Trajan's great bridge, built across the Danube to suppress the Dacians on the opposite bank, inspired in nineteenth-century travelers a melancholic sense of fallen greatness – a once mighty empire defeated by the forces of time and by the wantonness of barbarians who eventually overran these Roman *limes* (Best 1842: 313; Beattie 1843: 235). Traveling down the Danube and across history, references take on a martial tinge which seemed almost stamped onto the picturesque landscape itself. For example, William Beattie reminds the reader in his 1843 account:

> the hordes of Attila – the warrior knights of Charlemagne – the long array of Christian Pilgrims – the hardy bands of Gustavus Adolphus – the turbaned troops of Solyman the Magnificent – the victorious army of our own Marlborough, and the adventurous legion of Napoleon, have all marched in splendid succession, and left behind them tales and traditions which have become part of the scenery. (1843: 2)

Both as a border between powers and as a conduit for invading armies, the Danube has witnessed its share of European warfare. Its banks acted as the backdrop to one of Britain's greatest military victories: the 1704 Battle of Blenheim where the Duke of Marlborough led an allied army to victory against the French and their Bavarian allies (Beattie 1843: 22). At the 1526 Battle of Mohács, an Ottoman army led by Suleiman the Magnificent defeated Louis II and dissolved an independent Hungary. Beattie describes fleeing Hungarians cut down by the Turks 'who boasted that every Turkish scimitar on that day was red with Christian blood' (1843: 195). Further downstream, Beattie imagined the 'sepulchers of Gothic Warriors' accompanied by the few material reminders of Roman greatness (1843: 228). R. T. Claridge described the fortress at Widden (modern-day Vidin) as the largest in Bulgaria, and as having surrendered twice – to Austrians in 1689 and to Russians in 1828, each time washing the riverside with blood (1837:

168). Upon reaching the fortress of Ismail where the Danube splits into the channels of the delta, Adolphus Slade quoted Lord Byron's poem *Don Juan* in describing the 1790 Russian siege of the supposedly impregnable fortress as the 'scene of the fiercest assault and bloodiest slaughter in modern times' (1840: 201–2):

> There was an end of Ismael's hapless town!
> Far flashed her burning towers o'er Danube's stream,
> And redly ran her blushing waters down.
> The horrid war-whoop and the shriller scream
> Rose still; but fainter were the thunders grown
> Of forty thousand who had manned the wall.
> Some hundreds breathed – the rest were silent all

Victors often appropriated these battlefield confrontations as nationalist emblems. From the Russian side, the capture of Ismail inspired poet Gavrila Dershavin to compose what became the first Russian national anthem, which begins: 'Danube's swiftly flowing waters / Are at last in our firm hands' (translated in Thorpe 2013: 7). For the Turkish side, *Estergon Kalesi* is an Ottoman military march that celebrates Suleiman the Magnificent's capture of Estergon, a stronghold on the Danube northwest of Budapest, and the march continues to be popular in Turkey into the twenty-first century.

The bloody drama of the Crimean War also played out on the lower Danube's banks, and at the 1856 Paris Conference, the red river was very much on diplomats' minds and agendas. If the red Danube was intimately linked to the river's fractious past, a new international institution to govern the river promised to overcome that past and transform the river into a less violent and more civilized color.

The image from a distorted mirror

The Danube connects the heartland of Europe to the Balkans – known in nineteenth-century texts as the 'Near East' – and the Russian and Ottoman Empires beyond. Throughout the nineteenth century, this region played a liminal role in the western European imagination, presenting, as Lene Hansen describes, 'a borderline, a gate, a bridge, a crossroad, and a frontier' (2006: 87). This vision of the Balkans as a nexus between worlds echoed voices from the mid-nineteenth century. For example, French philologist and writer Cyprien Robert described the Slavs as an intermediary between 'Asia and Europe, between immobility and progress, between the past and the future, between preservation and revolution' (1852: 4). Therefore, while the traditional Danube ran east and transported liberalism and civilization downriver, a fear lingered in the European imagination that the river, like Hölderlin's

Ister, might be reversed. Unlike Hölderlin's river, this backward Danube threatened to bring disorder from a semi-familiar geography back into the European heartland.

Drawing on Edward Said's *Orientalism*, recent scholarship has proposed a Balkan variant of Orientalism as either a demi-Orientalization (Wolff 1994) or a 'colonization of the mind' in which the West intellectually appropriated the region without the formal trappings of imperialism (Goldsworthy 1998). Others have argued that Said's model offers a flawed lens through which to evaluate western Europe's engagement with the Near East. Fundamentally, they argue, Balkanism evolved independently of Orientalism and remains qualitatively different from Said's model of the West leveraging the power-knowledge nexus as a hegemonic tool of domination (Todorova 1997; Hammond 2008).

As Maria Todorova's work contends, neither the Balkans, the West, nor the relationship between the two should be essentialized as a homogeneous cultural imaginary – instead, identities shifted across time and space. Russians focused their interest on Bulgaria as an oppressed Slavic people, while French and British Romantics concentrated on Greece as the cradle of civilization. The future head of the Prussian general staff, Helmuth von Moltke, attributed any progressive trends he saw in the region to Russia, while the British often blamed regressive trends on Russian rule (Todorova 1997: 71). While many blamed the region's backwardness on the Ottomans, condemnation was far from universal. Englishman Henry Blount's 1636 account praised the 'Turkish disposition' as 'generous, loving, and honest' (Todorova 1997: 91). However, a geopolitical shift in the 1830s represented an important moment in the West's engagement with the Balkans, as British interests in the region altered from trade to a deep political interest (Todorova 1997: 95). The analysis of Danubian travelogues in this chapter bears out this politicization. Hence, by the 1856 Paris Conference, the Near East was not just a wild frontier for adventurers but had become a political geography where notions of civilization and political legitimacy were entangled in the riverscape.

Andrew Hammond's work on imagery in Balkan travel writings from the mid-nineteenth century to World War I builds on Todorova's scholarship and shows that, like the Orient, Western travelers viewed the Balkans as a place of mystery, degeneracy, savagery, chaos, and irrationality (Hammond 2008: 202–3). Unlike accounts of the opulent and sensuous Orient, travelers in the Balkans depicted the region as a hyper-masculine space without civilization or history. Hammond concludes that for the West, the Balkans represented 'less a secure marker of alterity than an unstable and unsettling process loosed from clear identity, an obscure boundary along the European peripheries where categories, oppositions, and essentialized groups are cast into confusion'

(2008: 204). In essence, rather than demarcating the self from the other, the Balkans played a much more unsettling role in the Western geographical imaginary – it presented a 'distorted mirror' with the potential to disturb order by upsetting established hierarchies and reversing the flow of civilization down the Danube.

Perhaps the most unsettling distorted reflection to travel back from the eastern reaches of the Danube was the vampire. The aristocratic blood-sucking monster was first popularized by John Polidori's 1819 book *The Vampyre* and later stamped onto the Western imagination by Bram Stoker's 1897 *Dracula*. Erik Butler maintains that the myth's appeal speaks to one trait uniting all vampires – 'the power to move between and undo borders otherwise holding identities in place. At this monster's core lies an affinity for rupture, change, and mutation' (2010: 2). Vampires rupture time by being at once ancient and futuristic in their ability to overcome death and decay; vampires rupture space by invading from the outside, seducing us with their uncanny allure. Analysts of the vampire as a nineteenth-century literary trope have also acknowledged the association between vampire stories and geopolitical fears that gnawed at western Europe (Senf 1988; Gibson 2006). Matthew Gibson's work on French and British vampires views these myths as a way for authors to express often unpopular views and give 'political commentary on the Eastern Question' (2006: 2). The vampire trope reveals a distorted self as at once human and monster that violates accepted civilized constructs of nature and politics.

Bram Stoker's *Dracula* links the disquieting specter of the distorted man to the Danube and the foreign lands bordering the Danube delta. Near the book's denouement, in hot pursuit of Dracula, the protagonists travel up the Danube because, as one character narrates, 'I felt sure that he must go by the Danube's mouth, or by somewhere in the Black Sea, since by that way he come' (1897: 340). Dracula came from the far reaches of the foreign east to 'invade' London and inspire unnatural behavior in young women. His supernatural ability to command the fog aided his flight back to his ancestral home in Transylvania – and only the intervention of the rational English protagonists with steamboats and railroads would finally stop the unnatural being from succeeding in his nefarious plans. Here, the foul fog and 'noxious fumes' repeatedly described in nineteenth-century accounts of the Danube swamps take on a supernatural quality, representing an unseen evil that expresses itself in the river's untamed characteristics.

Dracula the vampire gave form to the disquieting fear that instability could travel up the Danube from the Ottoman and Russian lands and unsettle the European political order. Attempts to tame the Danube delta, then, pushed back against this fear. This unease underlined the impetus of

European diplomats following the Crimean War to create a rational and scientific institution to civilize the Danube and forestall any economic and moral threats from traveling back upriver.

Conclusion

The 1856 Paris Conference hoped to tame the Danube for the benefit of global commerce and to maintain European order and stability. And for a time in the late nineteenth century, the European Commission of the Danube did transform Sulina on the delta into a civilized outpost buzzing with the multilingual activities of international bureaucrats, merchants, and engineers. However, fears that the Near East as a distorted mirror would unsettle European order came to fruition in the twentieth century as war and anarchy did travel to western Europe from the Danube valley in World War I and then again in World War II. By the time the Iron Curtain cut the Danube in half in the mid-twentieth century, political upheaval had erased the lower river's international identity and any 'civilizational' progress the commission might have achieved. Instead, the delta became the private domain of the Romanian dictator Nicolae Ceauşescu.

In the 1950s, in a distorted echo of Enlightenment projects to tame and control the river, Ceauşescu attempted to drain the swamps and transform the Danube delta into productive farmland. He aimed to make conquests from the wilderness as Frederick the Great had done in the eighteenth century. To accomplish this task, Ceauşescu's engineers designed a more rational riverbed for the Danube to correct the river's useless twists and turns and redirect its flow straight into the Black Sea. He put political prisoners against his communist regime to forced labor digging this grand channel. One of the prisoners, Romanian poet Andrei Ciurunga, wrote of this scheme to tame the river (translated in Thorpe 2013):

> History flows backwards now
> Gathering in its wide pages
> This terrible river
> Water spills from three mouths of the Danube,
> But from the fourth, blood

Hence, under Ceauşescu, it seemed that the Danube Commission's efforts to tame the river turned out to be nothing but folly, and the Danube once again became the red river awash in human blood.

This chapter detailed the nineteenth-century construction of the Danube in the Western geographical imagination as a connecting highway. Physically and metaphysically, the Danube as a conduit brought free trade and civilization from the West eastward and informed diplomatic efforts in 1855 and 1856 to establish peace in eastern Europe and create an international commission to manage the Danube delta. The political deliberations at Vienna and Paris will be discussed in the next chapter, but underlying these debates was a particular vision of what taming the Danube meant for stability in Europe. The international commission established to manage the delta aimed to secure the flow of civilization and progress from western European to the Near East. In taming the delta and transforming the swampy wasteland into a useful space for free commerce and civilization to flourish, the Danube Commission also intended to transform a chaotic space that threatened to destabilize the region into a rational space conducive to international cooperation. However, if taming the Danube delta was to free human society from the ravages of a red river and the powerlessness imposed by chronological time, then Ceaușescu's failed and bloody project to once again tame the delta reveals the hubris of our assumptions.

Notes

1 Scylla and Charybdis were two sea monsters that blocked Odysseus' journey home. Scylla was a six-headed man-eater on one side of the Strait of Messina, while Charybdis was a whirlpool threatening the other shore. Odysseus was forced to choose between the two and steered his ship toward Scylla, electing to sacrifice a few men to the monster rather than risk his entire ship sailing through the whirlpool.

2 'The cataracts of the Danube', *The Aberdeen Journal*, 4 October 1843.

3 Maria Theresa's efforts to blast the rocks that created the *Strudel* actually changed currents in such a way that the river's flow now shot vessels directly onto a different midstream rock called the *Wildriss* (Coates 2013: 51). This is a particularly good example of how the complex hydrology of the river often resisted ambitious and self-important political efforts to tame it. Schematic oversimplifications that ignored the river's complexity informed these failed efforts, and, echoing Timothy Mitchell's insights into technocratic governance, these failures simply created further justifications for bigger and grander projects to tame the river.

4 When he read about the floodwaters, Hungarian composer Franz Liszt remembered: 'I was suddenly transported back to the past … A magnificent landscape emerged before my eyes … it was the Danube rushing over the reefs' (Coates 2013: 47). Liszt's words highlight the prevailing tension in nineteenth-century imaginaries of the river – the dangerous river must be tamed for civilization, and at the same time, the river's perils were also central to its Romantic allure. The romance and tragedy of the dark, ominous river heightened artistic sensibilities as it also outlined the practical problems for progressive policymakers.

5 Slade speculated that the Ottomans were 'influenced by Russia' and 'determined to refuse leave' to Szechenyi's progressive project (Slade 1840: 200).

6 The 1878 Treaty of Berlin ended Ottoman authority in Europe, except for the small island of Ada Kaleh on the Danube near the Iron Gates. The island was accidently left out of the Treaty and remained under Turkish authority until after World War I and the Treaty of Trianon in 1920, when it became part of Romania. In the late twentieth century, the construction of the Iron Gates Dam submerged the island along with Roman archeological ruins along the gorge (Beattie 2010: 203).

7 Archeological records suggest that large towns, with populations of up to 10,000 people, arose between the Danube and Dnieper rivers between 5000 and 3500 BCE, five hundred years before cities on the Tigris and Euphrates. These towns established Europe's first long-distance trade route in *Spondylus gaderopus*, pink and white spiny oyster shells whose glowing beauty made them desirable items (Thorpe 2013: xvi).

8 'The reopening of the Danube', *Dublin University Magazine*, November 1854, 625–6.

9 'The reopening of the Danube', 626; Urquhart 1833: 164; 1851: 13–14.

10 The relative slowing of the rate of growth in trade was likely due to the revolutions of 1848 and the social and political turmoil they inspired in the Danubian principalities (Ardeleanu 2014: 235).

11 Gleason writes: 'the anti-Russian sentiment of the period bore Urquhart's stamp. More than any one man he was responsible for the character not of British policy but of British opinion about Russia during the growth of Russophobia to maturity' (quoted in Ardeleanu 2014: 136).

12 The measurements given here are in English as opposed to Venetian feet.

13 To address these navigation problems, the British foreign secretary Palmerston directed British emissaries to press the Russian foreign minister Count Karl Nesselrode to find a solution. To demonstrate British policymakers' eagerness to achieve results, Palmerston gave a speech before Parliament outlining the extensive correspondence between Britain and Russia on the subject (*The Morning Chronicle*, 20 August 1853; Hajnal 1920: 64). The body of correspondence between Cunningham, Lloyd, other British diplomats in the region, and officials in London from 9 February 1849 to 15 July 1853 was published, and is cited here as *Correspondence* 1853.

14 Slade writes that 'the old chateaux, the green vineyards, and the pretty villages of the Rhine, are wanting; but nature shows herself on the Danube in a grander mood, under wilder and more impressive forms. Here the atheist must acknowledge a God' (1840: 161).

15 Southeast Europe provided a particularly attractive destination for adventurous female travelers such as Julia Pardoe and Felicia Skene. Perhaps because of its proximity to Europe, the region at once challenged and reinforced the shifting narratives and imperialist assumptions of the nineteenth and early twentieth centuries (Hammond 2008).

16 The Danube featured not only in the Crimean War and the Balkan Wars but in all the bloodiest moments of the twentieth century. World War I erupted from

the Danube valley, and Mauthausen-Gusen, one of the most notorious Nazi concentration camps, was located on the Danube's bank. The Iron Curtain divided the Danube, and the river runs through Belgrade, which suffered extensive damage during the Yugoslav War, particularly from NATO bombings.

17 Lengyel starts his section on the red Danube with the observation that 'rivers, unlike flags, do not change their colors as they flow from one country into another' (1940: 139) – as this passage suggests, he believed that if we listened to the river, we would cease to divide it into political units and unite the river valley as a 'natural' political unit.

5

The 1856 Treaty of Paris and the first international organization

At the 1815 Congress of Vienna, the French representative Charles Talleyrand stated that the 'center of gravity of Europe is neither in Paris; nor in Berlin, but at the mouths of the Danube' (Hajnal 1920: 38). Here, Talleyrand did not envision the mouth of the Danube as the center of military power or economic wealth, but as a key geopolitical hotspot at the fringes of Europe that held sway over the future of European international society. The Danube as a connecting highway transported European power and civilization outward to command the eastern periphery, but at the same time the river is a fluid conduit that could easily flow backward and bring political instability upriver. In the mid-1850s, the Crimean War illustrated Talleyrand's worries by demonstrating how untamed and uncivilized geographies at the mouth of the Danube can throw the entire continent into conflict. This chapter details the establishment of peace in the wake of that conflict and the creation of a European commission to ensure a civilized and rational authority controlled the mouth of the Danube and the gateway to Europe.

The 1856 Paris Peace Treaty created the European Commission of the Danube as the first international executive body, and arguably the first truly international organization, with states holding joint authority over territory half a continent away. This chapter first considers the political context and the specific constellations of power governing the Danube at the Paris Peace Conference. Then, the chapter details discussions between diplomats on how to apply principles established at the Treaty of Vienna to the Danube. Specifically, I trace how competing understandings of the river as private property versus international commons were not resolved by the 1815 Vienna Treaty but continued to inform diplomatic disagreements over how to best manage the Danube. Finally, the last section examines the two commissions established by the 1856 Paris Peace Treaty – a riparian commission and the European Commission – and how the permanent riparian commission faded away while the temporary European Commission grew to become a unique and powerful international body. I argue that the creation and eventual success of the European Commission emerged from a combination of British and French geopolitical power at the end of the Crimean War and their understanding of the Danube delta as an untamed geography that required strong international guidance.

While it would be easy to brush over the creation of the European Commission as simply the application of the Rhine Commission model to a new river and the continuation of a global river governance regime, this would be an oversimplification that misses an important international political development. The Rhine Commission created a weak interstate model based on an understanding of the river as the private property of individual riparian states – and since the Rhine flowed through the heart of Europe, legitimate and civilized states held sovereign authority over its banks. However, the Danube was a different space in the European geographical imagination and required a different type of international body to manage it. The weak Rhine Commission model would have been insufficient to control the Danube as a liminal geography that connected European civilization to the disquieting East and to tame the Danube delta for the benefit of global commerce. To tame the Danube required a more powerful international commission with Britain and France, the foremost Europeans powers, at its helm.

The broader implication here is that the concept of the international did not develop from internal European politics but arose through European international society's engagement with the periphery and Europe's fears of untamed geographies and the instability such spaces might bring. Hence, early understandings of the Danube delta as 'international' implied a space without existing civilized authority and therefore necessitated an international authority to take over for the benefit of all. Underlying this understating of the international, then, is an argument that privileged a certain European form of territorial control based on the exploitation of nature as more civilized and more legitimate than others. In this way, the 'internationalization' of the Danube delta echoes imperialism in that both aimed to bring untamed territories under civilized European control.

Anglo-Russian competition and the Danube delta

The Crimean War highlighted the dominant fissures in mid-nineteenth-century European politics, with the retreat of the Ottoman Empire playing like a leitmotif over diplomatic activities until World War I. Ostensibly, the war began over a dispute regarding whether Russia's Orthodox Church or France's Catholic Church should be seen as the protector of Christians in the Ottoman Empire and thus hold the keys to Bethlehem's Church of the Nativity. However, the three-year war involved larger questions triggered by the Ottoman Empire's decline,[1] including Russia's ambitions south and west into the Black Sea and central Asia, Britain's expanding trade interests in the region, Germany's and Italy's national unification struggles,[2] and clashes between the preservation of the old social order and a new revolutionary nationalism threatening to overturn that order. The European Commission of the Danube, then, was created amid a whirlwind of geopolitical and social change. However, scholarly accounts of the Crimean War and its aftermath rarely offer analysis on the question of Danubian navigation. Most works that focus on the freedom of navigation at the Danube's mouth frame the episode as part of intensifying Anglo-Russian conflict throughout the nineteenth century (Urquhart 1833; Puryear 1931), or as a first stepping stone toward the intergovernmental global governance projects of the early twentieth century (Baicoianu 1917; Kaeckenbeeck 1918; Hajnal 1920; Chamberlain 1923). More recently, Romanian scholars have examined the role of the Crimean War and the 1856 Danube Commission in their own national history (Cernovodeanu 1986; Florescu 1998; Ardeleanu 2014; Munteanu 2015).

In the early nineteenth century, the Ottoman Empire controlled the Danube's mouth where the 2,860-kilometer river empties into the Black Sea. Upstream of Ottoman territory, a sizeable section of the Danube's navigable length passed through the Austrian Empire. The Ottoman Empire bled territory as its authority waned, and Russia took full advantage to pursue its ambition to establish a warm water port open to naval activity all year round – an ambition first planted in the Russian imperial imagination by Peter the Great in the seventeenth century. Controlling the Black Sea and the Dardanelles into the Mediterranean would affirm Russia's position as a global naval power (Lambert 2011: 37–40). In addition, a secure foothold along the Danube would allow Russia to increase its control over eastern Europe. With the 1812 Treaty of Bucharest, Russia became a riparian state along the Danube, and with the 1829 Treaty of Adrianople, Russia gained control over the entire Danube delta (Chamberlain 1923: 27). By controlling the delta, Russia also became responsible for maintaining freedom of navigation at the Danube's mouth according to the principles agreed at the Congress of Vienna.

Britain watched Russia's expansion and dreams of naval grandeur with concern. Eastern Europe, the Black Sea, and central Asia stood between Europe and Britain's prized possession of India. One important British concern was Russia's increasing capacity to hamper Britain's lines of communication and trade. As Lord John Russell polemically argued in Parliament, 'if we do not stop the Russians on the Danube, we shall have to stop them on the Indus' (quoted in Richardson 1994: 83). In addition to concern over central Asia, from the 1830s onward British commercial interests along the Danube increased, and merchants and diplomats familiar with navigation at the Danube's mouth increasingly complained of Russian neglect in keeping the shipping channels free from obstacles. As detailed in the previous chapter, international shipping was obstructed by sand and silt build-up, but also suffered from lawlessness on the delta and arbitrary quarantine measures.

Most accounts suggest that Russia actively neglected navigation at the Danube's mouth in favor of Russian trade out of Odessa, a Black Sea port roughly 200 kilometers north of the delta (see, for example, Chamberlain 1923: 36; Urquhart 1851: 14; Baumgart 1981: 126). However, as Constantin Ardeleanu's detailed scholarship shows, internal Russian politics complicated this assumption. While some, such as finance minister Count Egor Frantsevich Kankrin and select Odessa merchants, advocated for shutting down Danube trade at Sulina, important Russian policymakers including Tsar Nicholas I and Chancellor Karl Nesselrode did not advocate such an approach. In fact, military hero Count Mikhail Vorontsov even argued that Russia would gain from the growth of Danube trade. Hence, Ardeleanu concludes, 'available sources do not prove that an official policy was decided to hinder trade on the Danube' (2014: 167). Indeed, the British foreign secretary Lord Palmerston also dismissed the logic that obstructing trade at Sulina equated to gains for Russian trade at Odessa. He noted that 'it is plainly manifest that any such idea would be erroneous, and that prosperous commerce by the Danube would in no way interfere with prosperous commerce by Odessa' (*Correspondence* 1853: 24 September 1851). Tsar Nicholas I echoed these sentiments (Ardeleanu 2014: 168). Global demand would readily absorb any supply of cheap goods from the region. Hence, conflict over the Danube delta was not a simple function of economic competition between two growing superpowers.

In the early nineteenth century, the Anglo-Russian relationship included both conflictual and cooperative moments. Prior to the Crimean War, the verbal and secret agreement of 1844 between Britain and Russia stipulated that both would work to maintain the integrity of the Ottoman Empire, and Russia would consult Britain before making any moves against it (Puryear 1931: 6). Further, when the weight of complaints about Russia's obstruction of Danube shipping reached the upper levels of the British government, Palmerston directed British emissaries to press Count Nesselrode for a solution. To demonstrate his government's eagerness to achieve results, Palmerston gave a speech before Parliament outlining the extensive correspondence between Britain and Russia concerning Danube navigation between 1849 and 1853.[3] Count Nesselrode assured Britain that efforts were being made to clear the shipping channel and strict directives had been sent to local authorities. Later, British officials would express skepticism as to how hard Russia had actually tried to improve navigation on the Danube delta (FO 7/461, 1855: no. 314), but Russian efforts seemed sincere.[4] Hence, navigation difficulties on the Danube delta could not be reduced to simple economic or political jealousy. The unique hydrology of the river itself, as the Danube Commission would also experience after its inception, confounded simple technical solutions and contributed to the international confrontation over navigation on the Danube.

Furthermore, Anglo-Russian rivalry at the Danube's mouth involved ideological factors that shaped British and European perceptions. Iver Neumann argues that despite its status among the Great Powers at the Congress of Vienna, Russia 'experienced trouble maintaining its great power credentials' throughout the nineteenth century (2008: 138). This decline was a result of Russia's lack of social power in European international society as other states looked down on its illiberal domestic institutions and stagnant military. J. H. Gleason (1950) argued that between 1815 and 1841, anti-Russian sentiments were manufactured in Britain – a feeling based as much on competition for markets as a civilizational discourse against the policies of a reactionary Russia. In a prominent example, in 1854, the foreign secretary the Earl of Clarendon laid before Parliament the reason for Britain's involvement in the Crimean War:

> We cannot suppose that the intelligence and civilization of Central Europe would be any more a barrier to such encroachments than the intelligence and civilization of Rome were a barrier to the encroachment of the Huns. And, my Lords, the more we examine this question the more gigantic is the force it assumes. We are not now engaged in the Eastern question, as it is commonly called, but it is the battle of civilization against barbarism, for the independence of Europe. (HL Deb, 31 March 1854: vol. 132, col. 150)

Here, Clarendon argues that the 'Eastern Question' concerned something greater than simply economic interests at the edge of Europe. He elevates the conflict to a struggle to preserve European civilization against the encroachment of barbarism. While Clarendon does not specifically mention the Danube by name, the river is implied as the border between Rome and the Huns, the highway connecting central Europe and encroachments from beyond, and the line in the sand between civilization and barbarism. As I argued in the previous chapter, taming and rationalizing the Danube delta became a civilizational mission with the river as a conduit for civilization to flow east.

Alongside Britain, France also watched Russian advancement in eastern Europe with concern. In the mid-nineteenth century, Napoleon III sought to restore France to a position of prominence and to locate himself as the arbiter of the European balance of power (Richardson 1994: 80). Similar to Britain, France had colonial interests in the Mediterranean and the Middle East and did not want Russia to dominate lines of communication and trade in the Black Sea and Dardanelles. Additionally, with its history of republican politics and its support for Catholicism, France viewed reactionary and Orthodox Russia with suspicion (Figes 2012: 5–8). Military victory over Russia in the Crimea and a seat on the European Commission to govern the Danube delta would keep Russia contained and also advance French prestige on the European political stage.

Austria's involvement in the Crimean War resembled a complex balancing act – Austria aspired to play a central role in diplomatic negotiations without actually entering the war. In the early nineteenth century, Austria and Russia competed for influence in eastern Europe while cooperating under the Holy Alliance to maintain the conservative order. Russian intervention in the 1848 revolutions had checked internal forces that threatened the integrity of the Habsburg monarchy. However, the upper Danube was an imperial highway that bound Austrian lands together, and Russian control over the delta proved problematic for the transport of Austrian goods internationally. Austria stood in a central geographical location and aimed to check Russian advances up the Danube, but financial difficulties and the underlying social fissures that triggered the 1848 revolts weakened Austrian power (Schroeder 1972). Throughout the war, France and Britain hoped that Austria would join them against Russia, but Austria resisted and established diplomatic negotiations instead. Finally, Russia agreed to peace talks in Paris when Austria issued an ultimatum threatening to join the allies on the battlefield if Russia did not accept their terms (Baumgart 1981: 68–9). At the Paris Conference, when Emperor Napoleon III expressed regret that Austria had not participated in the war and therefore did not gain territory or power, Austrian foreign minister Count Karl Ferdinand von Buol[5] responded that Austria's intervention might have gained both, 'but it would certainly also have brought her a great increase and variety of troubles' (Hajnal 1920: 73).

Hence, the European powers entered the diplomatic negotiations to end the Crimean War with different hopes and fears about the post-war settlement. However, Britain, France, and Austria all aimed to check Russian power in eastern Europe, and in doing so, establish a more civilized authority to govern and tame the mouth of the Danube and ensure stability in European politics. With battlefield victory in the Crimea, Britain and France were in a position to impose such an authority.

History of cooperation and conflict on the Danube

The history of the Danube as a highway very much echoes that of the Rhine, where local authorities treated the river as private property subject to tolls and monopolies. Henrik Hajnal's account of the Danube's history tells of local medieval nobility who attached large metal chains across the river to regulate traffic and enforce tolls (1920: 8–9).[6] The custom of transshipping allowed local guilds to divide the river between them, and only boatmen from a particular guild could operate boats along each stretch of river. Even at the Danube's mouth, cargo had to be transferred to Ottoman ships to enter the Black Sea (Hajnal 1920: 22). Another practice known as staple rights required foreign boats to unload their cargo at local ports and display their goods for a set number of days so that local merchants had the first chance to buy. The guilds maintained towpaths and kept the waterway navigable. In exchange, merchants paid a toll to the guild (Hajnal 1920: 42; Chamberlain 1923: 20–1). These monopolistic rights enriched local authorities but hindered trade along the Danube.

In the eighteenth century, however, as trade increased and local authorities tamed the legendary natural dangers that hampered navigation along the Danube, states along the river signed bilateral treaties to expand the freedom to navigate the entire river. The 1718 Treaty of Passarowitz between Austria and Russia agreed that subjects of both empires could freely navigate and trade on the Danube. In 1739, Austria and the Ottoman Empire agreed to similar terms under the Treaty of Belgrade. In 1784, Russia and the Ottomans agreed to similar provisions and Austria was given most favored nation status (Hajnal 1920: 20–3; Chamberlain 1923: 26).[7] These reciprocal agreements regarded the Danube as the private property of riparian empires, and navigation rights were only granted to other nations at the discretion of each owner.[8] Despite these similarities between the Rhine and the Danube, the two rivers held different meanings in the European geographical imagination – unlike the Rhine, the Danube flowed from the center of Europe toward a liminal space between the known Europe and the uncivilized East. Hence, efforts to control the Danube were also efforts to tame this unstable conduit for fear that the uncivilized East might flow back upriver.

At the 1815 Congress of Vienna, the French representative Emmerich Joseph von Dalberg had proposed to include the Danube along with the Rhine, the Main, the Neckar, the Mosel, the Meuse, and the Scheldt on the list of international rivers. If passed, the principle that all nations had the same right to navigate and trade along an international river would have been extended to the Danube. However, Dalberg's proposal was rejected because the Danube lay beyond the territorial jurisdiction of the Congress. In addition, as I argued in Chapter 3, while in principle the Treaty of Vienna proclaimed the transboundary river as international commons, in practice states continued to dispute the international nature of the Rhine in favor of treating the river as a private highway. By the 1850s, however, diplomats interpreted the Treaty of Vienna as an affirmation of the principle that freedom of navigation and commerce should apply to all international rivers. When diplomats in 1855–56 turned their attention to navigation on the Danube, the proposed treaty text stated that 'the Lower Danube shall be subject to the general stipulations of the Treaty of Vienna in respect to the navigation of rivers' (PRO 30/22/18/8, 1855: no. 31). In the final days of the 1856 Paris Conference, the Austrian representative Count Buol argued that the peace conference should adopt a moral idea. The two moral ideas he believed the Congress of Vienna had adopted were the abolition of the slave trade and the free navigation of rivers (Thayer 1917: 39). Hence, by 1856, the Treaty of Vienna had become shorthand for the liberal and moral principle that transboundary rivers should be open to freedom of navigation and commerce for all nations. However, while diplomats agreed on the principle, the devil was in the details as they argued over how the principle should be applied and therefore continued to contest the meaning of the river.

Diplomats in 1855–56 looked to the Final Act of the Congress of Vienna as the legal precedent for applying freedom of navigation to the Danube, but the Rhine Commission established in 1816 included only riparian states. Aside from drawing up navigation regulations, the Rhine Commission had little power and met once a year as an appeals tribunal (Kaeckenbeeck 1918: 65–6). The untamed Danube offered additional challenges – both physical and moral – that required more robust international action.

First, immediate engineering works were needed to keep the delta's shipping channels free from silt and debris. Furthermore, in the long term, the Danube as a connecting river needed to be secured so that civilization could continue to flow from Europe outward. Hence, taming the Danube's mouth required a new kind of international body. In September 1850, British Vice Consul Charles Cunningham listed four ways to resolve the Danube's navigation problems: 1) the Russian government should undertake the project; 2) the Russian government should hire contractors; 3) a commission of all nations interested in Danube navigation should undertake the project; and 4) a commission should hire contractors for the project (*Correspondence* 1853: 30 September 1850). All four options – either a proactive Russia or a proactive commission – required a political force more powerful than the Rhine Commission. The next section will consider diplomatic debates at Vienna in 1855 and Paris in 1856 as they revealed how differing understandings of the river shaped the creation of the European Commission of the Danube.

A not-so-simple task: 'applying' the Congress of Vienna to the Danube

According to preliminary diplomatic agreements at Vienna and Paris, all European diplomats needed to do to ensure freedom of navigation on the Danube was to 'apply' the Congress of Vienna's principles to another river.[9] However, the matter of applying Vienna was much more politically and diplomatically volatile than the formal legal language implied, and similar to dynamics at Vienna four decades before, diplomats were divided on whether to interpret the river as private property or international commons. Not only was the Final Act of the Congress of Vienna inconclusive in adjudicating between these interpretations of the transboundary river and vague in how to enforce the principles of free navigation and commerce, diplomats in the 1850s also disagreed over whether the Vienna model applied to the Danube at all or whether the river required a completely different set of international principles.

Deliberations about the terms that would eventually dictate the end of the Crimean War began almost as soon as hostilities began. In December 1853, French, British, and Austrian representatives met in Vienna to discuss the four main war aims,[10] which eventually became the backbone of the 1856 Paris Treaty (Baicoianu 1917: 51–2). In August 1854, the allies sent a memorandum to the Russian representative in Vienna, Prince Alexander Gorchakov, to inform him of their four major war aims. Point two on the freedom of navigation on the Danube stated that relations between Russia and the Ottoman Empire could only be repaired if navigation at the Danube's mouth were freed from obstructions in accordance with the Treaty of Vienna (Geffcken 1883: 8). The memo continued: 'This goal seems most likely achieved if the land included in the Danube delta was declared neutral. Care for preserving and clearing the mouths should be entrusted to an organization ['une société'] that will be accountable to all the Powers' (quoted in Hajnal 1920: 70). The allies met again in December 1854 and sent a memorandum outlining the conditions for peace; Prince Gorchakov agreed to the points as a basis for negotiations. In March and April 1855, Count Buol, representative of the Austrian emperor, convened the Conference of Vienna with representatives from Britain, France, Austria, the Ottoman Empire, and Russia to discuss the memorandum.

The 1855 Vienna Conference

Already at the 1855 Vienna Conference, diplomats were divided over the international river as private property, shared property of the riparian states, or international commons. From the start, France and Britain interpreted the Danube as an international economic entity that promised the moral and commercial benefits of international trade for all nations. Ahead of the conference, French foreign minister Edouard Drouyn de Lhuys sent instructions to the French representative Baron de Bourquency maintaining that 'possession without control of the main mouth [of the Danube] brought, as to the navigation of this great river, moral and material obstacles, detrimental to trade of all nations' (Geffcken 1883: 8). Similarly, the foreign secretary the

Earl of Clarendon wrote to the British representative Lord Westmoreland that the allies should ensure the establishment of an independent authority to remove navigation obstacles, and that Russia should give up its rights since it had previously neglected its duties (Geffcken 1883: 9). The Danube as an international river, then, was the responsibility of all nations, and its maintenance was too morally and materially important to be left up to whoever happened to hold sovereignty over the banks.

At the first session at the Vienna Conference, Buol presented the second of four points worded in the following way: 'the freedom of the navigation of the Danube shall be completely secured by effectual means and placed under the control of a permanent syndical authority' (Kaeckenbeeck 1918: 85). On 21 and 23 March 1855, diplomats discussed this proposal. Russia upheld the river as private property and argued that only the sovereign had the right to grant navigation rights to shipping of other nations. Prince Gorchakov maintained that Russia had always been a good member of international society in granting 'the principle of freedom of navigation for all merchant flags' and had made efforts to remove navigation obstacles. And, he continued, if the word *syndicate* in Buol's proposed text 'implied the exercise of any right of sovereignty', then Russia must object since the delta was under Russian authority. Instead, to carry out the necessary engineering works, Russia wanted a body whose authority would be solely scientific and technical, and not political. Hence the neutral term European Commission was chosen instead (Geffcken 1883: 10; Kaeckenbeeck 1918: 88–9).

Austria, as a riparian state, advocated for interpreting the international river as joint property. The Austrian proposal divided the river into two segments: the upper and the lower Danube. On the upper Danube, Austria held sovereignty and intended to treat the river as an internal highway. The lower river's transboundary nature required a different solution. The Austrian proposal allowed for a European syndicate to establish regulations on the lower Danube, but the power to execute and enforce regulations would rest with a body comprised only of riparian states (Geffcken 1883: 9–10; Kaeckenbeeck 1918: 90). When Britain and France objected and pressed for positions on the executive committee, the Austrians responded that according to the model established at the Congress of Vienna, only the riparian states sat on river commissions. Here, divergence over how to 'apply' the Congress of Vienna reveals the unclear and politically charged nature of the seemingly straightforward proposal to extend principles already agreed in the Treaty of Vienna to the Danube. Certainly, all sides purported to endorse the principle of free navigation and commerce on the Danube, but how that principle translated to the design of the commission depended heavily on this contestation over what the Treaty of Vienna model meant.

For Britain, Austria's logic was unacceptable in that only the second executive commission would have actual powers to enforce free navigation and commerce on the lower Danube. This body needed British and French representatives to keep the Russians in line due to the history of Russian intransigence. In a note from the British representative Lord John Russell to Count Buol in March 1855, Russell wrote:

> Her Majesty's government can well understand why Russia who has always prevented the removal of obstructions to the free navigation of the Danube should object to English and French Commissioners, who would carefully watch her proceedings, but the ground on which Austria joins in and supports the objections of Russia is not intelligible. (FO 7/461, 1855: no. 273)

Further, in April 1855, Lord Russell sent another letter to Count Buol challenging Austria's logic that having French and British representatives on the executive committee would violate the precedent established by the Congress of Vienna:

> Having been attentively considered by her Majesty's government, who are of the opinion that if the navigation of the Danube is to be regulated in accordance with the Treaty of Vienna the Commission should consist of a Bavarian, an Austrian, a Russian, and a Turkish member, and the regulations should apply to the whole course of the Danube from the sea up to the point where it first becomes navigable and such an arrangement should require no further guarantee. If on the other hand there is to be a special arrangement to which Bavaria is not to be a party, and which is to apply only to that part of the river from the sea upwards to the point where it ceases to divide Austrian and Turkish territory, that is to the point where both banks are Austrian, *then the Treaty of Vienna is no longer the rule*, and the Commission to be appointed ought to contain an English and a French Member because England and France are deeply interested in having the channels of the River kept free and open. (PRO 30/22/18/4, 1855: no. 40, emphasis mine)

Here, Lord Russell specifically attacks Austria's logic regarding the applicability of the 1815 Vienna Treaty – if Austria wanted the exact same institutional model that was used for the Rhine Commission, then it would not be allowed to divide the river into two administrative segments and must invite a Bavarian representative onto the commission. Austria had adamantly opposed this. Following the logic behind Austria's own actions, Russell argued that establishing the Danube Commission was not a direct application of the Congress of Vienna, but the creation of something new – an independent, international body with power to oversee an international highway for the benefit of all nations. The final treaty language in 1855 favored Britain's interpretation: 'the freedom of the Danube and of its mouths shall be effectually secured by European institutions, in which the Contracting Powers shall be equally represented, without prejudice to the special position of the riparian Powers' (Kaeckenbeeck 1918: 91). In this language, all contracting powers would have a place on any institutions established to guarantee freedom of the Danube as an international river. However, the Vienna Conference collapsed without success, and the following year at Paris the entire debate would be rehearsed again.

The 1855 Vienna Conference failed due to disagreement over point three – the neutralization of the Black Sea. The British and French interpreted 'neutralization' to mean the demilitarization of the region, while Austria interpreted it as a system of balancing, with all powers keeping a naval presence in the Black Sea to deter Russia. Russia refused to accept the Anglo-French interpretation, and the British and French refused the Austrian plan (Baumgart 1981: 13). Lord John Russell resigned over the conference's failure, and George Villiers, 4th Earl of Clarendon, replaced him as the British representative in 1856. Edouard Drouyn de Lhuys also resigned as the French representative, and his replacement, Count Alexandre Walewski,[11] hosted the peace conference held the following year in Paris. By then, the allied victory at Sevastopol in September 1855 had elevated them to a stronger bargaining position.

The Anglo-French interpretation of the 'neutralization' of the Black Sea did have implications for their understanding of the Danube's mouth not as a military object to be conquered, but as a civilian space to be rationally administered through effective institutions. During deliberations, Austria proposed that Britain station ships of war at the Danube's mouth as a more effective means than any joint commission to guard against Russian intransigence and ensure freedom of navigation. Lord John Russell responded that ships of war would not be an appropriate remedy, since 'the evils complained of are not acts of violence which the presence of a ship of war could prevent but acts of willful omission which a member of the Executive Commission could watch and demand to have remedied' (FO 7/461, 1855: no. 273). Maintaining ships of war would effectively make the Danube delta a military object; instead Russell's words framed the international river as a civilian geography to be conquered and tamed not by warships but by the diligence of scientists, engineers, and bureaucrats.

The 1856 Paris Conference

Representatives from Britain, France, Russia, Austria, the Ottoman Empire, Sardinia, and Prussia convened at the 1856 Paris Peace Conference to establish peace after three years of war and roughly 640,000 deaths (Baumgart 1981: 216).[12] Like other diplomatic occasions of the century, intense contact between parties included social and formal functions day and night: 'intrigue, persuasion, eavesdropping went on at the breakfasts and dinners, at the balls, plays and receptions, in the drawing-rooms and even in the boudoirs' (Thayer 1917: 34). While the analysis here focuses exclusively on discussions about freedom of navigation on the Danube, these debates occurred around highly charged negotiations over post-war territorial and military adjustments and amid interpersonal rivalries. Indeed, like the International Rivers Committee at the Congress of Vienna, most scholarly works on the Paris Conference sideline discussions on the establishment of the Danube Commission in favor of detailing more contentious territorial and military issues.[13] At the same time, a sense of joint purpose united the diplomats and animated their efforts to restore peace and order to Europe. Guaranteeing freedom of navigation on the Danube was seen as part of this joint European effort.

At Paris, diplomats revisited arguments voiced the year before between Austria and Britain and France on the application of the 1815 Treaty of Vienna to the Danube. Territorial adjustments demanded by the first point of the peace terms meant that Russia was no longer a riparian state, and three new Danubian principalities – Moldavia, Wallachia, and Servia – were created under the suzerainty of the Ottoman Empire. Russia no longer had claims on the Danube, but Austria continued to insist on dividing it between the upper river under Austria's sole sovereign jurisdiction, and the lower river as a jointly managed transboundary entity. Ahead of the conference, the emperor sent strict instructions to his Austrian representatives to treat the river as two separate units. In the margins of one note, Emperor Franz Joseph wrote:

> There must be a very clear distinction made between the question of the Sulina and that of the Danube proper. On the former, all the powers have equal rights, whereas, on the latter, only the Riparian states have got a say in the matter. (quoted in Hajnal 1920: 72)

Hence, during discussions on the Danube, Count Buol insisted that the European Commission would 'affect only the interests of the navigation of the Lower Danube' (Kaeckenbeeck 1918: 93). Debate raged back and forth between Austria and Britain and France over this point in the sixth session (held 6 March) and the eighth session (held 12 March) (Parliamentary Papers 1856, LXI 2073). The French representative Count Walewski identified two distinct goals regarding the Danube: first, applying the principles established at the Congress of Vienna to the entire river; and second, removing obstacles to shipping in the delta. The peace treaty, he insisted, needed to address both, since the two aims were interlinked. Therefore, the river must be treated as one indivisible whole. In addition, the British representatives highlighted that since 'the condition assented to by the Belligerents referred to the Danube, it must be held to mean the entire navigable stream' and not just the lower Danube

(FO 27/1168, 1856: pp. 173–4, emphasis in the original). The Danube as a commercial highway must have consistent regulations throughout – it made little sense to divide the same river into private property and international commons subject to different rules and regulations.

Count Buol countered with assurances that Austria intended to uphold the principle of freedom of navigation along the entire river, but might be 'hampered ... by previous engagements and acquired rights which it has an obligation to take into account' (Parliamentary Papers 1856, LXI 2073: 36). By this statement, Buol was referring to an exclusive trade monopoly granted to the Danube Lloyd Navigation Company[14] until 1880, thus treating the river as private property that could be leased out by the Austrian government to commercial entities at will. According to Buol, Clarendon replied: 'You want Europe not only to clear the mouths of the Danube, but also to give you the exclusive right of trading there!' (Parliamentary Papers 1856, LXI 2073: 36; Hajnal 1920: 75). Both Britain and France objected to Austria's resistance – they insisted on applying the Treaty of Vienna's principles to the entire navigable length of the river, even if those principles were to be executed by two separate commissions. As Clarendon wrote in a report to Palmerston in London:

> Count Buol was asked whether the Belligerent Powers who alone had opened the navigation of the Danube and were about to take measures to rescue the freedom of its navigation by which Austria more than any other Power would have benefitted were likely to consent to his proposal which was to exclude them from the Danube and guarantee to an Austrian Company a monopoly of the traffic. (FO 27/1169, 1856: pp. 6–7)

After all, Austria had not contributed militarily to the allied victory in the Crimean War, and allowing Austria exclusive control over the upper Danube would give it unfair advantage, since the European Commission would work to improve navigation on the lower Danube for the disproportionate benefit of Austrian trade (Geffcken 1883: 11–12; Hajnal 1920: 74). Count Buol believed he stood on the losing side of this debate. In several reports to Emperor Franz Joseph, Buol first stressed that he had presented Austria's arguments for a divided river forcefully, particularly as the 'decrees of the Vienna Congress make no provision for interference by the European Powers' since only riparian countries had rights on the Rhine Commission. The other parties agreed. However, Buol maintained, the Austrian position of dividing the Danube could not be sustained as 'all the members being against us':

> I consider it a moral impossibility to assert that principles of the Vienna Congress can never be applied to the Danube. Such an assertion would call forth a unanimous cry of displeasure; it might even frustrate the whole work of the Peace Conference, and rob us of the fruits of the freedom of the mouths

of the Danube ... In conclusion, I humbly beg Your Majesty to bear in mind that it is far better to grant this freedom of our own will and accord, than to wait till we are forced to do so. (quoted in Hajnal 1920: 77)

Some have questioned whether Buol's inability to stand his ground reveals a weakness of character or even treasonous pro-British leanings. However, the political weight of Europe stood against him. In addition, as Buol's comment concerning the adoption of moral ideas at major conferences suggested, he believed in the value of liberal, universal ideas. A free Danube would be in line with these values. In response to Buol's letters, on 16 March 1856, Emperor Franz Joseph gave his consent to the application of the Treaty of Vienna to the entire river. During the tenth session on 18 March, Buol acquiesced to the proposed treaty language and agreed to the creation of two commissions (Parliamentary Papers 1856, LXI 2073: 43). Buol's notes suggested that the European Commission would complete its task within two or three years and thus end foreign interference on the Danube delta in favor of an executive commission of riparian states (Kaeckenbeeck 1918: 97).

The 1856 Treaty of Paris

The final text of the 1856 Paris Treaty applied navigation principles established at Vienna to the Danube. Unlike the Treaty of Vienna, which was a general declaration of principles, the Paris Treaty was more concrete in specifying how to ensure navigation along the Danube. Article XV stipulated that navigation on the Danube should not be impeded. Tolls would be collected to maintain navigation, and police and quarantine regulations would be established and would hinder navigation as little as possible. To enact Article XV, a temporary European Commission of all parties to the treaty – Britain, Austria, France, Prussia, Russia, Sardinia, and the Ottoman Empire – would plan the engineering works and draft the code of navigation at the Danube's mouth. In addition, 'the flags of all nations shall be treated on a footing of perfect equality' along the entire river, following the principles of the 1815 Treaty of Vienna (Chamberlain 1974 [1918]: 27; Kaeckenbeeck 1918: 98–9). Article XVII established the second, permanent riparian commission with delegates from Austria, Bavaria, the Ottoman Empire, Wurtemberg, and the Danubian principalities. Hence, with the 1856 Treaty of Paris, the first international organization was born in which non-riparian states exercised authority over a geographical space a continent away.

However, the establishment of the Danube Commission should not be considered a complete victory for the British and French interpretation of the Danube as international commons. In fact, in the end, the Paris Treaty did split the river. The delta became an international geography under the joint jurisdiction of all parties that signed the Paris Treaty. In principle the upper Danube would not be an internal Austrian space (as Austria had hoped) and freedom of navigation for all would apply. However, in practice, this segment of the river remained the common property of riparian states, particularly Austria, which continued to defend its right to manage the upper Danube without interference. Two commissions were established to manage these different understandings of the Danube – a European Commission comprised of all the treaty's signatories including Prussia and Sardinia to clear the mouth of the Danube, and a permanent executive commission of riparian states to prepare regulations, remove impediments, and take over the management of the delta after the temporary commission was dissolved. This tension between the river as a private or international space continued to inform cooperation over the Danube. While geographical imaginaries of the Danube as a connecting river that must be tamed for European civilization enabled the international definition of the delta and hence the creation of the 'temporary' European Commission, as I will discuss in the following section, contingent political developments also played a role in why the second commission never gained traction while the European Commission became permanent.

Throughout the debates at Vienna and Paris, all parties agreed to apply the Treaty of Vienna to the Danube, but disagreed over what the Danube as a transboundary river meant and therefore what 'applying' the Treaty of Vienna meant. In addition, early in the discussion, diplomats discussed the nature of the commission as a political or technical entity. In response to Russia's early insistence on the scientific and technical nature of the commission, Baron Bourqueny argued at the 1855 Vienna Conference that 'it was impossible to divest of all political character a question which had been raised to the importance of a European guarantee'. While this comment was largely ignored, Bourqueny pinpoints a pivotal insight about the Danube Commission and international organizations in general – these are deeply political bodies designed to exert control over a sphere of international life. To treat these commissions as merely technocratic or scientific is to willfully neglect their nature as political sites, which in itself is a political statement that aims to apportion power and resources in certain ways at the exclusion of others.

How the European Commission became permanent

The conflict over whether the Danube should be considered private property or international commons did not end with the signing of the 1856 Paris Peace Treaty – instead, the dueling interpretations of the river continued to haunt the commissions established to implement the Treaty. Despite diplomatic agreement in 1856 on the universal applicability of Articles 108 to 117 of the Final Act of the Congress of Vienna to the Danube, Austria continued to resist and held onto its exclusive power over the upper Danube as the private property of riparian states. Austria's recalcitrant position echoed Dutch resistance to the Treaty of Vienna and its application to the Rhine. In contrast, Prussia, which maintained a restrictive interpretation of the Treaty of Vienna with respect to the Rhine, pushed for a liberal interpretation of the Danube as international commons (Kaeckenbeeck 1918: 100). The shifting interests of the parties and their geographical position on the river shaped how they understood it.

This section explores post-formative politics after the establishment of the riparian commission and the European Commission to control the Danube. While the 1856 agreement created a permanent riparian commission, British and French dominance and the contingent politics within the body led to its dissolution. Conversely, while the 1856 agreement agreed to create a temporary European Commission with the single purpose of clearing the shipping channels on the delta, the overall mission to tame the Danube delta for global commerce and the river's stubborn hydrology that resisted simple engineering solutions transformed a temporary commission into a permanent one. Indeed, the river's resistance to simple solutions contributed to the growth of the European Commission's power and authority, and by the early twentieth century, the European Commission as an international organization held independent financial, judicial, and policing powers over the Danube delta.

The Riparian Danube Commission and political impasse

The riparian commission – with Austria, Bavaria, Turkey, Württemberg, and the three new Danube principalities of Servia, Moldavia, and Wallachia – convened in Vienna in November 1856 with the Austrian representative chairing. One of the committee's main tasks was to draft articles of navigation. In addition, the commission established three subcommittees: the first to formulate plans for freedom of navigation; the second to determine duties, quarantines, and other regulations; and a third to prepare a strategy for the elimination of navigation obstacles along the river.

Immediately, Austria dominated discussions on the articles of navigation and pushed to restrict rights for non-riparian countries. This included a scheme for toll collection to be managed solely by riparian states and the continuation of the Austrian monopoly over regular steam services along the upper river (Hajnal 1920: 83). Austria proposed language stipulating that navigation for vessels coming from or going to the high seas should be free for all nations, but that 'the use of the river navigation, properly so called, between the ports of the Danube without going on to the high seas, is reserved to the vessels of the riparian countries of the river' (Kaeckenbeeck 1918: 102). This disregarded the 1856 Paris Treaty and the notion of equality for flags of all nations. Further, Austria was suspicious of other members and attributed resistance to its proposals from states such as Servia (modern-day Serbia) to the interference of outside parties such as France. Discussions came to an impasse in February 1857 when the European Commission wrote to the riparian commission asking for a copy of the body's meeting minutes as both commissions ought to coordinate policies regarding the same river. Bavaria, Württemberg, and Servia agreed to the request, but Austria refused to comply, adjourned the meeting, and rebuffed subsequent requests to reconvene. By the following year, all representatives had left Vienna and the riparian commission never resumed (Hajnal 1920: 83–5). Perhaps the Austrians preferred to dissolve the commission rather than be outvoted by the smaller riparian states.

A conference of European powers met in Paris in August 1858 to review the riparian commission's draft articles for Danube navigation. The British representative Lord Cowley objected to the articles' blatant disregard for the principles established by the Vienna and Paris agreements. In addition, the French representative argued that all tributaries of the Danube should be open to free navigation without monopolies, as France had recently canceled a concession with the Moldavian government based on this principle. In response, the Austrian representative Baron Hübner argued that Austria and the riparian commission did not need the consent of other European powers to implement the navigation articles. Further, Hübner argued that a restrictive interpretation of freedom of navigation had been applied to the Rhine, with regular service rights reserved for riparian states. Technically, Hübner was correct.[15] However, Lord Cowley had the backing of all the others and retorted that just because the Rhine Commission wrongly applied the Vienna principles did not mean it should be used as a precedent for the Danube Commission or as proof that only riparian states had the right to free navigation along an international river. Following the British lead, the French representative Count Walewski also declared that the parties should follow the principles established at Vienna rather than the subsequent – and wrong – application of the Treaty on the Rhine (Kaeckenbeeck 1918: 105–7; Hajnal 1920: 85–7). Here, the weight of geopolitical power behind Britain and France informed a certain interpretation of not only the Danube but also previous diplomatic efforts. However, the Austrians continued to stall rather than reconvene the riparian commission to address the changes the others had demanded. Almost a decade later in March 1866, Austria continued to prevaricate rather than reconvene the commission (Hajnal 1920: 88).

Hence, echoing post-1815 arguments along the Rhine, the conflict between Austria and other European powers over whether the Danube was the private property of riparian states or international commons continued past the signing of the 1856 Paris Peace Treaty. The specific dynamics of this conflict resulted in the dissolution of the Riparian Danube Commission, which the Paris Conference had intended as the permanent interstate body on the Danube. British and French victory in the Crimean War allowed them to push through their understanding of the Danube as an international highway and strengthen the European Commission to tame the river for global commerce.

The European Commission and the unruly river

Despite continued arguments over which principles and precedents would govern the upper Danube, even Baron Hübner admitted that with respect to the Danube's mouth, 'a new state of things' had been created (Kaeckenbeeck 1918: 110). If the Danube delta was envisioned as a lawless space that required rational government, and local authorities were either unwilling or unable to achieve this, then a capable and proactive international body would be needed to tame the delta for global commerce. This geographical imaginary informed the creation of the European Commission, but the development of the commission from a temporary to a permanent body was also helped along by the dynamics of the river itself.

The European Commission first convened on 4 November 1856 and started work immediately with none of the delays associated with the riparian commission. The European Commission conducted an engineering survey, built embankments, jetties, and even a lighthouse, and created a lifeboat service. The depth at the Sulina channel improved from nine feet in 1857 to 17.5 feet in 1861 to 19 feet in 1871 (Chamberlain 1923: 54). However, taming the Danube was not a simple task and the complex hydrology of the delta resisted one-time technical solutions, despite pre-war British rhetoric about how 'simple' it would be to clear the silt and debris. The Paris Conference had originally stipulated that the European Commission would operate temporarily for two year to clear the navigation routes in the delta, but the magnitude of the engineering project required the commission to be extended again and again to continue its battle against the sand and silt. In 1865, the commission was granted a five-year extension; in 1871, it was granted another twelve-year extension; and in 1883, the commission was given a twenty-year extension that would be automatically renewed every three years after that (Blackburn 1930). This effectively made the European Commission a permanent international body. Hence, contrary to what the 1856 Paris Peace Treaty might have intended, the supposedly permanent riparian commission disappeared while the temporary European Commission of the Danube grew as an institution.

Indeed, the river's hydrological complexity not only allowed the European Commission to become a permanent body but extended its power and authority in order to develop and execute larger engineering projects to tame the river. First, to finance the growing scale of engineering works and infrastructure improvements, the commission contracted loans guaranteed by the member states (except Russia) and levied duties based on tonnage to repay these loans.[16] This ability to borrow on the international market made the commission financially independent. Second, to maintain order and enforce regulations, the commission gain not only regulatory capacity but also policing and judiciary powers. It created sanitation and quarantine measures, regulated lighterage services, managed the hiring of qualified pilots, and established navigation regulations that were 'binding not only in policy matters but also before the civil courts' (Chamberlain 1923: 57). To enforce its independent authority, the commission hired two international officers stationed at Sulina – an inspector general of the lower Danube and a captain of the port. Hence, as the complexity of the commission's engineering projects to tame the river grew, its powers also grew. It evolved from a temporary body with a single purpose to clear the shipping channels into a quasi-territorial authority with employees, courts, a flag, financial independence, and control over the use of force.

Hence, the steady expansion of the European Commission's powers affirmed its mission to control the unruly red Danube and tame the delta's channels for global commerce. By the early twentieth century, liberal thinkers such as Leonard Woolf praised the European Commission as an impressive achievement in international governance and the first international executive body (Woolf 1916: 21). This book draws heavily from secondary sources by Chamberlain, Kaeckenbeeck, and Hajnal that date from this period of liberal optimism, when experts in international law looked to the European Commission as a model for international government. Writing in 1930, historian Glen A. Blackburn even described the commission as being 'at the twilight of statehood' and 'something quite extraordinary in European history' (1930: 1154).

Conclusion

This chapter detailed the creation of the 1856 European Commission of the Danube as the first international organization in which a non-state body gained independent authority over a contested space. In analyzing the debates and negotiations surrounding the application of the 1815 Treaty of Vienna to the Danube, I have outlined how cooperation and conflict transcended supposedly critical junctures and continued before, during, and after the signing of treaties and creation of international bodies. Rather than a straightforward story of normative progression or consolidation, the application of the 1815 Treaty of Vienna to the Danube was very much shaped by power politics, historical contingency, and the complex hydrology of the river itself. However, it was geographical imaginaries of the Danube as a connecting river that constituted the political possibilities available to diplomats at Vienna in 1855 and Paris in 1856. The construction of the Danube's mouth as an untamed, anarchic geography cast the European Commission not only as an economic and engineering project but as a moral enterprise to tame the forces of irrationality and anarchy on the margins of Europe. Indeed, this construction of the Danube clarifies why the European Commission on the Danube strengthened in the late nineteenth century while the riparian commission dissolved.

In the mid-1850s, as General Charles George Gordon traveled down the Danube, he noted the difficult tasks ahead for the newly created commission. Over the winter of 1856–57, he met several of the commissioners including Major Stokes for Britain, Colonel Besson for France, and Prince Stourdza as the second Turkish commissioner. In a letter dated 15 April 1857, Gordon wrote to a friend 'what the Danube Commission is about no one knows' (1884: 136). However, as the European Commission commenced its tasks, this early uncertainty melted away. By the early twentieth century, when American missionary John Augustine Zahm traversed the Danube delta on his way to Baghdad, he described the great works accomplished by the commission 'for the betterment of this great international waterway' (1922: 33). In the more than six decades that separated Gordon's letter and Zahm's reflections, the Danube Commission had transformed from an uncertain venture into a success and triumph of rational engineering over the anarchic forces of nature and politics.

However, the glow of success did not last. Following World War I and the dissolution of the Habsburg Empire, the European Commission was finally extended to the entire navigable length of the river from Ulm in Germany to the Black Sea. But with the end of World War II, the Danube was once again divided – not between the upper river as private property and the delta as an international space but by the Iron Curtain. One commentator in 1951 lamented:

> Unstable like the waters they are set up to control, the international regimes which have from time to time been constituted for Europe's international waterways have been in a state of almost constant flux since the first attempt to secure freedom of navigation was made by the Congress of Vienna in 1815. (G. L. 1951: 419)

As these reversals suggest, how one views the lessons of history depends on where one stands. For the optimistic liberal internationalists of the early twentieth century, the European Commission of the Danube represented the advancement of international society against the forces of chaos and irrationality. However, for a world on the verge of a terrifying nuclear standoff, the commission was just another failed experiment in the dustbin of European history. Perhaps the beginning of the twenty-first century has recovered some of the liberal optimism of the early twentieth century, with a united Europe and a new integrated regime to manage the Danube signed in Sofia, Bulgaria, in 1994. However, any attempt to construct a teleological story to summarize the successes and failures of international regimes along Europe's waterways is likely to be overturned by future events. Indeed, fears that the Danube might flow backward, bringing dangerous people and ideas into the heart of Europe, still linger in western European imaginaries of the far side of the Mediterranean.

Notes

1 When Tsar Nicholas I asked Austrian Chancellor Klemens von Metternich in 1833 what he thought of the Turks as the sick man of Europe, Metternich is said to have responded, 'Is Your Majesty addressing the doctor or the heir?' (Palmer 1972: 261). As Metternich's quip suggests, the question before European powers was whether to prop up the sick man and hope he lived or start dividing up his possessions in anticipation of his eventual death.

2 Both Prussia and Sardinia participated in the Crimean War and subsequent peace conference in hopes of enhancing their positions in unification struggles.

3 'Steam navigation of the Danube', *The Morning Chronicle*, 20 August 1853; Hajnal 1920: 64.

4 For example, in 1845, Count Nesselrode sent inspectors to investigate the military governor of Bessarabia, General Pavel Ivanovici Fedorov, to resolve the lawlessness of the Danube delta. In 1847, Tsar Nicholas I personally sent another investigator. However, these inspectors were unable to resolve the situation, as the administrative corruption of the remote Danube delta ran deep (Ardeleanu 2014: 170). Similarly, technical solutions such a steam digger failed to resolve the silt build-up due to the hydrological complexity of the delta (Ardeleanu 2010).

5 Historians have judged Count Buol harshly, describing him as a liberal Anglophile unfit for the importance of his position as foreign minister and blaming him for the decline of Austria foreign policy after Metternich. Historian Roy A. Austensen contends that this dim view is not entirely justified. A careful analysis of Buol's career suggests that while he did have pro-British leanings, he was an able statesman and had strong ideas about Austria's position in Europe. But he inherited problematic legacies from his predecessors and faced a divisive domestic situation within the Empire (Schroeder 1968; Austensen 1973: 180–7). His general approach was to move closer to France and Britain, and he saw

Austria's role in the peace negotiations as a moderating influence on French and British war aims (Austensen 1973: 190).

6 Hajnal describes twelfth-century documents from the Austrian town of Stein that list the treasures flowing upriver, including raw silk, gold, silver, oil, laurel leaves, saffron, cinnamon, pepper, and ginger. Prince Leopold levied taxes on these goods – taxes that he pocketed. These documents also show that taxes were levied on female slaves exported to Turkey (Hajnal 1920: 111).

7 Emperor Joseph II had the agreement published along with a list of things that would sell well in the Ottoman Empire, and he actively subsidized and encouraged companies to take advantage of the Eastern market (Hajnal 1920: 116–17).

8 For example, Britain and Austria signed a signed a treaty with the Ottomans in 1839.

9 For example, the Austrian representative Baron Prokesch's proposal at the Vienna Conference starts: 'The Act of the Congress of Vienna ... having established in its articles 108 to 116 the principles intended to regulate the navigation of rivers which traverse several States, the Contracting Powers mutually agree to stipulate that, for the future, these principles shall be equally applied to the lower course of the Danube...' (Kaeckenbeeck 1918: 90).

10 The four war aims were: 1) that Russia would end its protection over the Danubian principalities (Moldavia, Wallachia, and Servia); 2) freedom of navigation on the Danube for all nations; 3) the end of Russian power ('neutralization') on the Black Sea; and 4) the Christian population in the Ottoman Empire to be placed under European protection.

11 Walewski was widely acknowledged as an illegitimate son of Napoleon Bonaparte, and Clarendon wrote that his intellect was 'not of an order to fit him for the management of the foreign affairs of France at a moment of great crisis' (Conacher 1987: 45). The antagonism between Clarendon and Walewski was palpable and even noted in official reports (Hajnal 1920: 73).

12 Baumgart's history of the Crimean War draws from a variety of sources to estimate the total casualties to include illness and battlefield-related deaths: French 95,000; British 22,000; Russia 470,000; Ottomans 45,000; Sardinians 2,000.

13 For example, P. Schroeder's *Austria, Great Britain and the Crimean War* (1972), Winfried Baumgart's *Peace of Paris 1856* (1981), and J. B. Conacher's *Britain and the Crimea, 1855–56* (1987).

14 The Austrian Lloyd Company was founded 30 April 1836 through government concessions and took over the Austrian Danube Steam Navigation Company (Hajnal 1920: 145).

15 Hübner even brought up the argument that the Treaty of Paris interpreted free as meaning 'merely the preservation of navigation from such impediments' as natural barriers, and did not grant 'to all the subjects of non-riparian states an equal right of navigation that was enjoyed by the subjects of the riparian state, and in turn for which there would be no reciprocity' (Kaeckenbeeck 1918: 109).

16 At first, the Ottoman Empire advanced the commission funds, but through a convention signed at Galatz on 30 April 1868, the signatories of the 1856 Paris Treaty agreed to guarantee the loans of the commission (Kaeckenbeeck 1918: 119).

6

Civilizing the imperial river: constructing the Congo

I have many things given me long ago from the white men's land, and I have often wished to see those who could make such wonderful things. I am told you people make all the cloth, the beads, the guns, the powder, plates, and glasses. Ah! You must be great and good people.

Chief Makoko according to Henry Morton Stanley, 1885

Then I saw the Congo, creeping through the black
Cutting through the forest with a golden track

Nicholas Vachel Lindsay, 1915

Diplomats gathered at the 1884–85 Berlin Conference looked to access Africa's resources and markets but without sparking violent competition among themselves and without upsetting the balance of power in Europe. To do so, diplomats aimed to apply previously established European models of cooperative river management to the Congo basin. However, the Congo as an object of cooperation held very different meanings than the Rhine or Danube for diplomats at Berlin and the wider European public. If taming the Danube controlled the liminal space between the civilized European self and a semi-familiar near periphery, taming the Congo was to impose European civilization on an entirely foreign geography. This chapter charts the construction of the Congo as a colonial highway that would bring commercial rationality and civilization to an empty space. However, the Congo as an untamed colonial object would also reveal deep anxieties in the European geographical imaginary about Europe's own civilizational and moral superiority.

The Congo is an unusual river – many miles before voyagers reach its mouth from the open seas, a dark yellow stream invades the blue waves, pouring 40,000 cubic meters of water per second into the sea. In addition, unlike most tropical rivers, the Congo's flow fluctuates curiously little with the seasons. These characteristics stem from two hydrological quirks. First, much of the Congo runs its course on a plateau, but in the final 350 kilometers the river drops nearly 300 meters, sending the water rushing with incredible force toward the ocean. Second, unlike other rivers such as the Amazon, the Congo flows in a semi-circle, draining from lands both above and below the equator. The equator roughly divides dry and wet seasons, so the water draining into the river is roughly equal all year round. There are two main social consequences of these hydrological quirks. First, anyone navigating upriver from the ocean hits a barrier of cataracts roughly 400 kilometers inland. This makes the Congo largely an inland river, and the largest trading centers along the river at modern-day Kinshasa and Brazzaville sit at the top of the cataracts. Second, this final section created a navigational barrier for European empires that wished to trade upstream but also holds immense hydroelectric potential due to its force and consistency (Hochschild 1998: 17).

However, the Congo's hydrological peculiarities did not in themselves create a different imaginary of it as an international river. Instead, unlike the other rivers discussed in this book, Europeans envisioned the Congo as a disconnected geography cut off from the normal politics of European society. The Congo basin as an abstract and foreign space allowed European colonizers to construct a conceptual emptiness and populate it with European goods, morals, and institutions. This chapter will first detail this act of conceptual erasure and how explorers, legal experts, and cartographers combined epistemic forces to construct emptiness along the Congo. Then, I will outline the commercial rationality that diplomats intended to impose upon this emptiness. In doing so, I argue that exporting civilization to Africa not only erased the Congo but also contorted Europe's own messy experiences with economic and political development into a generalizable and idealized model that could be applied across the globe.

Finally, I will explore how taming the Congo was central to the colonial project, but also how fears that the river might reverse rationality and uncivilize those who went upriver reflected late nineteenth-century European anxieties about their own seemingly invincible global status. Throughout, the analysis highlights how European imaginaries of the Congo centered on Europe itself, and reveals a colonial arrogance built on collapsing time and terrestrial space into the same civilizational and development continuum. This understanding of the Congo shaped European diplomats' enthusiasm for exporting European river institutions to the untamed African interior, but also contributed to its failure.

Imagining emptiness along the Congo

The 1884–85 Berlin Conference began with an act of erasure: diplomats and policymakers at Berlin envisioned the Congo as a conceptual blankness.

Much debate surrounds the use of *terra nullius* as a legal justification for nineteenth-century European imperial expansion, and these legal arguments were part of a larger repertoire of justifications and rationalizations for imperial acquisition (see, for example, Todorov 1984; Fitzmaurice 2007; Benton and Straumann 2010). However, this perceived absence of legitimate occupation by indigenous societies contributed to a larger conceptual blankness that shaped European diplomats', politicians', and the wider public's understanding of their political and civilizational role in West Africa. This act of erasure also omitted local social structures and histories from diplomatic consideration at the Berlin Conference, and made possible the application of European practices, guidance, and institutions to this empty space.

This vision of the Congo basin as empty space was constructed by experts – explorers, cartographer, and legal authorities – the foremost in their field, with the epistemic authority to shape European leaders' understanding of the Congo. Few at the conference had ever set foot in the Congo, and diplomats depended on information from those with better epistemic claims to know the river through direct observation, scientific measurements, and learned legal considerations. The following sections detail how these experts were able to erase the conceptual, geographical, and legal status of peoples and geographies along the Congo basin. In each category, I identify one prominent expert who actively shaped Europeans' understanding of the Congo basin. These experts, however, were not standalone agents in this story; they were products of their historical milieu and part of an underlying epistemic confidence in human society's ability to deploy a full range of technical tools to dissect, analyze, and tame the Congo.

Henry Morton Stanley and conceptual emptiness

In the late nineteenth century, Henry Morton Stanley was an acknowledged expert on the Congo basin. From 1874–77, the Anglo-American Stanley, financed by the *New York Herald* and the *Daily Telegraph*, traveled from Zanzibar to Boma on the West Coast of Africa along the entire length of the Congo (van Reybrouck 2014: 33). On a previous trip, he had encountered David Livingstone on the shore of Lake Tanganyika and supposedly uttered the immortal line, 'Dr. Livingstone, I presume?' Upon his return to Europe from traveling the length of the Congo, the French press compared Stanley's exploits to Hannibal's and Napoleon's (Hochschild 1998: 31). In the 1880s, now financed by King Leopold II of Belgium, Stanley returned to the Congo to explore the river and establish stations along its navigable length. Based on his experiences, Stanley published two best-selling travelogues of the Congo, which were translated into several languages: *Through the Dark Continent* in two volumes (1878) and *The Congo and the Founding of Its Free State* in two volumes (1885). In addition, he frequently authored newspaper articles and gave speeches about the commercial potential of the Congo.

Stanley joined the Berlin Conference as a technical expert on the American delegation. As one of the only people in attendance who had spent extensive time in the Congo, he held diplomats across Europe mesmerized by his vivid descriptions of the river and its environs. Throughout his writings and talks, Stanley portrayed the Congo basin as a moral and historical emptiness to be filled with the light of European civilization and commerce. In his 1885 book, Stanley describes the river as possessing 'extreme historical barrenness' without the classical associations elicited by other African rivers such as the Nile and Niger. He writes in his typical melodramatic fashion:

> No grand event is connected with its name; nothing has ever been performed in connection with the Congo to make its history popularly interesting to those who are not engaged in commerce or some special study of it. No military, naval, or scientific enterprise of any magnitude is associated with its name. (Stanley 1885, I: 102)

When Stanley does allude to the river's history, it is a colonial history, since Portuguese explorer Diogo Cão claimed the Congo's mouth with stone pillars in 1482. He describes the 'dismal local history that arouses a gruesome feeling when we recall the slave-trading days' – a history that would be erased with the civilizing light of Europe's antislavery campaign. In another example that depicts the Congo's perceived emptiness, Stanley tells a companion in *Through the Dark Continent*:

> Now, look at this, the latest chart which Europeans have drawn of this region. It is a blank, perfectly white ... I assure you, Frank, this enormous void is about to be filled up. Blank as it is, it has a singular fascination for me. Never has white paper possessed such a charm for me as this has, and I have already mentally peopled it, filled it with most wonderful pictures of towns, villages, rivers, countries and tribes. (Stanley 1878, II: 449)

Here, Stanley not only suggests to readers that the Congo is blank, but that the European imagination should fill it up, and throughout his narrative he fills this imaginary emptiness with European products: both material and ideational imports. Both the emptiness and the need to fill it culminates in the spread of commerce along the Congo as a civilizing project – a mission that the Berlin Conference considered its foremost aim. The Congo as a colonial and commercial artery would carry not only the material markers of civilization, but the habits and scientific mentality that transformed savage societies into civilized ones. Stanley's account effectively moved many Europeans to imagine how they would fill the conceptual emptiness along the Congo with commerce and civilization, including the man with the most influence on the region's future – King Leopold II of Belgium.

Sir Travers Twiss and legal emptiness

Jurists at the Berlin Conference also shaped the Congo's conceptual emptiness with legal arguments. Sir Travers Twiss's credentials as a British and international jurist were impeccable. Educated at Oxford in the 1820s, Twiss served as the Drummond Professor of Political Economy at Oxford, Professor of International Law at King's College, and London and Regius Professor of Civil Law at Oxford. In addition, he was named Queen's Advocate General and Vicar General to the Archbishop of Canterbury. In 1872, Twiss retired to Basel and self-imposed exile amid a social scandal in London – he had entered a sham marriage with a prostitute whom they had tried to pass off as Polish nobility. Twiss attended the Berlin Conference as a technical expert and prominent international jurist advising the conference on international law (Sylvest 2008; Fitzmaurice 2009). Despite his retirement from British legal circles, Twiss held particular sway over the British delegation and was influential among other delegations as well. According to legal historian Andrew Fitzmaurice, Twiss's views on international law were not remarkable nor uniquely British; his legal interpretations harmonized readily with those of jurists from Germany, France, Italy, and the United States (2009: 147).

While Twiss maintained that international law should defend the weak state against the strong, he upheld two sets of international legal codes: first, the law of nations between civilized European states, and second, a moral and natural law with and between African and East Asian powers. Africans, he wrote, could not be held accountable to European international law as indigenous peoples had no knowledge of these laws. However, Africans could not be ignorant of natural rights and laws, as these laws do not depend on civilizational status. Hence, even the most isolated African societies remained bound by natural law. While perhaps intended to release African polities from European legal obligations, in reality this separation between the two legal standards created a hierarchy that celebrated the material and moral progress emanating from the West while erasing Africans' legal status in the law of nations (Sylvest 2008: 409; Pitts 2012: 118). This legal position reflected prevailing nineteenth-century understandings of the international legal distinction between civilized and uncivilized states.

This view of Africa's legal agency allowed Europeans to maintain Africans' legal competence when it suited them, but relegate Africans to legal nonexistence when required. In published arguments prior to the Berlin Conference, Twiss wrote in support of Leopold II's schemes along the Congo by taking the position that:

> A nation, which by any just means enlarges it dominions by the incorporation
> of new Provinces with the free will of their inhabitants, or by the occupation

of vacant territory to which no other Nation can lay claim, is pursuing the legitimate object of its Being, the common welfare of its members. (quoted in Sylvest 2008: 409)

Hence, Twiss suggests that one could occupy Africa by either proving it was vacant territory or by obtaining the free will of the inhabitants. Leopold and his assistants attempted to do both. In the early 1880s, Twiss helped Stanley obtain the 'free will' of inhabitants along the Congo by concluding as many treaties as possible with local chiefs. Twiss and Stanley established more than 400 treaties in four years; some chiefs signed away their sovereign rights for reams of cloth, uniforms, and bottles of gin (Hochschild 1998: 71; van Reybrouck 2014: 51). While some legal scholars questioned whether 'uncivilized tribes' possessed sovereignty that they could sign away, many legal scholars at the conference and afterwards supported Twiss's position with respect to the legality of these treaties (Craven 2015). However, despite the existence of political authorities that had the competence to sign away their sovereign rights, territory along the Congo was effectively legally empty at Berlin and African leaders were not invited to the conference where their legal status was a major topic of discussion. Africans were legally bound and not bound; both paths led to dispossession.[1]

Subsequent legal scholars would pinpoint the Berlin Conference as a pivotal international moment when Africans were stripped of their competence as legal actors, and Africa was transformed into a 'conceptual *terra nullius*' ripe for European conquest (Anghie 2005: 91). As a prominent jurist at the conference, Twiss's arguments shaped the accepted understanding that the Congo basin was *terra nullius* without pre-existing international legal status – an emptiness into which European positive law could extend with the civilizing guidance of European institutions. Adding to Stanley's accounts and the emptiness he described for an awe-struck European public, leading legal experts at Berlin provided in technical language a legalistic justification for the Congo basin's emptiness.

Cartographers and geographical emptiness

To enforce the emptiness that Stanley and legal scholars constructed, European cartographers portrayed the Congo basin as a geographical emptiness through the use of white space. Prior to the mid-eighteenth century, unexplored spaces on maps were not left blank but filled with imaginary animals and landscape or descriptive texts. Only with Jean B. B. d'Anville's 1749 map of Africa did the convention of blank spaces become the cartographic norm. Local narratives did describe the social and political structures that populated this supposed geographical emptiness, but mapmakers excluded non-Western knowledge as unscientific and therefore unreliable. Only accounts with the epistemic authority of meticulous scientific measurements could be used in cartographic reproductions. Hence this imagined emptiness 'desocialized space' and erased the geographical existence of those along the Congo (Basset 1994: 324).

At the Berlin Conference, the map hanging in the conference hall was the Congo section of the 63-sheet map of Africa that Regnault de Lannoy de Bissy created for France's Service Géographique de l'Armée (see Figures 6.1 and 6.2). Lannoy de Bissy was a French officer in the Corps of Engineers who had frequented Algeria since childhood and developed an interest in the African continent. In 1872, he was appointed commander of a French engineering unit in Algeria. Inspired by David Livingstone's death in May 1874, he embarked on his grand project to map the continent. He later wrote that 'the general map which summarized the results of his [Livingstone's] journeys over so many years was so reduced in scale that it gave no idea of the importance of the lands he had visited' (quoted in Loiseaux 2016: 2). Working with a network of correspondents to supplement existing explorers' accounts, Lannoy de Bissy meticulously mapped explorers' routes

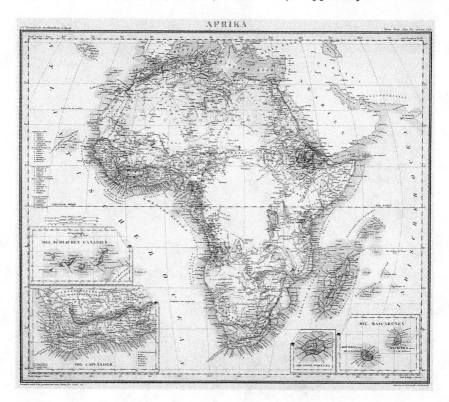

Figure 6.1 Map of Africa, 1861

Figure 6.2 Sketch of Berlin Conference with map of Africa in the conference hall, 1885

so that fellow Europeans could understand the scale of their undertakings. Hence, the project was a genuine attempt to understand the physical world. However, the mapping project was also an introspective European one; the subject was the great deeds of European explorers rather than the African continent itself.

The finished map reflected Lannoy de Bissy's painstaking efforts to translate all scientific knowledge of Africa onto cartographic space. Different local names for features and descriptive sentences were used to supplement the detailed geographical renderings. Lannoy de Bissy also relied on a transnational network of cartographers, including the British Ernst George Ravenstein, the Belgian Lieutenant Van de Velde, and the Italian Federico Bonola stationed in Cairo (Loiseaux 2016: 9–10). He relied on Stanley's accounts for the Congo section and left much of the region blank. For cartographers, the blank spaces signified gaps in reliable, scientific knowledge and the vast amount of exploration needed to fill the blankness. Only by way of technical expertise could the Congo basin be made legible. In this way, this seemingly 'scientific' blankness took on political consequences as the visibility of an entire river basin became dependent on one method of knowing at the exclusion of local knowledges. Once displayed at the Berlin Conference, diplomats interpreted this cartographic emptiness not as a neutral epistemic uncertainty but as an argument about the ontological emptiness of the space and an invitation to fill it with European practices and institutions.

The Congo basin was not the only geographical object to be erased through the science of cartography. Cartography had been key in the legitimation of empires (Branch 2011). For centuries before the Berlin Conference, the poor and powerless have been mapped out of existence. In an earlier imperial example, seventeenth-century English surveyors omitted Irish cabins from maps not because of lack of knowledge, but as a deliberate act of erasure and an expression of London's political and religious authority. Likewise, in the eighteenth century, the poor in London and Native Americans in Virginia experienced the same disappearing act (Harley 1988: 292). In fact, King Leopold II consciously used geography in the service of his territorial ambitions in the Congo. In April 1884, he launched the journal *Le Mouvement Géographique*, which produced maps, research, and news articles with the stated purpose of supporting Leopold's Congo agenda (Nicolai 1993).

Scholarship in critical geography has explored cartographic depictions not as representations of reality but as arguments about knowledge, power, and authority (Ó'Tuathail 1996; Dalby and Ó'Tuathail 1998; Dodds, Kuus, and Sharp 2013). Gearoid Ó'Tuathail, drawing from Jacques Derrida and Ferdinand de Saussure, compares maps to texts where 'language is a phenomenon that charts and affixes objects in space, just like a map' (1996: 528). Both maps and texts use patterns and spatial arrangements to render the world legible; both denote acts of power in their ability to elevate a single understanding of the world above others. In addition, Ó'Tuathail likens maps to panoramic friezes where the viewer or knower stands apart from and above the scene, suggesting an objective, scientific distance between the mapmaker and the unitary and stable world she renders. The map is a snapshot in time that is then frozen and accepted as timeless truth. Geographical features such as rivers, however, change their physical position, width, and depth yearly according to spring melts, and daily according to tides and weather. Hence, the river is a fluid geography not conducive to mapping. But once cartographers affix the river onto a cartographic plane, its position becomes a fixed fact – any deviation from that fact becomes abnormal, costly, and in need of human intervention. Maps that sought to standardize and rationalize assumed an objective cartographer who used scientific methods to convey detached truths.

The not-so-empty space

At Berlin, European diplomats saw the vastness of their ambitions in the Congo's emptiness. The visual clarity of the empty African map crystalized for Europeans the task before them. The emptiness was not necessarily a physical emptiness but a conceptual one devoid of existing institutions and histories. Once naturalized, the emptiness became an invitation or even a challenge to explore more, to fashion better maps, and to deploy more robust institutions to fill the blank spaces.

Despite this construction, the Congo was not empty but rich in historical traditions and political institutions. Hundreds of years before the arrival of Europeans on the Congo, while they did not have formalized writing, the societies that inhabited central Africa developed a sophisticated drummed language (*langage tambourine*) through which tonal messages – often amplified by rivers – could travel up to 600 kilometers in a day (van Reybrouck 2014: 20). In his book *Muntu* (1961), literary scholar Janheinz Jahn dubbed these drummers the 'official historians of Africa'. Local communities along the Congo also developed rich cultural traditions in their relationships with the river as a living entity – for example, communities of the lower Congo conceptualized the river as *Mamy Wata*, a half-woman, half-fish goddess that brought riches and good fortune to those faithful to her. Indeed, her followers who converted to Christianity reportedly had to have *Mamy Wata* cast out of them before embracing Christ (Tshimanga 2009: 29–30).

Since the mid-fourteenth century, hierarchical structures of authority over defined territories along the Congo developed into kingdoms such as the Kongo, the Lunda, the Luba, and the Kuba. Importantly, since the late fifteenth century, these local historical narratives and political institutions had been entangled with and co-constituted alongside inter-imperial European and global histories of exploration and expansionism along with the spread of Christianity. After the Portuguese first landed in 1491, the son of the local ruler, Nzinga Mvemba, converted to Christianity, became Afonso I, and relied on prosperous trade with Europe to maintain his control over the Kongo Empire for the next four decades (van Reybrouck 2014: 22). In the eighteenth century, civil wars broke out in Kongo due to disagreements over not only who would rule the kingdom, but also constitutional limitations to the monarch's power. As historian John Thornton charts (1993), these disagreements centered on two divergent founding myths of the Kongo – the king as conqueror and therefore absolute monarch, and the king as blacksmith and therefore a forger of alliances and a conciliatory figure selected by popular acclaim. These civil wars also resulted in large numbers of Kongolese being transported across the Atlantic in the slave trade – and Thornton narrates how Kongolese political philosophy on the constitutional limitations of monarchy also traveled with them to the Caribbean, where it influenced the Haitian Revolution.

These brief vignettes cannot possibly do justice to the diversity and sophistication of the history, ideas, and institutions that filled from this supposedly 'empty' geography. Indeed, by 1885, the Congo basin had become an international site of competing ideological and material interests, as missionaries, explorers, and merchants of all nations vied for wealth and influence. The blindness of those at Berlin toward the historical and political complexity of the Congo basin also blinded them to the geopolitical realities they faced and, as will be examined in the next chapter, contributed to their failure to establish a Congo River Commission.

The tools of empire: civilization, peace, and commercial rationality

In the European geographical imagination, the Congo represented a civilizational tool that would bring commerce, rationality, and morality to the empty African interior. While some historians have debated the relative importance of commercial versus ideological rationales in fueling the scramble for Africa (for example, Crowe 1942), my analysis stresses the ways in which commerce and ideology were interlinked and reinforced one another as a hallmark of rational European civilization. Since the Enlightenment, liberal political thinkers had viewed the practice of commerce itself as an instrument that trained the mind and brought civilized institutions to untamed societies. Hence, establishing commerce along the Congo as a colonial highway promised both wealth and civilization, both material and moral gains for international society.

Central to European understandings of commerce and colonialism in the late nineteenth century was the combination of civilizational standards with a universal and totalizing notion of societal progress (Bowden 2009). The classical Standards of Civilization refer to legal mechanisms that barred societies that did not meet certain civilizational requirements from gaining full membership status in the international society of states (Gong 1984; Bowden 2014). This standard implied both a hierarchy between uncivilized and civilized polities and an avenue for progression from uncivilized to civilized status. This understanding of human progress allowed European powers to colonize the periphery under the banner of the 'white man's burden' not only to civilize but to subordinate and extinguish 'peoples and cultures deemed inferior' by remolding these societies in the European image (Bowden 2009: 129).[2]

Hence the term *civilization* was not just a descriptive term referring to the multiple civilizations across space and time, but became a normative universal standard that collapsed space and time along a single continuum. As various critical theorists have pointed out (for example, McClintock 1995; Agnew 1996; Chakrabarty 2008; Rao 2020), this singular continuum necessitates a geographical outlook that centers western Europe as the most temporally and civilizationally advanced space, and conflates terrestrially distant spaces with a temporally distant European past. Put simply, Europeans viewed uncivilized societies as *backward* precisely as the term suggests – as occupying a place behind current European developments along the same timeline with the same destination. This conflation of time and terrestrial space enabled Europeans to give benevolent assistance modeled on their own experiences to help backward societies progress toward a European civilizational standard. Doing so aimed to erase these societies' 'uncivilized' characteristics and recast them in the European mold. Doing so also created an idealized and simplified version of the European experience as a model for emulation. By focusing on European understandings of the Congo, I argue that nineteenth-century Standards of Civilization not only erased local sociopolitical histories and agency along the river, but it also contorted Europe's own historical development into a totalizing benchmark to measure civilization and progress.

Building the benchmark: commerce and civilization in European thought

Prominent political thinkers of the eighteenth and nineteenth centuries relied on the European experience to advance the Enlightenment notion that commerce had a civilizing influence on societies. David Hume's 1777 *Political Discourses* describes how commerce creates 'happiness', 'prosperity', and 'greatness' for people and nations alike. Remarkably, he ends the chapter on commerce with the following question:

> What is the reason, why no people, living between the tropics, could ever yet attain to any art or civility, or reach even any police in their government, and any military discipline; while few nations in the temperate climates have been altogether deprived of these advantages? (Hume 1994: 230)

Hume speculates that a probable cause of this geographical difference in civilizational attainment is the climate in the tropics. Due to the tropical heat, Hume muses, Africans likely have less need for clothes and shelter, and therefore, did not naturally develop the inclinations, inventions, and industries required to manufacture or trade in these goods. The tropical climate, Hume also speculates, means these populations have fewer needs and hence fewer possessions, which in turn diminishes these societies' need for policing or a military to protect their possessions. Hence, Africa's unlucky climatic conditions hindered the development of private property and trade, which limited its civilizational progress. Here, Hume compares an idealized European experience with an imagined and homogeneous African (or even 'tropical') one, and attempts to explain Africa's deviation from the European norm with a combination of racial prejudice and geographical determinism.

In the nineteenth century, John Stuart Mill famously highlighted commerce as a civilizational standard and marker of social progress. In his essay on civilization published in 1836, Mill argued that commerce is a hallmark of the advanced society: 'in savage life, there is no commerce, no manufacturers, no agriculture, or next to none; a country rich in the fruits of agriculture, commerce, and manufacturers we call civilized' (1836: n.p.). Here, commerce stands alongside the rule of law, complex cooperation, and mutual protection in large-scale political units as what distinguished the civilized from the uncivilized polity. These characteristics go together as part of a civilizational bundle – for example, Mill marveled at the complex cooperation and coordination entailed by large commercial and manufacturing enterprises. For Mill, civilization was a progressive, but not necessarily unidirectional, move toward increased wealth and sophistication. Advanced civilizations – and in Mill's mind, England was the most advanced – had a duty to aid uncivilized societies in their progress along the civilizational continuum (Souffrant 2000; Jahn 2005). If capitalism and commerce created the conditions for civilization, then spreading commerce to the periphery was one way to help those societies advance. Even in the 1848 *Communist Manifesto*, Karl Marx and Friedrich Engels echoed Mill's civilizational discourse in arguing that the bourgeoisie, 'by the rapid improvement of all instruments of production, by the immensely facilitated means of communication, draws all, even the most barbarian nations, into civilization' (1848: n.p.).

Into the mid-twentieth century, Joseph Schumpeter continued to investigate the precise link between commerce and civilization through the cultivation of rationality. He wrote, 'it is the everyday economic task to which we as a race owe our elementary training in rational thought and behavior – I have no hesitation in saying that all logic is derived from the pattern of economic decision' (1994 [1942]: 122–3). Here, Schumpeter draws a direct intellectual line from the capitalist concept of the monetary unit to the development of modern mathematics and 'the spirit of rationalist individualism'. Hence, capitalism not only leads to the accumulation of wealth but also a rational habit of mind that produces civilized behaviors at the individual and societal levels. Combined, these theories on the link between commerce and civilization centered on an idealized and homogenized European experience with the expansion of commerce – a foreshortening of the messiness of Europe's actual history with capitalism. This idealized experience was then upheld as a universal standard against which other societies were measured.

Some theorists went even further to link commerce with not only civilized manners and institutions but also international peace. Immanuel Kant's third definitive article elevates universal hospitality, which arose through free trade and the free exchange of ideas, as essential for perpetual peace. Perhaps more so, Montesquieu's writings held early kernels of what would later become the capitalist peace theory – a line of argument that Norman Angell would later develop as part of his argument for how to end the structural threat of war. In an often cited passage, Montesquieu argues:

> Commerce cures destructive prejudices, and it is an almost general rule that everywhere there are gentle mores, there is commerce and that everywhere there is commerce, there are gentle mores ... the natural effect of commerce is to lead to peace. Two nations that trade with each other become reciprocally dependent; if one has an interest in buying, the other has an interest in selling, and all unions are founded on mutual needs. (1989 [1748]: 338)

In this passage, Montesquieu highlights two facets of the capitalist peace theory: economic interests and socialization. He argues that interest in trading goods encourages peaceful relations between two polities, but beyond the mutual material gain, there is something in the act of the commercial transaction that moderates human enmity and civilizes. Therefore, aside from an increase in wealth, the practice of commerce itself generates the 'spirit of commerce' that forges peaceful characteristics within a society and creates more rational and agreeable relations between peoples. Interests and socialization mutually reinforce one another to underpin the capitalist peace – the practice of commerce has the potential to transform the character of an entire people through both the increase in material gain and the rational relations it produces. However, for capitalist peace to spread globally, the practices and institutions of commerce must also take root in the periphery, and Europeans imperialists believed it was their duty to export these blessings of commercial civilization to the heart of Africa. The Congo as an imperial highway would help them do so.

All the world's a fair

The dreamscape of commercial rationality's utopian and internationalist promise can best be seen in the late nineteenth-century World's Fairs that captivated the Western imagination. For the West, these spectacles celebrated science and progress and solidified the unification of all global development into the same civilizational continuum. Riding on the exuberance of early industrialization and a sense of wonder at the world's growing interconnectedness, London held the first World's Fair in 1851 and boasted more than six million visitors, including Queen Victoria on several occasions. The fair's stated purpose was to 'forward the progress of industrial civilization' (Findling 1990: xvii). The term *fair* harkens back to medieval marketplaces of trade and joviality – a romanticized emblem of early capitalism. But this new breed of fairs was less a market for the exchange of goods – at the 1851 Fair, no prices were affixed to the commercial items on display. Rather, these new fairs were self-conscious showcases for the marvels of Western commercial civilization. The religious tone of medieval fairs had been replaced by the just as dogmatic ideology of scientific progress. This ideology, captured by exhibits such as the History of Labor in Paris 1867 and the History of Civilization in Paris 1900, depicted history as a linear and unidirectional advance toward what historian Robert Rydell calls a 'utopian' future (1984: 4). While these World's Fairs touted commercial progress, they also expressed two interrelated themes: the internationalism generated by peaceful coopera-tion between all peoples and the imperial impulse to close the civilizational distance between the West and the periphery.

These internationalist and imperialist themes were built into the very fabric of early World's Fairs. While the home country always occupied the largest exhibition space, these displays often depicted foreign geographies and exotic colonial riches. The London Colonial and Indian Exhibition in 1886 showcased Britain's most prized colony, while British exhibitions in Sydney and Melbourne in 1879–81, Calcutta in 1883, and Kingston in 1891 placed imperial wealth and progress on display for a global audience. Similarly, French World's Fairs routinely featured their North African colonies and the Dutch their holdings in the East Indies. The 1878 and 1889 Paris exhibition included 'negro villages' that put human beings on display for the European public. Chicago's 1893 Columbian Exposition introduced fairgoers not only to innovations in urban planning, art, and architecture, but to the latest advances in anthropology that depicted nonwhites as barbaric and childlike (Rydell 1984: 40). In Belgium, Leopold II used two expositions in Antwerp in 1885 and 1894 to demonstrate the civilizational progress he personally had brought to the Congo. In a public relations *tour de force*, Leopold's 1894 exhibition charmed visitors with displays of bountiful raw material, intricately carved ivory, drawings from native children, a model steamer to navigate the Congo, and modular homes as exemplars of European technology to be exported to the region (Figure 6.3; Findling 1990: 133). These displays consolidated the conflation of time and terrestrial space in the Western geographical imagination as societies in the periphery were portrayed as children in need of European guidance and civilization.

Alongside these colonial exhibits, the World's Fairs also promoted a sense of internationalist optimism that technology and scientific advancements could reach across national divides to unite humanity. In the guidebook to Paris's 1867 World's Fair, Victor Hugo exclaimed: 'Down with war! Let there be alliance! Concord! Unity! O France, adieu … thou shalt no longer be France: thou shalt be Humanity! No Longer a nation, thou shalt be Ubiquity!' (quoted in Chandler 2006: n.p.). At the 1867 Paris World's Fair,

Figure 6.3 Congolese village at the Antwerp World's Fair of 1894

for the first time exhibits were not only organized by nations but also by transnational groupings. Group X in this classification included 'articles whose special purpose was meant to improve the physical and moral conditions of the people' (Findling 1990: 38). One subtle way of showcasing technology's promise for uniting humanity was through elaborate landscaping designs and water features that awed audience through the control of nature. World's Fairs competed with one another to create ever more impressive landscaping – such as the Champ de Mars in Paris in 1978 and the Midway in Chicago in 1889 – as the backdrop to society's narrative of commercial and civilizational progress. Mastery over water was also prominent, and the engineering project to tame the Danube's floods created a series of canals as the perfect location for the 1873 Vienna Fair (Findling 1990: 48). Visitors to the 1878 Paris Exposition marveled at its sophisticated hydraulic displays that pumped the Seine's water through 37 kilometers of pipes to beautify the entire exhibition hall. The Seine's tamed flow was made useful in powering the elevators and cooling the Palace of Industry; it also created an 18-meter water display that wowed visitors (Findling 1990: 64). Winning the battle against nature, these displays promised, would unite humanity and lead the world toward a future of progress.

Alongside the Fairs themselves, organizers also held international congresses on important transnational topics of the day to generate a sense of international unity and progress. Of course, their declarations of international brotherhood centered European civilization as the vanguard of universal aspirations – it not only collapsed the rest of the world into followers who needed to be helped along by European benevolence but also painted an idealized vision of the European experience itself as a unified march toward peace and prosperity. In these World's Fairs, time and space came together and were systematized into the same progressive narrative, with the world united under a single developmental logic.

Stanley, the Congo, and the commercial civilizing mission

If bad geographical luck had left tropical Africa without clothing, private property, and civilization, it was Europeans' moral duty to bring the civilizing arm of commerce to succeed where nature had failure – all while lining their own pockets. Both were morally laudable. Stanley used precisely this logic when he spoke to crowds in Manchester in October 1884 on the importance of bringing civilization and Christianity to the Congo. He asked the crowd to imagine how much they would profit from manufacturing the cloth needed to supply every inhabitant in the Congo with just six outfits – two for Sundays and four everyday ones – and a burial shroud for each family. Christianity would civilize the naked natives of Africa, but Stanley also calculated the profits would be £16 million each year of Manchester calico at two pennies a yard (*Daily Mail*, 25 November 1884). The English were not alone; French textile interests also supported expanding colonial activities into Africa in search of virgin markets for manufactured goods (Wright 1995 [1974]: 293). Hence, commercial profit and the civilizing mission were not opposing aims; rather, they reinforced one another.

Commerce as a vehicle for both profit and moral advancement permeates Stanley's travelogues as he invites Europeans to imagine the Congo as a highway into an unexplored geography full of untold and untapped economic potential. He writes:

> There are 5250 statute miles of uninterrupted navigable water, which may by overcoming a little trouble at one rapid be increased to 6000 miles in the Upper Congo section of the Congo basin. The area through which these navigable channels flow is over 1,000,000 square miles superficial extent, and is throughout a fertile region unsurpassed for the variety of its natural productions. (1885, II: 366)

Like Europeans who first saw the economic potential of the Rhine and Danube rivers as natural roads to lands overflowing with bountiful resources, Stanley advertised the Congo as a lucrative market waiting to be accessed. He described one million Africans living among an abundance of 'ivory, palm-oil, palm kernels, ground-nuts, gum-copal, orchilla-weed, camwood, cola-nuts, gum tragacanth, myrrh, frankincense, furs, skins, hides, feathers, copper, India-rubber, fibre of grasses, beeswax, bark-cloth, nutmeg, ginger, castor-oil nuts', and others raw material (1885, II: 368). The fact that the Congo was already waiting for them as a ready-made highway to expand commerce gave the picture a sense of natural inevitability, as if the river had one purpose. Stanley purposely downplayed the navigational hazards of the lower Congo – he describes it as 'a little trouble at one rapid' – but anyone familiar with the lower Congo's 32 impressive cataracts would dispute this characterization. It would take Leopold II's enslaved workers nine years to construct 366 kilometers of the Matadi–Kinshasa railway to bypass the cataracts. The grave human costs of railway construction are detailed in Roger Casement's 1904 report revealing Leopold's abuses, Joseph Conrad's *Heart of Darkness*, and Adam Hochschild's *King Leopold's Ghost*. However, by depicting the Congo as an ideal navigable river that led to a fertile land, Stanley invited Europeans to fill the empty space with their commercial desires.

Expanding commerce was an important objective of the Berlin Conference. At its opening session, host and German Chancellor Otto von Bismarck gave this rationale for the gathering: 'all the Governments invited share the wish to bring the natives of Africa within the pale of civilization by opening up the interior of that continent to commerce'. By doing so, European would encourage Christian missions, end the slave trade, and give inhabitants the means to instruct and improve themselves (Gavin and Betley 1973: 129). Hence, the conference's objectives became the three Cs – commerce, civilization, and Christianity. These were not three separate items on a checklist but a package that mutually enforced one another in pushing Africa toward progress and civilization. Commercial activity was the central driver. As Bismarck also noted in his opening remarks, 'the fundamental idea of this program is to facilitate the access of all commercial nations to the interior of Africa' (Gavin and Betley 1973: 129), after which civilization and rationality would follow. Commerce, then, was vital for the Berlin Conference as a civilizing practice that benefitted both the colonizers and the colonized.

Perhaps the moment in Stanley's account that best captures the interplay between European commercial and moral aims in Africa is an exchange with Chief Makoko. In his narrative, as Makoko gave Stanley and his boats safe passage along the river, he supposedly told Stanley: 'I have many things given me long ago from the white men's land, and I have often wished to see those who could make such wonderful things. I am told you people make all the cloth, the beads, the guns, the powder, plates, and glasses. Ah! You must be great and good people' (1885, I: 330). There is a hint of awe in this statement, as if Makoko desired increased contact with Europeans so he too could become both good and great. Whether or not Makoko ever uttered these admiring words, they reflect Stanley's vision of European civilizational superiority as both commercial and moral. Commercial enterprise makes a society both *great* in the magnificent products invented, the complex productivity engendered, and the prosperity created, but also *good* as a moral condition that naturally follows from increased commercial activity. Here, Stanley's narrative reinforces Hume, Montesquieu, and Mill. Commerce is not just a means to a material end – the practice of commerce is also a moral practice that fosters rationality, enlightenment, and progress.

Breaker of rocks: taming the Congo as imperial expansion

Like the Rhine and the Danube in the European geographical imagination, the Congo was also a natural commercial highway that would bring free trade, industry, and civilization to the peoples along its shores. However, unlike the Rhine as an intra-European road and the Danube as a connecting highway between Europe and the near periphery, the Congo invited Europeans to a foreign geography beyond the boundaries of their known world – a geography where traditional maps had always warned of monsters. For many, the Congo basin represented an abstract space removed from regular politics, and served as a testing ground for their individual mettle and for their civilizational convictions. Taming the Congo, then, represented the totalizing triumph of their personal and civilizational assumptions and the final victory of Western rationality against the mythical monsters that lurked in the unknown. In domesticating the Congo, European man could finally become the measurer of all things. However, the Congo as an exceptional and dislocated geography also had the potential to throw into doubt Europe's civilizational assumptions and its confidence in humankind's ability to conquer barbarism.

Measurer of all things

Stanley begins the narrative of his journey up the Congo in the service of King Leopold II with a reproach of previous travelogues along the river. These accounts described the river in flowery language but without scientific accuracy, anthropomorphizing it as locked in a quarrel with the sea. These accounts created dramatic prose – for example, describing the river 'with deep and indented frowns in his angry face, foaming with disdain and filling the air with noise' (Stanley 1885, I: 5) – but neglected to record the depth and speed of the river's mouth. Stanley expressed frustration with these accounts' lack of useful technical and scientific data, only identifying one account by Captain James Kingston Tuckey as giving reliable information. 'For the first time,' Stanley wrote admiringly of Tuckey's journals, 'the

Lower Congo was shorn of all myth and fable, and was described with an accuracy that cannot be much excelled even in the present day' (1885, I: 7). Here, Stanley promises his readers a rational and scientific account of the river without superstition or myth. Throughout his books, Stanley carefully details precise facts and figures – providing charts with the depth of the river, the speed of flow, distance traveled, and estimated population of natives. Even his analogies evoke a sense of industrial utility and technological progress as he compares the Congo's mouth to a valve as a part of a mechanized system. In doing so, Stanley used scientific rationality to sweep away the illogical myths that surrounded the Congo.

Further, Stanley describes Western society's relationship with the river as a battle, echoing the way Johann Tulla had described engineering plans along the Rhine and Frederick the Great along the Oder. He wrote admiringly of Dutch engineering works along the banks of the lower Congo as 'an industrial war against flood encroachment', and Stanley intended to carry forward this war against 'the impetuous current' (1885, I: 83). Here, Stanley amplifies the Enlightenment mission to tame nature to a colonial scale as he declares with full confidence:

> We feel still that it is a dangerous river to be trifled with. It has awful power when ruffled by impeding rocks, or when its waves rise up, remonstrant to the breeze, and fall heavy and sullen. But we also have power now – power gained by knowledge and harsh experience. We will brave the giant stream with steel cutters driven by steam! (1885, I: 80)

Stanley's message here is clear: the Congo may be irrational and dangerous but it is no match for the power of European civilization and technology. The river will yield to European steel and steam. This passage also demonstrates the conflation of European time with territorial space as the knowledge, experiences, and ultimate victories of past European battles against the untamed river can now be brought to bear on this foreign geography.

European civilization's use of technology to conquer nature – both the river and the untamed human populations that inhabited its banks – is best encapsulated by another of Stanley's vignettes. Along the Congo's north bank, Stanley and his men established the town of Vivi. While building a garden[3] and wooden huts, they removed large boulders with crowbars and sledgehammers, and then pulverized some of the rock to build foundations for a road. Stanley describes native populations looking on with curiosity and amazement, and claims that for this display of control over nature, the chiefs along the river gave him the name *Bula Matari* or 'breaker of rocks'. He portrays the Vivi chiefs as 'wonderingly looking on while I taught my men how to wield a sledge-hammer effectively, [and they] bestowed on me the title *Bula Matari* – Breaker of Rocks – with which from the sea to

Stanley Falls, all natives of the Congo are now so familiar' (1885, I: 147–8).
A bit further upriver, while his engineers were again working to break rocks
for road construction, Stanley again claims the name *Bula Matari* and relays
that the natives had already heard the name, which 'travels much faster
up-river than I can' (1885, I: 237). And if readers were in any doubt of
Stanley's self-portrayal as a conqueror of Africa, he compares his new name
to that of Scipio Africanus, the famous Roman general who earned his
name by defeating Hannibal in the Second Punic War. The name reveals
not just Stanley's but European civilization's understanding of itself as the
hero who would tame the Congo's dark banks, and through technological
superiority, bend the rocks and the river to their will.

Order, knowledge, and control

Stanley's ambition to measure, know, and tame the Congo reflected the
wider late nineteenth-century European determination to order and rationalize
the universe through the natural and social sciences. While botany and
fossil-filled cabinets of curiosities had enthralled European publics since the
seventeenth century, the publication of Darwin's *Origin of Species* in 1859
ignited heightened debate on natural history and society's evolution toward
the fittest human stock (MacKenzie 1988: 36). Museums, botanical gardens,
and World Exhibitions displayed natural and cultural artifacts from all
corners of European empires. At the same time, European scientists weighed
and cataloged the universe at the atomic level with the publication of the
first periodic tables by Russian Dmitri Mendeleev in 1869 and German
Lothar Meyer in 1870. Cataloging and categorizing the natural world quickly
spread to the study of human societies, as anthropology, ethnography, and
statistics sought to order and improve human societies within national
borders and beyond (Hacking 1990; Franey 2001).

The co-implication between the natural and social sciences and empire
quickly grew as explorers sought to analyze exotic plants, animals, and
societies in unknown lands at the fringes of empire.[4] European explorers
raced to be the first to discover a river's source, an unknown species, or
a native tribe, with the added bonus of naming the discovery, such as the
Rhinoceros *oswellii* named after Cotton Oswell, one of David Livingstone's
companions (MacKenzie 1988: 39; Donovan 2006: 41). Scientific exploration became a political enterprise to tame, control, and rationalize nature.
As Hungarian anthropologist Emil Torday wrote in 1913 on his views of
the natives along the Congo, 'it is only by studying a man that you can
understand him and only by understanding him that you can rule him' (1913:
290). For Torday and other colonial explorers, understanding the African
native was akin to understanding the lion or rhinoceros, and European

society's ability to study, catalog, and rule helped legitimize its colonial expansion.

Indeed, hunting as a metaphor for human mastery over nature has been a cultural and political trope since antiquity. Assyrian King Ashurbanipal immortalized his lion hunts in stone as an emblem of state power and royal obligations to protect the people. John M. MacKenzie (1988) charts the social and symbolic significance of hunting in the nineteenth century as an elite 'sport' – as European elites consolidated power over the political and natural worlds, hunting changed from an activity to provide sustenance and protection into a symbolic practice of aristocratic legitimacy. English Romantics may have embraced hunting as a glorification of nature, but very little about pheasant covers, grouse moors, deer forests, or bird blinds are in fact natural – instead, the trappings of the hunt affirm hierarchies within society as 'natural' and naturalize humankind's domination over its environment. Taken to the colonial scale, white hunters in Africa played and continue to play out the same rituals of domination, hierarchy, and conquest over the African landscape and its peoples. By the twentieth century, the entire continent of Africa would be synonymous with big game in the Western imagination.

On the ground, European control was less all-encompassing, but rivers as colonial highways provided the ideal material and ideational launching point for European ambitions. It is no accident that Stanley's journey of colonial conquest followed the Congo – shorelines and navigable rivers have been the arteries of European power projection since European explorer-conquerors' first dreams of colonial empires. Lauren Benton describes European colonial control not as absolute command of contiguous territory but as control over 'narrow bands, or corridors, and over enclaves and irregular zones around them' (2010: 2) – empires of garrison towns and trading posts often connected by pathways of water. Navigable waterways allowed Europeans to penetrate deep into the Americas, Asia, and Africa, often first as explorers, followed by traders, armed escorts, and flags, all to secure untamed spaces for the home empire. To explore the banks, discover the source, and map the river, then, was both a material and symbolic practice of European domination.

Rivers such as the Congo invariably became a military road and symbol of colonial power – steamboats upriver carried guns, colonial officials, and the decrees of faraway kings to transform the people and landscape of the Congo basin. After Leopold imposed devastating rubber quotas on communities along the river, populations simply left the riverbanks and moved beyond the reach of colonial authorities. Between 60 and 90 percent of residents in one of the oldest trading posts along the river – Lukolela – disappeared between 1891 and 1901. As one witness said, 'We ran away because we could no longer live with the things they did to us. Our village chieftains were hanged, we were murdered and starved. And we worked ourselves to death in order to find rubber' (van Reybrouck 2014: 94). Hence, while European colonial control over central Africa's 'emptiness' was far from absolute, the ideal colonial river allowed Europeans to project their military and political superiority far into the heart of darkness.

A mirror into the heart of darkness

While Europeans embraced the Congo basin as a conceptual emptiness into which the West could bring the civilizing influence of commerce, currents of disquiet rippled through European imaginaries of the river. Joseph Conrad's *Heart of Darkness* (1899) unmasked the tensions between commercial rationality and European civilization's existential anxieties by reversing the narrative of the Congo as a natural highway that promises to bring commerce and civilization to Africa. Rather than a river that transports European goods, ethics, and institutions to the African emptiness, Kurtz as the epitome of European civilization[5] traveled upriver to find his own irrationality and existential darkness. Unlike the invading armies that threatened to march upriver along the Danube, the Congo's threat to European civilization was more abstract and pervasive. But like the ambitious mapping projects of European cartographers, Kurtz's journey into darkness was also an introspective one that centered on Europe's own nagging doubts about its moral and civilizational superiority. *Heart of Darkness* does not claim to be about the Congo itself. For Conrad as much as others, the Congo was an abstract and blank backdrop, and Europe remains the key protagonist. However, rather than Stanley's civilizing story of how the river would lead to commercial wealth and moral advancement, Conrad's story takes us somewhere else entirely and inverts the ideal river as a commercial highway and civilizing tool.

Alongside liberal optimism about the moral and material benefits of commerce, a darker understanding of the commercial possibilities of the colonial river hounded the European imagination. 'By the end of the eighteen sixties,' observe Robinson, Gallagher, and Denny in their history of the Victorians' scramble for Africa, 'this optimistic idealism was cooling, as disappointment piled up and the millennium of peace, brotherhood, and free trade receded' (1978: 3). In Europe, Karl Marx's powerful account of historical materialism, in which capitalist oppression inevitably led to world revolution, inspired social backlash against the exponential accumulation of commercial wealth. By the end of the nineteenth century, Conrad's *Heart of Darkness* had exposed the moral and existential doubts that began to seep into the myth of Europe's commercial civilizing mission in Africa.

While Montesquieu's writings largely supported the civilizing influences of commerce, his works are notoriously unclear and often included statements that directly contradict one another (Howse 2006: 3). Almost as soon as he argues for the salutary and pacifying effects that commerce has on society, he modifies the argument by distinguishing between how commerce affects relations between nations and how it affects relations between individuals. Of individuals, he writes:

> The spirit of commerce produces in men a certain feeling for exact justice, opposed on the one hand to banditry and on the other to those moral virtues that make it so that one does not always discuss one's own interests alone and that one can neglect them for those of others. (Montesquieu 1989 [1748]: 339)

Here, Montesquieu situates commercial values in opposition to moral virtues. The rational calculations that Schumpeter had celebrated for their ability to train the mind also force us to neglect the public good for private gain. An individual obsessed with commercial profitmaking becomes exacting and miserly. Taken to the colonial context, Montesquieu's qualifications against the civilizing effects of commercial rationality morph into new moral uncertainties, as if the dislocation caused by the foreign-ness of the Congo had torn asunder the moral fabric of European society. Adam Hochschild describes this effect: 'men who would have been appalled to see someone using a *chicotte*[6] on the streets of Brussels or Paris or Stockholm accepted the act, in this different setting, as normal' (Hochschild 1998: 121). Or as station chief Georges Bricusse recorded in his diary in 1895, Africa desensitized him to human cruelty and suffering: 'And to think that the first time I saw the *chicotte* administered, I was pale with fright. Africa has some use after all. I could now walk into fire as if to a wedding' (quoted in Hochschild 1998: 123). For Bricusse, Africa as an exceptional geography out of time and space eroded the social and moral norms of polite European society. Of course, Leopold's heavy-handed policies and ruthless extractive practices created the permissive environment for these atrocities, but there was also the sense that the Congo was another reality that existed outside of European moral boundaries.

Conrad's *Heart of Darkness*, written fifteen years after the Berlin Conference, exposes these moral anxieties through the looking glass of a trip up the Congo. Conrad's tale separates the trader's commercial rationality from Kurtz's metaphysical despair and opposes the two realms. Upon meeting Kurtz, the narrator Marlow has a discussion with the manager over his 'unsound methods'. While Kurtz's methods do seem unhinged, the irony is that the commercial story Marlow charts on his trip from the coast to the inner station is full of unsound commercial methods – the emaciated bodies of the dying workers along the unfinished railroad that Stanley had promised would tame the river for commerce, and the violence perpetrated against the land and the people in exchange for a 'precious trickle of ivory'. Marlow sees the irony in the manager's comments and defends Kurtz. He then muses to his readers, 'Ah! But it was something to have at least a choice of nightmares' (1899: n.p.). For Marlow, both the commercial butchery and Kurtz's butchery were appalling nightmares, but at least Kurtz's actions were raw and authentic. The commercial butchery perpetrated along the Congo was just as morally unhinged as Kurtz's, but masked by the false sheen of rationality and civilization.

The dark seductress

The moral anxieties Europeans saw in the Congo basin as a dislocated and exceptional geography led to a return to narratives of the river as magical and alive – a dark seductress that corrupted the hearts of European heroes who sought to tame her. Literary scholar Tim Youngs' analysis compares Conrad's and Stanley's understandings of the emptiness on the African map. Stanley longed to fill up the blank space: 'I have already mentally peopled it, filled it with the most wonderful pictures of towns, villages, rivers, countries, and tribes – all in the imagination – and I am burning to see whether I am correct or not' (quoted in Youngs 1994: 1). Stanley's vision led to a utopia of his own making, with the river as a highway that transported European goods and civilization to Africa. Conrad's personal story starts with the same emptiness on the map: 'When nine years old or thereabouts ... while looking at a map of Africa of the time and putting my finger on the blank space then representing the unsolved mystery of the continent, I said to myself ... "When I grow up, I shall go there"' (quoted in Hochschild 1998: 140). He wove this autobiographical reflection into *Heart of Darkness* by giving Marlow the same desire to explore 'all the blank spaces on the earth' (Conrad 1899: n.p.). However, as Marlow grew up, the white space became filled with something more sinister:

> It had become a place of darkness. But there was in it one river especially, a mighty big river that you could see on the map, resembling an immense snake uncoiled, with its head in the sea, its body at rest curving afar over a vast country and its tail lost in the depths of the land. And as I looked at the map of it in a shop-window, it fascinated me as a snake would a bird – a silly little bird. (1899: n.p.)

Here, the river is no longer a rationalized topography on a map or an enticing emptiness waiting to be filled. Instead, it has taken on life as a menacing snake with three-dimensional physicality. The river embodies a dark magic as it charms Marlow and reverses the traditional story of society's conquest of nature. Instead, nature in the form of the river-snake seduces society and holds rational civilization under its malevolent spell.

The same narrative of spellbound European explorers unable to resist the irrational allure of foreign rivers echoes in travelogues and fiction. At the turn of the nineteenth century, Scottish explorer Mungo Park's obsession with navigating the Niger and visiting the mythical city of Timbuktu lured both him and his son to mysterious deaths along the river. After returning from his first trip, the Niger seemed to haunt Park. Despite fame and a happy family, Park told his friend, the novelist Walter Scott, that he 'would rather brave Africa and all its horror' than live his days in the 'lonely heaths and gloomy hills' as a country doctor (quoted in Holmes 2008: 222). Dr. David Livingstone, the most famous missionary to Africa, was fixated with finding the source of the Nile, disappeared into central Africa, and died there. But perhaps the most colorful expression of this sense of reversal can be found in the works of Victorian novelist H. Rider Haggard. His novel *She: A History of Adventure* was first published in magazine installments in 1886–87 and became one of the bestselling books of all time. *She* tells the tale of European explorers who journey up a mysterious river to the interior of Africa to find a beautiful, all-powerful she-demon who holds men spellbound. The metaphor here is palpable. The untamed – and feminine – nature of the African interior holds the power to reverse civilizations, returning even the most civilized Europeans to the state of irrational barbarism.

Conclusion

Like their predecessors at Vienna and Paris earlier in the nineteenth century, diplomats at the 1884–85 Berlin Conference did not deliberate in a social vacuum – instead, their diplomatic considerations were enabled and influenced by prevailing intellectual and social undercurrents. These forces, embodied by explorers, legal experts, and cartographers, portrayed the Congo basin as a conceptually empty space, waiting to be filled with the civilizing influence of European commerce and institutions. Like the Rhine and Danube rivers, the Congo was also an economic highway that would carry free trade and civilization, but unlike the Rhine and Danube, the Congo represented a foreign and disconnected space as much in the European imagination as in physical reality. Hence, controlling the Congo symbolized a totalizing control over politics at the core and periphery, and the establishment of a global hierarchical order with Europe at its apex. To achieve this, the colonial geographical imaginary conflated time with terrestrial space to unify the world along the same developmental and civilizational continuum – and it was the duty of Europeans to help uncivilized places and peoples progress along that continuum. The Congo represent a God-given natural highway to bring commercial rationality and civilization to Africa. However, the abstract and foreign Congo also represented European fears of reversal and the revelation of a darkness at the center of European civilization.

In either reading of the Congo, the imperial geographical imagination centered the narrative on Europe itself. This is best seen in the way the Thames, an otherwise unimpressive river in a small corner of the earth, was elevated to mythical status as the center of an imagined network of monumental rivers. The Thames was a universal river that connected the imperial core in London to the mighty rivers of the periphery. In Rudyard Kipling's *The River's Tale* (1911), he connects the Thames to the Romans, the Phoenicians, the Norse, and the Greeks, reinforcing the river's classical status. Percy Shelley's friend Thomas Love Peacock described the poet watching the Thames and imagining a journey 'up and down some mighty stream which civilization had either never visited, or long since deserted: the Missouri and the Columbia, the Oronoko and the Amazon, the Nile and the Niger, the Euphrates and the Tigris' (quoted in Holmes 2008: 233). The Thames as an imperial river disregards the logics of time and space to subsume the past and the periphery under its totalizing influence.

While Joseph Conrad's *Heart of Darkness* is remembered for the atrocities it describes along the Congo, readers often forget that the book starts and ends on the Thames estuary as a vessel at anchor awaits the tides. Conrad describes the scene through an impressionistic narration that captures the river's gauzy beauty and draws a link between Europeans in Africa and Roman soldiers who first arrived on the banks of the Thames to colonize the dark, untamed forests filled with barbarian peoples. He writes that 'nothing is easier for a man who has, as the phrase goes, "followed the sea" with reverence and affection, than to evoke the great spirit of the past upon the lower reaches of the Thames' (Conrad 1899: 4). Historian Simon Schama writes of Conrad's temporal highway: 'to go upstream was, I knew, to go backward: from metropolitan din to ancient silence; westward toward the source of the waters, the beginnings of Britain in the Celtic limestone' (2004: 5). Here, the Thames is a river of memories – a road that in connecting both time and terrestrial space also unifies the world entire.

Notes

1 Anthony Anghie explains that 'the ability of natives to enter into such treaties was paradoxical, given that they were characterized as entirely lacking in legal status … international lawyers granted the natives such status, quasi-sovereignty,

for the purpose of enabling them to transfer rights, property, and sovereignty' (2006: 745).

2 In his erudite analysis of Europe's efforts to bring civilization to the periphery, Bowden argues that despite differences between European states and empires, there is a startling consistency in the way they understood the civilizing mission: 'What becomes evident is that there is a certain consistency and continuity across time and space, irrespective of which particular European nation is acting in the name of civilization and administering the civilizing' (2009: 130).

3 'Then I bethought me of a garden – the place looked so devoid of grace and completeness without it – and for the sake of giving a finish to the plan a long oval was drawn which should represent an enclosure wherein...' (1885, I: 147). Stanley's desire to build a garden – a bit of order, familiarity, and civilization in a strange land – echoed travelers along the Danube delta who also longed for a garden. The desire for a garden in foreign spaces echoes in many travelogues and reflects Western travelers' nostalgia for the sense of ordered mastery over nature that animated European gardens.

4 In Richard Owen's address to the British Association for the Advancement of Science in 1858, he declared, 'No empire in the world had ever so wide a range for the collection of the various forms of animal life as Great Britain ... Never was there so much energy and intelligence displayed in the capture and transmission of exotic animals by the enterprising traveler in unknown lands and by the hardy settler in remote colonies, as by those who start from their native shores of Britain' (MacKenzie 1988: 37).

5 Conrad writes that Kurtz was educated in England, his mother half-English, his father half-French, and 'all Europe contributed to the making of Kurtz'. This description reflects Conrad himself, who was born in Poland, spent years in the French and British merchant marines, and finally made Britain his home.

6 The *chicotte* was an instrument of punishment used in Leopold's Congo – a whip made of sun-dried hippopotamus hide cut into spiral strips. Twenty-five lashes typically would render a person unconscious; a hundred or more would be fatal.

7

The 1884–85 Berlin Conference and the international organization that never was

If the 1815 Rhine Commission and the 1856 European Commission of the Danube could be considered accomplishments in institutional creation and international governance, then the abortive International Commission of the Congo proposed in the text of the 1885 General Acts of the Berlin Conference was certainly an international disaster. Liberals and internationalists who celebrate the creation of the Rhine and Danube commissions as markers of international progress (Woolf 1916; Chamberlain 1923; Kaiser and Schot 2014) leave out the Berlin Conference and the circumstances surrounding the non-creation of the Congo Commission. By highlighting diplomatic efforts to civilize the Congo basin as a failure of global governance, this chapter challenges assumptions that institutional models have a natural teleology as they spread from one geographical and political context to another, becoming more robust and established. Geographies such as the Congo basin are not 'naturally' empty or international, just as they are not 'naturally' conducive to international management through institutions. Instead, it was the co-constitution between social and material factors that imbued the Congo with political meaning, and therefore allowed or precluded certain institutional possibilities.

On the surface, diplomats at the Berlin Conference seemed to face the same dilemma as diplomats at the 1856 Paris Conference – whether to tame an uncivilized geography through private sovereign control or as an international commons. However, unlike the Danube, which was laden with the bloody history of clashing civilization, the conceptual emptiness of the Congo represented new opportunities for European colonizers to transplant progressive European civilization and institutions to a blank canvas. Consequently, the European powers that advocated for the Danube delta as an international space now changed their tunes and maintained that the Congo and the Niger rivers were private colonial territories.

This chapter details European diplomats' efforts at the Berlin Conference to bring European normative and institutional models to the Congo basin. In doing so, I contend that the primary consideration of the conference was not the Congo itself but the balance of power in Europe. The first section details the threat posed by inter-imperial competition to power balances within European international society, and argues that King Leopold II of Belgium's shocking territorial gains in the Congo were a direct result of maintaining this delicate balance. The chapter then explores the two European models that diplomats hoped to transplant from Europe to West Africa – the establishment of freedom of navigation and commerce along the Congo and the creation of an international commission to govern and improve the river for global commerce. However, I argue that, unlike the Rhine and the Danube, the Congo represented a particular colonial geography in the European geographical imagination – first, in the conceptual emptiness Europeans envisioned along the river, and second, in its primary importance as a token in European balance-of-power politics. Combined, these framings resulted in the imposition of ill-fitting models from Europe's historical development onto the morally and politically 'empty' spaces of the periphery – a pattern for global development that continues to play out in the twenty-first century.

The final section explores the Berlin Conference's failure to transform the Congo into a peaceful, non-sovereign, and neutral space for the benefit of international commerce. While diplomats were sincere in their efforts to establish a neutral and effective international body on the Congo, the dynamics of colonial competition forced Europeans to accept Leopold's ambitions as being in line with European practices. Further, I argue that the Berlin Conference highlights the policy failings that emerged from the European geographical imagination, both in its conceptualization of the empty colonial river as well as its assumption that Europe was a geography of generalizable and universal political possibilities. Ultimately, the non-creation of the International Commission of the Congo rested on European understandings of both the 'empty' Congo basin and the applicability of the European past to the colonial present – both were acts of erasure that sidestepped the historical complexities of both the periphery and Europe itself.

European politics at the 1884–85 Berlin Conference

German Chancellor Otto von Bismarck opened the Berlin Conference on 15 November 1884 by listing the major policy objectives for the gathering: first, to establish freedom of commerce on the Congo; second, to establish freedom of navigation on the Congo and Niger rivers; and third, to establish a principle for effective occupation. However, what Bismarck left unsaid was the real purpose of the conference: to access Africa's lucrative resources without upsetting the balance of power in Europe. Like the cartographers who worked to map the great deeds of European explorers and Conrad's book that uncovered the heart of European darkness, the Berlin Conference was less about West Africa than it was an inward-looking diplomatic conference to resolve European anxieties about the potential for intra-European conflict over colonial possessions.

From the time explorer Diogo Cão first claimed the Congo's mouth with stone pillars in 1482 to the mid-nineteenth century, European interest in western Africa rested primarily in maintaining a string of coastal trading posts. Explorers who tried to navigate the Congo ran into hydrological barriers: a deep canyon and impossible cataracts greeted European ships roughly 400 kilometers upriver from the Atlantic. However, the discovery that rubber, ivory, palm oil, and groundnuts could be turned into profitable raw materials for a quickly industrializing Europe catapulted inland Africa into the geopolitical limelight (Crowe 1942: 12). In 1883, according to the Privy Council for Trade, the British ran a trade deficit with the West Coast of Africa, importing £910,741 of palm oil and £298,488 of nut oil (FO 403/47, 1884: no. 17). Although still cumbersome, steamboats that could be disassembled and carried past the cataracts in pieces gave locomotion to inland exploration and trade. Advances in weapons technology also enabled Europeans to make further conquests upriver.

Fourteen states, including the United States and the Ottoman Empire, attended the Berlin Conference held between November 1884 and February 1885. Of those, four major European states – Germany, France, Britain and Portugal – and one association – King Leopold II's International Association of the Congo (IAC) – competed for influence. Since the fifteenth century, the Portuguese had claimed the territory at the Congo's mouth, but in the 1870s, the French rushed to secure territorial concessions using Italian-born explorer Savorgan de Brazza to negotiate treaties with local chieftains along the lower Congo. Leopold II of Belgium surreptitiously pursued his own territorial ambitions with the aid of British-born American journalist Henry Morton Stanley. When confronted with increasing French and Belgian encroachment, the Portuguese sought to reinforce their claims by negotiating a treaty with Britain. The proposed 1883 Anglo-Portuguese treaty affirmed Portuguese sovereignty between 5°12' and 8° south latitude in exchange for granting Britain most favored nation trading status and establishing a joint Anglo-Portuguese commission to manage the river (Crowe 1942: 20). At first, the British had proposed an international commission, but the Portuguese insisted on a two-state Anglo-Portuguese commission – a stipulation that fanned French and German fears that Britain and Portugal intended to shut them out of the lower Congo. French and German objections meant the treaty was never ratified, and Bismarck convened the Berlin Conference in an effort to settle matters through multilateral rather than bilateral negotiations.

Britain had few interests along the Congo itself beyond free trade, but its political maneuvers over the Congo were informed by its determination to keep the neighboring Niger firmly under British control. Earlier in the century, British explorer Verney Lovett Cameron and even Stanley had attempted to negotiate treaties in favor of British control, but ultimately Britain had little interest in colonizing the Congo. However, Britain was very much interested in the Niger, and as Percy Anderson, a member of the British delegation at Berlin, declared, 'we must take our seat as the Niger Power' (Pakenham 1991: 241). Hence, Britain was happy to uphold the principle of freedom of navigation and commerce on both rivers, but when it came to the question of a commission, Britain adamantly insisted on treating the two rivers differently. While an international commission should be established to govern the empty Congo basin, Britain asserted that it had sufficient control over the lower Niger to be able to guarantee freedom of navigation and trade without a commission (Maluwa 1982: 378; van Reybrouck 2014: 53). As the chairman of the National Africa Company Lord Aberdare wrote to the foreign secretary Earl Granville:

> The trade of the Lower Niger and its tributaries has been entirely the creation of British enterprise, after long efforts and many failures. The 100 factories now on the river are exclusively British, and it would appear unreasonable to subject it to the same authorities as the undeveloped and unowned waters of the Upper Congo. (FO 403/46, 1884: no. 32)

Here, Aberdare argues that the Niger was under the purview of British sovereignty, but the Congo, because it was 'undeveloped and unowned', should be placed under an international commission. This definition of what constitutes international spaces echoed arguments about the lack of civilized authority on the Danube delta and framed the international as only imaginable in relation to – and as the opposite of – legitimate sovereign control over a territory's natural and human resources. But this framing also created an opening for an unowned international space to become a domestic one once a legitimate colonial authority was established and able to exercise effective occupation. Hence, in order to maintain control over the Niger, Britain conceded control over the Congo to Leopold, and in return, Germany, Belgium, and the United States gave their support to Britain on the Niger question.

France's main objectives at the Berlin Conference were to challenge British control over the Niger while defending its growing claims over the lower Congo, particularly along the north bank where de Brazza had been busy building trade links and negotiating treaties with local chieftains. Portuguese, British, and IAC activities threatened these claims, and the French feared that the Anglo-Portuguese treaty was a British attempt to gift the lower

Congo to Portugal because Portugal was less of a threat to British interests in West Africa than France. The French arrived at Berlin in what they believed was a strong bargaining position. Bismarck and the French ambassador to Berlin, Baron de Courcel, had just concluded a Franco-German alliance in late 1884. In exchange for its cooperation with Germany in West Africa to establish free trade along the Congo, Germany had agreed to back France in Egypt (Crowe 1942: 63). However, true to his reputation, Bismarck was a slippery ally, and at Berlin he sided more often with Belgium and Britain than he did with France. The French were not pleased. At one point, during discussions about the Congo's neutrality during war, an angry Courcel shouted at the German and British delegates: 'Do you take us for robbers?' (Pakenham 1991: 250).[1] Ultimately, the territorial question was negotiated in private meetings between French and Portuguese delegates and Leopold's representatives, Eugene Pirmez and Emile Banning. The French ended up with the north bank of the middle Congo from Brazzaville to the village of Manyanga, and the Portuguese kept Nokki and the enclave of Cabinda on the north bank. These concessions kept the French and Portuguese happy while Leopold walked away with the largest territorial prize.

For Bismarck as the conference's host, the Congo was a smokescreen. The historiography on Bismarck largely suggests that he was not interested in colonial expansion but rather in what manipulating the politics of African colonialism could do for him in Europe (Taylor 1955; Eyck 1964; Richter 1965; Crankshaw 1981).[2] According to one account, Bismarck once pointed at a map of Germany sandwiched between France and Russia and proclaimed: 'This is my map of Africa!' (Taylor 1955: 221). Even if apocryphal, the story nicely illustrates Bismarck's conception of the conference and its importance for the balance of power in Europe and Germany's survival. In addition, two domestic factors may have spurred Bismarck's fleeting interest in German colonies in Africa. First, Bismarck needed to court domestic economic and ideological pro-colonialism constituents for electoral purposes. As Bismarck wrote to his Vice Chancellor Karl von Boetticker, 'the whole colonial business is a swindle, but we need it for the election' (quoted in Richter 1965: 282). Second, he wished to drive a wedge between Germany's Prince Wilhelm and Britain (Crankshaw 1981: 396). Bismarck used outrage over the Anglo-Portuguese treaty and his subsequent orchestration of a conference on West Africa to drive this wedge. 'What Bismarck really wanted, of course, was not colonies but a quarrel about colonies,' wrote German historian Werner Richter, who then concluded that history punished Bismarck by giving him both a quarrel and a set of second-rate colonies (1965: 283–4). Hence, for Bismarck, norms and institutions on a river half a world away were primarily leverage for geopolitical maneuvers in the heart of Europe.

Despite the Berlin Conference's main focus on balance-of-power politics among European powers, one objective unified the European competitors – transforming the Congo into a conduit for free navigation and trade to bring European civilization to a backward continent and enrich themselves in the process. Further, tales from the adventures of David Livingstone and Henry Morton Stanley had ignited the public imagination and contributed to the salience of moral objectives at Berlin, starting with the abolition of the slave trade – a practice that Europeans had first adopted to an unpresented extent and now rejected as morally abhorrent and carried out by uncivilized Arabs. In his opening speech, Bismarck took up Livingstone's famed three Cs for Africa – commerce, Christianity, and civilization – to give the proceedings a sense of moral purpose. Indeed, it was this sense of moral purpose that also closed the distance between the desire for balance within European international society and its projection outward as a civilized model and influence. In essence, establishing a peaceful balance in Europe through diplomatic agreement rather than war and civilizing the Congo's emptiness with free trade validated both the superiority of European civilization and the necessity of its expansion outward.

The personal ambitions of King Leopold II

The Berlin Conference exposed a tension within European international society in the late nineteenth century between inter-imperial competition and the impetus to avert violent conflicts that might destabilize Europe. Into this delicate balancing act walked King Leopold II of Belgium, who desired nothing more than to make the liberal and increasingly democratic Belgium into a formidable colonial empire. Leopold's obsession with colonies led him to scan the world for possibilities. At first, he looked toward North Africa or South America, and was frustrated by the Belgian government's aversion to colonies. He lamented to his aides that 'Belgium doesn't exploit the world … it's a taste we have got to learn' (quoted in Hochschild 1998: 38). It might be easy to attribute Leopold's fixation to his unhappy home life, but the notion that colonies would bestow him with power, wealth, and, most of all, prestige emerged from the larger context of late nineteenth-century European international society, in which all states, large and small, competed to divide the world and gain prominence through colonial expansion.

In the decades before the Berlin Conference, Leopold had set events in motion on three fronts – legal, diplomatic, and humanitarian – in his bid to transform the Congo basin into his own personal colony. Adam Hochschild's engaging scholarship (1998) describes how Leopold took careful steps to conceal his machinations from the international community abroad as well as Belgian leaders at home. To ensure the legality of his claims,

Leopold employed Stanley and legal scholar Sir Travers Twiss and instructed them to conclude as many treaties as possible with local chieftains to cede sovereignty to Leopold. Earlier European treaties with locals had rented land for payment, but Leopold now wanted the treaties not only to sell him the land in perpetuity but also to cede all rights to it. He made this wish clear in a letter to one of his employees:

> The text of the treaties Stanley has signed with the chieftains does not please me. It should at least contain an article stating that they relinquish their sovereignty rights to those territories. ... This effort is important and urgent. The treaties must be as brief as possible and, in the space of one or two articles, assign all rights to us. (quoted in van Reybrouck 2014: 50)

Hence, Leopold went from renting land from indigenous populations to claiming sovereign rights over that land. Even if the chieftains could have understood the English and French terms used to draft these treaties, it is unlikely that they understood the gravity of the 'rights' they were asked to sign away.

Diplomatically, through his US agent Henry Shelton Sanford, who hosted and charmed his way into the heart of American politics, King Leopold secured American recognition for his Congo claims ahead of the Berlin Conference. Sanford shrewdly compared Belgian interests in the Congo to America's support for establishing Liberia. He likened Leopold's treaties with African tribes to seventeenth-century Puritan treaties with the Native Americans. Sanford even invited President Chester A. Arthur to his orange plantation in Florida in order to win the administration's support. All this lobbying bore fruit – the USA issued a statement in April 1884 announcing 'its sympathy with and approval of the humane and benevolent purposes of the International Association of the Congo, administrating, as it does, the interests of the Free States there established' (quoted in Hochschild 1998: 81).

Next, Leopold secured French recognition before the Berlin Conference with a shrewd ploy that offered the French *le droit de préemption* to be the first to buy the Congo in case Leopold could not sustain the financial burden of managing such a vast holding (van Reybrouck 2014: 52; FO 403/46, 1884: no. 31). This device satisfied France that the Congo would never fall into British or Portuguese possession, and in return, France backed Leopold's claims. In exchange for British recognition, Leopold supported British claims along the Niger. Finally, Leopold even won over Bismarck, who had at first described Leopold's proposal to incorporate the Congo into a new state as a 'swindle' and sarcastically compared Leopold to an Italian 'who considers that his charm and good looks will enable him to get away with anything' (Hochschild 1998: 83). However dimly Bismarck may have viewed Leopold's character, he saw British, French, and Portuguese ambitions in West Africa as far greater threats to Germany's position in Europe. This played to Leopold's advantage and by the opening of the conference, Bismarck was approaching other delegations on behalf of Leopold's claims to the Congo (FO 403/48, 1884: no. 18).

But perhaps Leopold's most clever ruse was the humanitarian sheen he gave to his plans in the Congo – a humanitarian front that concealed his ambitions and allowed him to give eloquent lip service to Europeans' sense of moral purpose in Africa. A decade before Berlin, Leopold had established the International African Association (IAA) as a philanthropic organization. At its first conference, Leopold proclaimed: 'to pierce the darkness which hangs over entire peoples, is, I dare say, a crusade worthy of this century of progress'. He went on to describe Belgium as a neutral and satisfied state with peaceful and humane intentions, and maintained that he, Leopold, had 'no other ambition than to serve her [Belgium] well' (quoted in Hochschild 1998: 44–5). In a published statement he insisted on

> the completely charitable, completely scientific and philanthropic nature of the aim to be achieved. It is not a question of a business proposition; it is matter of a completely spontaneous collaboration between all those who wish to engage in introducing civilization to Africa. (quoted in Anstey 1962: 59)

A few years later, Leopold established another organization that he deviously called the International Association of the Congo (IAC). The names IAA and IAC were designed to be confusingly similar. As Leopold instructed his agents, 'care must be taken not to let it be obvious that the Association of the Congo and the Africa Association are two different things' (quoted in Hochschild 1998: 65). Diplomatic missives from the conference bear out this confusion and often simply referred to 'the International Association' rather than the organization's full name (see, for example, FO 403/46, 1884: no. 31). In addition, Leopold's public relations campaign worked to conceal any evidence that his activities were not entirely in the service of promoting civilization and free trade. When he published his treaties with chieftains, Leopold carefully omitted clauses that gave him monopoly over trade along the river (Hochschild 1998: 78). Leopold's publicity ruse worked. By the time of the Berlin Conference, business interests such as the Manchester Chamber of Commerce were asking the British Foreign Office to support the 'earnest efforts of His Majesty the King of the Belgians to establish civilization and free trade on the Upper Congo' (FO 403/46, 1884: no. 69). On the eve of the Berlin Conference on 22 October 1884, the *Daily Telegraph* printed a piece that lauded Leopold:

> Leopold II ... has knit adventurers, traders and missionaries of many races into one band of men, under the most illustrious of modern travelers [H. M. Stanley] to carry into the interior of Africa new ideas of law, order, humanity, and protection of the natives.

Leopold did not set foot in the conference room at Berlin, and yet he walked away as the biggest winner. Credit and blame for the failure to establish an international commission to govern the Congo, however, cannot be solely laid at the feet of one man. Not only did European representatives not hamper him, delegates even applauded Leopold at the conference's signing ceremony as the man who would bring order and civilization and guarantee free trade in the heart of Africa. The IAC's flag which increasingly flew over Leopold's Congo was deep blue with a yellow star – the blue represented the darkness of Africa while the star represented the light of European civilization. While Europe's colonial empires engaged in power politics to check one another's ambitions in West Africa, Leopold emerged with the Congo Free State as his personal colony.

Bringing European institutions to Africa: two models

In order to prevent violent conflict over the Congo, European diplomats at Berlin aimed to bring two models from European international society to Africa – first, the principle of freedom of navigation and commerce on an international river; and second, the establishment of an international commission to manage and regulate the river for the benefit of humanity. While all parties agreed on the need to guarantee freedom of navigation and commerce and to ensure 'the proper and orderly development of European commerce in Africa' (Maluwa 1982: 375), diplomats remained divided between the river as private property – in this case, private colonial conquest – and international commons. However, unlike the Rhine as an internal European river and the Danube as a connecting river between Europe and the near periphery, the Congo represented a different type of abstract space in the European geographical imagination. This conceptual emptiness underscored two main barriers to the successful transplantation of European models – first, the absence of European-style sovereign authorities to control the banks; and second, the Congo's symbolic place as a mere token for the balance of power in Europe. These differences made the application of European models nonsensical. However, as I will contend in the remainder of this chapter, European confidence in the universality and generalizability of their own past experiences made the two models the only imaginable blueprints at the Berlin Conference.

Model one: freedom of navigation and commerce

All parties at Berlin agreed that the longstanding European principle of freedom of navigation and commerce along international rivers should be applied to West Africa just as it had been applied to the Rhine through the 1815 Treaty of Vienna, extended to the Danube with the 1856 Treaty of Paris, and to the Parana and Uruguay rivers in 1853.[3] The conference started with the British delegation's general declaration attempting to define freedom of commerce on the Congo. The declaration stated that flags of all nations should have access to the river and its tributaries, with no monopolies, no import and transit duties, and no taxes except 'as may be levied as compensation for usual expenditure on trade, and, under this head, shall be equally borne by natives and foreigners of every nationality' (Gavin and Betley 1973: 129–30). According to this definition, which was accepted by the USA, Germany, Italy, and Belgium, the Congo as an international commercial highway was open to free trade and should not be privatized through colonial conquest. The French and Portuguese disagreed, but they were outnumbered.

However, while this definition made sense along transboundary European rivers as exceptions to the general principle of sovereign control over the banks and surrounding territories, applying the principle in an abstract colonial space with limited sovereign control and no boundaries to traverse raised the question of why stop at the river. If the colonial river was a commercial thoroughfare, then why not the entire basin of all navigable rivers in West Africa? British diplomats pushed the general declaration even further – if the river is an international highway, then the principle should also be applied to the coastline between Gabon and Angola, since boats had to navigate these waters to reach the Congo from Europe. The Americans wished to stretch the logic further still – to extend the principle of freedom of commerce to the entire continent between the Congo and the Indian Ocean (Gavin and Betley 1973: 90–3). Here, Bismarck interjected and announced that the Berlin Conference's agenda only included the Niger and Congo rivers and would leave the question of navigation on other waterways and land-based routes to subsequent discussions (Gavin and Betley 1973: 129–30). However, while these proposals to extend the principle of freedom of navigation and trade were largely rejected,[4] they did illuminate the absurdity of applying principles developed in the context of European international society to an 'empty' colonial geography devoid of European-style state authorities.

Another indication that the 'empty' colonial river differed from European transboundary rivers was the distinction between freedom of navigation and freedom of commerce. While the two might have been separable along the Rhine and Danube, the two could not be separated in the Congo since European commerce depended exclusively on the ability to freely navigate along the river and its tributaries. Without navigation, there was no commerce. Indigenous trade was not even part of the equation. Again, in the absence of existing sovereign authorities, European norms of transboundary river governance made an awkward transition to West Africa. However, diplomats did not deviate from their plans.

The moral river

Diplomatic discussions surrounding the internationalization of the Congo differed from previous conversations concerning the Rhine and Danube in the paternalistic moral tone of the proposals. Here, the Congo was not just a commercial highway that brought rationality and civilization in its wake but a self-consciously imperial tool to impose legitimate authority and moral values on an otherwise blank canvas. In West Africa, commerce would not be trusted to 'naturally' do its civilizing work as on the Rhine and Danube, but morality had to be brought in through stricter European guidance. This moral tenor is reflected in Granville's instructions to the British representative Edward Malet on the moral limits of free trade along the Niger and Congo:

> I have, however, to direct your attention to the consideration that commercial interests should not, in the opinion of Her Majesty's Government, be looked upon as exclusively the subject of deliberation; while the opening of the Congo market is to be desired the welfare of the natives should not be neglected; to them it would be no benefit, but the reverse, if freedom of commerce, unchecked by reasonable control, should degenerate into license (FO 403/47, 1884: no. 28)

In other words, because the native Africans were backward and in need of guidance, 'free' trade should not be *laissez faire* but governed by the understanding that European commerce along the Congo was part of a bundle of civilizational practices that ought to be tempered by moral concerns. In accordance with these moral concerns, diplomats at Berlin often discussed the 'reasonable controls' that ought to be applied to two degenerative commercial activities that could hinder Africa's progress along the civilizational continuum: the trade in slaves and in alcohol.

The desire to end the slave trade permeated discussions on free trade. The Portuguese took credit for introducing 'the seeds of civilization into Africa' and highlighted, without any intended irony, the 'sacrifices which she [Portugal] has made to arrive at the total suppression of the Slave Trade in those territories' (Gavin and Betley 1973: 239). The Italian ambassador enthusiastically backed the proposal for all powers to suppress slavery and declared that this 'high treason against humanity should be comprised, like piracy, amongst crimes against international law, and punished as such' (Gavin and Betley 1973: 239). These statements of moral indignation were underhandedly directed at the 'Arab' slave traders who captured the late nineteenth-century European imagination as the perpetrators of this vile practice. Hence, free trade on the Congo should be the virtuous flow of European goods, wealth, and ideas rather than this evil practice. All parties agreed and the General Articles of the Berlin Conference included a statement that the Congo basin should not be used as 'a market or means of transit for the trade in slaves, of whatever race they may be', and that all Powers vowed to punish those who did (Article 9).

In addition to trade in human beings, diplomats at the conference also questioned whether the 'traffic in spirituous liquors' was acceptable on an international river. First raised by Italy, efforts to limit the trade in alcohol were taken up by the Portuguese representative António de Serpa Pimentel, who proposed the prohibition of liquor and spirits as well as 'wooden collars, whips, and other instruments of torture made use of by slave-proprietors' (Gavin and Betley 1973: 239). The sentiment was later echoed by representatives from Britain, Belgium, and the USA at the fifth meeting. As Percy Anderson of the African Company noted in a submitted report to the conference, 'It would be a disaster for the humane cause and a reproach to all civilized nations if the result of contact with foreign commerce should give birth to a passion amongst the native which would demoralize and degrade them.' While his company stood to make financial gains from increased Congo trade, these gains would not be worth 'the return to barbarism of these countries' (Gavin and Betley 1973: 223–4). These moral qualifications to free trade also played into Leopold's ambitions in the aftermath of Berlin. In 1889, Leopold called an antislavery conference in Brussels to discuss the prohibition against the trade in slaves and liquor; in actuality, he was strapped for cash to finance his Congo schemes and wanted to override the prohibition against levying tariffs in the Congo as agreed to in Berlin (Craven 2015: 56). The 1890 Brussels Conference Act gave Leopold what he wanted wrapped in the veneer of humanitarian purpose, and he was allowed to levy a 10 percent import tariff in contravention of any notion of freedom of trade agreed to at the Berlin Conference.

These moral qualifications revealed that European diplomats had a very specific notion of what freedom of navigation and commerce along the Congo meant. It highlights the differences between the Congo as an abstract colonial geography and the Rhine or Danube rivers as concrete commercial roads grounded in European history and politics. While untapped commercial possibilities did elicit interest, European commerce along the Congo was seen first and foremost as an overt civilizing tool that would remake the emptiness of the Congo based on European values, behavior, and institutions.

Model two: the international river commission

The second European model that diplomats aimed to apply to the Congo was an international commission that would regulate navigation on the river and ensure free trade. After all, freedom of navigation and trade meant very little without effective implementation, and an international river needed a practical body to maintain navigation lanes and create and enforce regulations. Looking to the Rhine and Danube commissions as models, diplomats at Berlin worked to create a similar body. However, this act of transplanting European institutional models to Africa faced two looming problems. First, as I have discussed previously, the Rhine and Danube commissions were not analogous – the 1815 Rhine Commission was a weak interstate consultative body involving only riparian states, while the 1856 European Commission of the Danube developed into an independent international body with non-riparian states exercising authority over territory a continent away. These commission were shaped by distinct context-specific configurations of power and were products of differing geographical imaginaries of each river. Hence, to maintain that there was one European institutional model to apply to the Congo would be to ignore the complex history of these European river commissions.

Second, European geographical imaginaries of the Congo as an abstract colonial space presented legal and geopolitical barriers to an international commission. Prior to Berlin, the British Foreign Office had recognized that the Congo basin's lack of 'well-defined territories of civilized States' might be a problem for establishing a cooperative institution to manage the river. After all, how do you create an interstate body without states in the first place? As Granville noted, 'the problem there to be solved is the application of the general principles of the Treaty of Vienna to the very different circumstances that present themselves in Africa' (FO 403/46, 1884: no. 15). Granville's comment suggests that while he understood that implementing European models in Africa would be different, he underestimated how insurmountable that difference might be. Not only were there no well-defined 'civilized' states in the Congo basin, but European understandings of the Congo as conceptually empty and ready to be remade invited colonization and privatization rather than an international commission.

At Berlin, all states agreed in principle on the creation of an International Commission of the Congo based on the Rhine and Danube models. However, in grouping the Rhine and Danube commissions together, diplomats concealed disagreement on whether the Rhine model or the Danube model should be followed – would the new commission be a powerful body capable of independent action like the Danube Commission, or would it be a weak body whose actions relied on the consent and consensus of riparian states?

In other words, the lack of well-defined territorial states along the Congo might be resolved in two different ways – either by a civilized European power controlling and colonizing that space and ensuring freedom of navigation and commerce, or by an international body administering the Congo as an international space. However, while diplomats in 1856 chose to internationalize the Danube delta, the context of African colonization elicited a very different reaction from key European states – these states' colonial ambitions elsewhere in Africa made it all but impossible to prevent colonial control in this instance. Hence, Europeans saw the 'empty' Congo as an enticing invitation to colonial rule and flipped the argument to advocate for a weak international commission.

While both Portugal and France committed themselves to the principle of freedom of navigation and trade along the Congo, they wanted the principles to be administered under their sovereign powers as colonial owners of the river. In response to the general declaration for freedom of navigation and commerce, the Portuguese representative Count de Launay stated that as of the Berlin Conference, there were no dues imposed on commerce, but there was in West Africa the 'absence of that constant and effective governmental protection which is justly looked upon as compensation for taxes collected' (Gavin and Betley 1973: 136). In other words, taxes are part of the civilizational package. The trade that diplomats wished to protect was not local trade but future European trade, and therefore freedoms meant nothing without a competent authority to establish and promote that trade. Riparian colonial powers would impose taxes in exchange for 'effective governmental protection', and only with this protection could Europeans enjoy freedom of navigation and commerce in practice. Indeed, the enduring legacy of the conference, the idea of effective occupation, was based on this logic. As noted in the previous chapter, Africa became a 'conceptual *terra nullius*' to be ceded to any power that could offer effective and moral administration (Anghie 2005: 91).

Rejecting the Danube Commission model

The 1856 European Commission of the Danube loomed as a controversial model for diplomats at Berlin. Ahead of the conference, the British Foreign Office wrote to Mr. Sanderson, British representative on the Danube Commission, for him to explain 'the manner in which, in practice, effect is given to the decision of the European Commission of the Danube' so that the same model could be applied to the Congo (FO 78/3724, 1844: no. 50). Sanderson replied with details on how the commission managed financial affairs, established regulations, and enforced those regulations on the Danube delta. He described how the commission coped with its tricky role of enforcing international navigation regulations and adjudicating between competing states (FO 403/46, 1884: no. 90). This correspondence suggests that the British were ready to replicate the independent Danube Commission on the Congo, but not all parties agreed.

While Belgium, Germany, and Britain advocated for a strong, independent commission with full powers to regulate navigation and commerce, Portugal and France pressed for giving the body as little power as possible (Crowe 1942: 131–3). In addition, Russia and Austria-Hungary, which had objected to the European Danube Commission in the first place, now supported Portugal and France's position. The Russian delegate to Berlin, Count Pyotr Kapnist, began the fifth meeting on 18 December 1884 by rejecting the universality of the Danube Commission model. He argued that diplomats at the conference had a 'tendency to enlarge and generalize the range of the Acts relative to the Danube … and to turn these Acts and these resolutions into doctrine of international law'. Further, the Danube Commission was not an application of the Final Act of the Congress of Vienna, but an exceptional circumstance due to the lack of effective sovereign control on the Danube delta. Hence, the Danube model's application to the Congo should be considered the exception rather than the rule, since the model would not be applied to the Niger. The Austro-Hungarian delegate Count Szechenyi agreed (Gavin and Betley 1973: 174–83). They were not wrong. Here, Kapnist at once rejected the Danube Commission as an established model and humbled the British, whose insistence on an independent commission on the Congo contradicted their objectives on the Niger. Britain as the strongest advocate for an independent commission was caught in the net of its own colonial ambitions.

In the end, despite stated intentions to follow the Danube model, diplomats at Berlin stepped away from the Danube Commission. This is particularly clear from the conference's decisions in two key areas – the commission's independent authority and its ability to borrow money. First, on the question of the commission's authority, the conference concluded that it would only be independent of territorial authorities 'where no Power exercises sovereign rights'. In places where sovereign authority already existed, the Commission would 'concert its actions (*s'entendra*)' with that power (General Act, Article 20). However, the Berlin Conference itself installed sovereign powers over the Congo basin, as all states recognized Leopold's IAC and Congo Free State as sovereign authorities over the upper river.[5] Portugal and France also held sovereign rights over sections of the lower Congo. The international commission would have to coordinate its actions with all three powers (Banning 1927: 28–9; Crowe 1942: 134). Hence, even if the commission had been established, it would have been subservient to the three colonial powers and would have had little latitude for independent action. This legal language made the Congo Commission a diplomatic formality that would never leave the pages of the General Acts.

Second, the ability to borrow money on the international market marked out the 1856 Danube Commission as a unique institution in European politics and allowed it to finance the expensive engineering works needed to clear the delta's shipping channels. According to the General Acts of the Berlin Conference, the Congo Commission would take on similar functions as the Danube Commission – to remove any hindrance to freedom of navigation, to collect the standardized fees needed to do so, to draft navigation regulations, and to police the river (Gavin and Betley 1973: 188–9). The Danube Commission was able to take on these expensive projects because it was able to borrow money, with its debts guaranteed by the commission's participating states. If the Congo Commission was to achieve similar results, it would also need funds to cover startup costs. At first, Bismarck had suggested that the Congo Commission's loans be guaranteed in the same way as those of the Danube Commission, and Britain and Belgium agreed. However, France and Portugal objected and won out. The final wording stated that the Congo Commission could negotiate loans but only 'in its own name' and 'exclusively guaranteed by the revenues raised by the said Commission' (General Act, Article 23). Undoubtedly few private investors would risk granting a loan to a new international commission on an unknown continent without a guarantor. In effect, this language left the Congo Commission without viable funding.

By limiting the proposed International Commission of the Congo's ability to operate independently of sovereign state authority and to borrow money, the Berlin Conference implicitly reverted to the Rhine Commission model of transboundary river governance. However, the Rhine Commission was a weak interstate body that depended on the power of riparian states to guarantee freedom of navigation and commerce – and in the case of the Congo, European-style sovereign states simply did not exist. Hence, to replicate the Rhine Commission on the Congo would have been impossible, and in the end, the General Acts of the Berlin Conference created just such an impossible international commission on paper.[6]

Diplomats' intentions of transplanting a civilized European model for river management to the Congo dissolved in the contradictions latent in an institutional blueprint that simply did not work in the new geopolitical context of European colonial ambitions in Africa. The intensity of colonial competition impeded efforts to adopt the Danube Commission model, and the absence of European-style sovereign states along the banks meant the Rhine model would also be impossible. Once the diplomats at Berlin recognized the IAC's sovereignty over the Congo, and the organization became synonymous with the Congo Free State, Leopold had finally secured his colony. The meaning of the Congo that won out, then, was not the river as an international highway open to all, but as a blank territory and invitation for colonial conquest and subjugation.

The failings of the 1884–85 Berlin Conference

Historians have long condemned the Berlin Conference as a complete failure. Rather than free trade and a neutral space in the Congo basin, Sybil Crowe noted that in the aftermath of the conference, monopolistic economic systems emerged, and Belgium gained exclusive control over the Congo basin (1942: 4). Adam Hochschild highlights that instead of commerce and civilization, the Belgian Congo became Leopold's gruesome personal colony and saw the deaths of up to 10 million Africans (1998: 278–80). In Thomas Pakenham's scathing judgment of the treaty, he writes that 'there were thirty-eight clauses to the General Act, all as hollow as the pillars in the great saloon' (1991: 254). While the conference failed to secure two of its three stated objectives, other scholars focus on the final objective of establishing a principle for effective occupation and pinpoint the Berlin Conference as a pivotal global moment when Africans were stripped of their competence as legal actors (Anghie 2005: 91).

One interpretation of the conference's failure to establish lasting institutions on the Congo might be that it was simply a fig-leaf for naked colonial ambition, and that diplomats were disingenuous in their efforts to establish free navigation and trade and an international commission. A decade later, Stanley wrote that the Berlin Conference reminded him of 'the way my black followers used to rush with gleaming knives for slaughtered game during our travels ... I do not blame them at all; on the contrary, I think it admirable, necessary and inevitable. The starving white man must be satisfied, or he will become ugly' (Stanley 1896). However, official records of the conference suggest that diplomats put real effort into applying norms and institutions from European international society to the Congo.

Legal scholar Mathew Craven describes the conundrum surrounding scholarship on the conference: how could it be both a complete failure and also a pivotal moment in the colonial history of Africa? He squares the circle by arguing that the Berlin West African Conference was both an anti- and pro-colonial enterprise that, like Foucault's carceral system, created 'an institution whose effect might be traced through the confounding of its own expectations' (2015: 35). Rather than setting out to divide the Congo basin, diplomats at Berlin genuinely intended to create an international, neutral, and non-sovereign space along the river. To deter colonization, diplomats took away the economic incentive for would-be colonizers by stipulating in Article 4 of the General Act that no import or export duties would be levied on goods except for a non-discriminatory fee to cover the expenses of maintaining navigation. Hence, diplomats attempted to make colonizing the Congo as economically unattractive as possible. And yet securing freedom of commerce required infrastructure – ports, roads, and railways – that could only be built and maintained by a sovereign power (Craven 2015: 55). In particular, the turbulent hydrology of the last 350 kilometers of the lower Congo before it reaches the Atlantic highlighted the extensive and expensive infrastructure that would be necessary to make the Congo viable as a commercial highway.

However, while the General Acts were designed to solve the rational cooperation dilemma by shifting the cost-benefit calculations away from colonization, they failed to account for the complex brew of non-economic logics that drove Europeans in the scramble for Africa.

The tragedy of Great Power politics

While Leopold bears a large portion of the blame and infamy for the terrible atrocities that devastated the 'international' river, Bismarck was right in the sense that contestation over the Congo was about Great Power politics in Europe, and Leopold was in the right place at the right time to reap the rewards of an intra-European stalemate. It is possible that some attendees at the conference genuinely believed Leopold's smokescreen; after all, he had charmed, manipulated, or blackmailed his way to recognition from America, France, and Germany even before the conference began. Throughout the negotiations on the abortive Anglo-Portuguese treaty, Leopold had engaged in an amiable exchange of correspondence with the British secretary of state Lord Granville, who remained sympathetic to Leopold even after British public opinion and Parliament turned against him after the revelation of his pre-conference agreement with France (Crowe 1942: 78; Anstey 1962: 173–4). However, the main players at Berlin believed Leopold because it was convenient not to dig deeper.

It did not take much reflection to see through Leopold's scheme, and the warning signs were everywhere. In addition to his enemies in Belgium, and Bismarck, who had his deep suspicions of Leopold, observers on the ground in the Congo also voiced their skepticism toward his supposedly humanitarian plans. As an example, Nowell Salmon, British rear admiral and commander-in-chief of the Cape of Good Hope and West Africa Station, wrote to the Secretary of the Admiralty on 22 March 1884 describing a brief journey he had taken up the Congo:

> The Association or Comité of Stanley is still pushing on at enormous expense above Stanley Pool; the traders are much puzzled at their proceeding, for while

professing purely philanthropic motives, it is acquiring territory and making trading treaties...

Whatever may be the ultimate object of the International Association, I cannot believe that the Stanley route, with its alternative river and land stages will ever become a trade route, even now any one going to Stanley Pool will prefer walking the whole distance ... The Congo is no doubt a grand river to look at but above Boma its navigation is ordinarily difficult and even dangerous ... Banana [a port at the Congo's mouth] seemed a busy place: there were lying there four steamers: I cannot, however, think the trade is sufficient for so many and such expensive establishments as have been formed on the river. I have no doubt that part of the present activity is the result of the action of the International Association. (ADM 123/86, 1883–84: pp. 156–8)

During his short trip, Admiral Salmon noted two major contradictions between Leopold's stated goals and his actions. First, the IAC declared only non-political, philanthropic motives, so why were its agents furiously signing treaties that required local leaders to give up full sovereignty over their land? Second, the IAC repeatedly stated that free trade was an animating feature of its activities, so why was it fixated on such a problematic and unprofitable river? From the Atlantic coast to Stanley Pool, the river ascends 300 meters through cataracts that barred navigation – any railroad built from the Atlantic to Stanley Pool to bypass the cataracts would have to traverse through jagged canyons. Not only would this be difficult, but there was no indication that there would be an economic return on the investment. The invention of rubber tires was still several years in the future,[7] and as Admiral Salmon noted, there was not enough trade to warrant Leopold's interest in the Congo as a major commercial artery. As Salmon insinuates, something else was afoot that could not be explained by the innocent line of simply promoting and protecting free trade.

Salmon was not the only one suspicious. The British assistant under-secretary of the Foreign Office, Thomas Villiers Lister, saw copies of Leopold's treaties that reached the British Foreign Office. He wrote to Granville in May 1884 asking him not to recognize the IAC as an independent power at the upcoming conference as the USA had foolishly done and as the French had greedily done. Lister argued that Leopold was perpetuating a fraud and asked Granville to beware of the 'shabby and mischievous trick which the King [Leopold] has played' (quoted in Stengers 1971: 162). Great Power politics at Berlin, however, made British recognition of the IAC imperative.

Indeed, despite Leopold's duplicity, he was not playing an unknown game. In the late nineteenth century, the French, the Portuguese, and the British had competed to sign treaties up and down the West African coast. These treaties forced indigenous leaders to cede their land or become protectorates.

The British sent Colonel E. H. Hewitt, and Admiralty records reveal land signed away for a pittance and treaties with Xs marked next to a long list of chieftains' names. 'A French man of war anchored off the bar of the Cameroon River ... made a treaty with King Passall to cede the country to the French; payment to be made to him of £2000 or £3000 pounds and an iron house' (ADM 123/86, 1883–84: pp. 81, 91). Savorgan de Brazza for the French along the Congo, Joseph Thomson for the British in Northern Nigeria, and Carl Peters for the Germans in East Africa all busily signed treaties with local populations (Craven 2015: 40–1). Hence, while Leopold's treaties with native chiefs were strange given the IAC's claim to be a purely humanitarian organization, his actions merely reflected common European colonial practices.

Hence, the logics of European power politics and colonial competition fueled Leopold's ambitions and enabled his success. Put bluntly, France did not want the Congo to fall into British or Portuguese hands, Britain did not want the Congo to fall into French hands and did not wish to give up the Niger, Germany did not want the European balance of power to shift too much in any direction, and Britain, Germany, and the USA all wanted the Congo to become an efficient and civilizing colonial highway. Given these priorities, recognizing the IAC and its control over the Congo seemed like a win-win situation for all, as the Great Powers achieved their aims without the expense of developing the river themselves. But what seemed like a successful example of international cooperation was flawed in fostering two irreconcilable understandings of the Congo – as a humanitarian conduit to bring European free trade and civilization to Africa and as a token in the balance of power in Europe. In the end, the Congo could not successfully be both.

Blind spots in the European geographical imagination

If the Congo's context was so different from the creation of the Rhine and Danube commissions, the puzzle remains as to why European diplomats at Berlin insisted on these institutional models. Here, I contend that as much as the abortive International Commission of the Congo represented the failures of Great Power European politics, it also revealed the failings of the European geographical imagination – both in its understanding of the Congo as an abstract, empty space and in its understanding of European historical development as a universal model applicable to different temporal and spatial settings.

First, as I have argued before, the Congo basin was in no sense conceptually empty. Instead, by the 1880s, the river was bustling with entangled global processes and the contradictory meanings these processes engendered. If

British Admiralty records were any indication of on-the-ground realities, the Congo basin resembled a schoolhouse game where colonial empires, religious organizations, explorers, traders, and indigenous groups formed tangled alliances and competed for influence. European activities must have perplexed some locals as representatives of the French, Portuguese, and the IAC scrambled to sign as many treaties and raise their flags over as much territory as possible. Legitimate authority was up for grabs. In response to a request from the Portuguese Governor of Angola to act against Stanley's suspicious activities, the British responded that they had no power to intervene against an American citizen acting on behalf of a Belgian monarch (ADM 123/86, 1883–84: p. 142).

African representation of any sort was missing from the Berlin Conference, and Stanley, who attended the conference as a technical expert, was the only attendee who had spent extensive time in West Africa. Hence, how diplomats understood the Congo basin – as a blank space to be mapped, divided, and shared among European commercial empires – rested on fundamentally different ontological assumptions than how West Africans saw the river on which they lived. In reports from the Senior British Officer to the West Coast Division Angus MacLeod, one humorous story illustrates these divergent worldviews. MacLeod wrote to Admiral Salmon that he had seen a French flag displayed by a local chief and approached him about it. In response, the chief 'told us that the Holy Fathers at Landoma gave him the French flag a couple of months ago; he said that he hoisted any colors given to him and offered to display English ones there and then if I would supply him' (ADM 123/86, 1883–84: pp. 50–1). For the chief, a flag was just a piece of cloth. For European colonial empires, it meant much more. A gulf of meaning separated the Europeans from their African interlocutors on the importance of cloth flags, paper treaties, and ink lines to be drawn on a map in Berlin. Diplomats' inability to see beyond the emptiness they wanted to see created the perfect opportunity for Leopold.

Second, diplomats at the Berlin Conference understood their local European geography as a site of universalizing possibilities. Using European river commissions as institutional models offers a specific narrative about the generalizability of European solutions grounded on a geographical imaginary of Europe as a universally representative space whose past experiences were applicable to the present in the colonial periphery. This imaginary combined with the conceptually empty Congo to create a sense of continuity and extension from the European experience outward. Here, it was not just European understandings of the Congo that were problematic, but also European understandings of its own history which gave its narrative of progress a sense of inevitability and universality.

For diplomats at the Berlin Conference, European experiences in creating the 1815 Rhine Commission and the 1856 Danube Commission served as a prototype for other untamed rivers. As these commissions brought order and civilized cooperation to Europe's transboundary rivers, so a similar body would also bring commerce and civilization to the Congo. In his treatise on the rights and duties of nations in times of peace, Sir Travers Twiss charted the history of international law governing transboundary rivers. Prior to the nineteenth century, nations had jealously guarded their exclusive rights to rivers, levying tolls that impeded navigation and commerce. But the 1815 Congress of Vienna, in one of its 'most beneficial arrangements', declared that transboundary navigable rivers, with respect to commerce and navigation, should be open to vessels of all nations. Hence, imperial rights over these rivers ceased and European laws adapted to 'less selfish views' (Twiss 1884: 240). The 1856 Treaty of Paris extended these rights to the Danube and into the public laws of Europe. While he does discuss the uneven process of implementing the Rhine and Danube commissions, Twiss's general narrative suggests a story of progress from fractious competition to a civilized approach that allowed 'nature to cement the peaceful relations of mankind, by facilitating their mutual intercourse' (Twiss 1884: 241). Published in 1884, the book's introduction addresses the 'Congo Question' and Twiss's narrative of progress directly speaks to the Berlin Conference and the extension of European legal institutions into the colonial emptiness.

Here, Twiss constructs a universal narrative of political progress based on the European experience of institutional creation and consolidation. It directly equates the European past to the Congo's present and sketches for diplomats at Berlin a global history of their responsibilities. Hence, despite differences in circumstances, diplomats at Berlin did not question the orthodoxy that European institutional models would benefit this untamed river on the colonial fringe. Their inability to imagine beyond the European as universal enabled Leopold to walk away with a personal colony 76 times the size of Belgium.

Conclusion

Without a doubt, the outcome of the 1884–85 Berlin Conference did not bring freedom of commerce and civilization to the Congo basin, and the human cost of Leopold's Congo has been extensively detailed elsewhere. The aim of this chapter was to explore the factors that hindered the successful establishment of the International Commission of the Congo and hence enabled Leopold to gain exclusive control over large swathes of the Congo basin.

One overriding observation of diplomatic conversations at Berlin is how little the actual Congo basin mattered – instead, deliberations were inwardly focused on concerns about the European balance of power and aspirations for spreading European civilizational, trade, and moral virtues. The Congo's conceptual emptiness, so carefully described by cartographers, legal experts, and explorers, transformed it into an abstract backdrop for diplomats' more tangible fears and ambitions at home. Unfortunately, this use of the Congo as an inert background at best or the malevolent heart of darkness at worst continues to dominate Western representations of the river. Like Conrad, modern narratives such as Maya Jasanoff's *The Dawn Watch* (2017) continue to use the river as a poignant backdrop to explore Western agency and Western-dominated processes of globalization. At the Berlin Conference, this inward focus created an irreconcilable disconnect between the European models that diplomats had hoped to bring to the Congo and the different political and geographical contexts in which they operated. In particular, two differences hindered the success of European models – first, the absence of well-defined European-style sovereign states as riparian powers, and second, the Congo as a mere token in a larger political game over colonial control and preserving the precarious European balance. These differences made the transplantation of European normative and institutional models, which were developed in the context of specific European histories, impossible.

A lingering puzzle is why diplomats at Berlin insisted on applying the Rhine and Danube models to the Congo despite some acknowledgment that the context of the Congo differed so dramatically from European transboundary rivers. I contend that this insistence stemmed from two blind spots in the European geographical imaginary – first, its conceptualization of the Congo basin as an abstract and empty colonial space that ought to be filled with European values and practices, and second, its understanding of Europe as the center of generalizable and universalizable political possibilities. These two blind spots created a conceptually empty space along the Congo that European institutional models were destined to fill, despite the fact that the Rhine and Danube commissions emerged from very different geographical contexts and under different configurations of power. Hence, following Agnew (1996), diplomats projected Europe's temporal development onto terrestrial space and placed their confidence in the applicability of European models in the colonial periphery.

The next chapter will bring our story of the taming of nature into the twentieth century and explore in detail this prevailing confidence in the applicability of European development models to all geographies.

Notes

1 To be more precise, he shouted in French: 'Nous prenez-vous pour des brigands?'
2 Scholars are divided on whether Bismarck had a long-term colonial strategy. A few historians view Bismarck's 1884–85 colonial acquisitions, which included territories five times the size of the German *Reich*, as intentional imperialism or even a long-term strategy (see Townsend 1930; Pakenham 1991). However, Wehler (1970) and others argued that Bismarck used imperialism to distract from domestic issues at home or as a chip in European power politics.
3 As this book focuses on European conferences and treaties establishing international river commissions, it does not discuss the application of the Treaty of Vienna to the Parana and Uruguay rivers in 1853. This could be an illuminating additional study for future research.
4 One victory in expanding the principle was the adoption of the Belgian representative Emile Banning's proposal to treat terrestrial routes constructed alongside unnavigable sections of the Congo as part of the international thoroughfare (Banning 1927: 28).
5 The USA, Germany, Britain, Italy, Austria-Hungary, the Netherlands, Spain, France, Russia, Sweden, Norway, Portugal, and the Belgian government all concluded treaties with the IAC, recognizing it.
6 Article 17 of the General Acts of the Berlin Conference officially established an International Commission of the Congo, and all signatures to the General Acts would have one representative on the commission. The commission would have the power to 'decide what works are necessary to assure the navigability of the Congo in accordance with the needs of international trade', fix tariffs and dues, administer the revenue from tariffs and dues, establish quarantines, and appoint officials (General Acts, Article 20).
7 At the time of the Berlin Conference, there was no indication that the Congo colony would be profitable. The first pneumatic tire that could be easily manufactured was patented in 1888. The pneumatic tire required rubber – a natural resource that was plentiful in the Congo – and made the Congo colony lucrative. The most egregious stories of abuse and criminal violence in Leopold's Congo, and later the Belgian Congo, emerged from the extraction of rubber.

8

History is a river: the taming of nature into the twenty-first century

Rain came from above as God willed it, in plenty or otherwise, and nobody could stand face to face with God and demand adequate rain, but one could go up to a canal officer and demand water, all he had to do was enlarge the outlet.

Prakash Tandon (quoted in Gilmartin 2015: 144)

One year before the opening of the Suez Canal in 1869, German philosopher Ernst Kapp wrote in anticipation of the canal's opening: 'with the completion of this correction ... the human mind will finally achieve mastery over even this disadvantage of nature it has suffered with for thousands of years' (quoted in Blackbourn 2006: 165). For Kapp and others, large-scale engineering marvels such as the Suez Canal provided evidence of society's progressive trajectory and the eventual fulfillment of the Enlightenment promise that humanity stood together as masters over nature. Here, Kapp lauds the triumph of human science over the imperfections of nature – or one might even say the mistakes of God – for the advancement of global commerce. This faith in human society's ability to overcome all barriers and 'correct' nature's errors framed not only nineteenth-century optimism toward international progress but continued to shape the thinking of twentieth-century policymakers toward taming the river and its role in the state's domestic and international legitimacy. By inspiring the first international organizations, this mission to tame nature also continued to inform twentieth-century international society's quest for order.

This chapter tells the story of international society's aim to construct the ideal river in the twentieth century. It begins by tracing the Rhine, Danube, and Congo rivers' role in World War I and the diplomatic deliberations at the 1919 Paris Peace Conference that finally seemed to settle the question of whether Europe's transboundary rivers were private property or international commons. Standing at 1919, it would seem that a century of cooperation along transboundary rivers had finally culminated in a victory for liberalism and progress. I dispute this narrative of progress by showing how 1919 might be interpreted otherwise, and argue that narratives of institutional success and failure depend very much on where in history we stand and the thickness of our analytical blinders.

The second half of the chapter traces Enlightenment confidence in science's ability to tame the river for economic wealth and moral progress. I show how controlling the river continued to inform a state's domestic and international legitimacy, first as a tool of imperial dominance, but then adopted by post-colonial states as a symbol of their rising status and self-sufficiency. While there is a wealth of global examples from which to draw, I focus on the megadam as a monumental symbol of the continuation of a certain way of imagining the ideal river as a conduit for liberal economic progress. In doing so, I suggest that throughout the twentieth century, advances in technology and in international institutions are two facets in the same larger ambition to unite humanity through the taming of nature.

The Treaty of Versailles and the triumph of the international river

The continuation of the story of global river governance with the 1919 Treaty of Versailles reaffirms international diplomats' use of the ostensibly neutral and progressive aims behind river management as a political tool to tame the dangerous forces of international relations.

Austro-Hungarian gunboats on the Danube fired some of the first shots of World War I as they bombarded the Serbian capital Belgrade. The Danube became a militarized border as Serbians mined the river to prevent supply ships from using it to reinforce Austria-Hungary's potential ally Bulgaria. The European Commission of the Danube continued to operate until Romania entered the war in August 1916 on the side of the Allied Powers. Romania's entry into the war meant the Dardanelles were closed to the commission, cutting off its supply of funding and fuel from western Europe and ending ongoing engineering works (Chamberlain 1923: 126). With the outbreak of war in Romania, the Central Powers established a new Danube Commission based on the Rhine Commission. The new body included only riparian states and had a supervisory role rather than executive powers as before. With eventual Allied victory, this body was also disbanded, and a provisional Danube Commission was established in April 1919 under the command of British naval officer Sir Ernest Troubridge. The temporary commission went to work assisting with the distribution of relief goods and the restoration of commercial shipping on the Danube (Temperley 1920: 311; Popper 1943: 241).

The Rhine and Congo rivers' involvement in World War I was less dramatic. A legal quarrel arose on the Rhine as the Allies disputed the transport of sand, gravel, stone, and scrap metal to Germany along the river.

The Dutch, however, argued that the material would be used for civilian rather than military purposes, and was therefore protected under the 1868 Mannheim Act (Chamberlain 1923: 266–8).[1] In the Belgian Congo, the colonial government[2] mobilized the colony's military and police force, the *Force Publique*, which fought on three fronts in Cameroon, Rhodesia, and East Africa (van Reybrouck 2014: 132). More importantly, the Congo's rich copper mines supplied the British and American war effort. Artillery shells used on the European front had brass casings made of 75 percent Congolese copper (van Reybrouck 2014: 136). The increase in copper exports made a fortune for the Belgian government-in-exile – a government often pitied as an unlucky victim of German aggression in general narratives about World War I. In war as in peace, the Congo basin's abundant natural resources remained a curse that fueled the global economy of death while enriching its colonial masters.

The 1919 Paris Conference and technocratic impartiality

World War I exposed the weaknesses of the Rhine and Danube commissions as cooperative forums amid a global conflict, and their commitment to technocratic aims did not prevent them from being overrun by geopolitical forces. The 1919 Paris Peace Conference envisioned a new liberal world order to prevent future conflict, and the strengthening of institutions such as the Rhine and Danube commissions would play an important role in that order. However, diplomats at Paris worked to obscure the politics behind this liberal international vision with claims that the conference proceedings embodied an ostensibly technocratic and neutral process.

The victorious Council of Four – Britain, the United States, France, and Italy – dominated the 1919 Paris Conference. At its second meeting on 25 January, the conference created four commissions: one to assign responsibilities and penalties; a second to assign reparations for damages; a third to discuss international labor regulations; and a fourth to discuss international control of ports, waterways, and railways. While all four commissions were considered technical bodies that would devise appropriate measures based on data collection, rational deliberation, and scientific expertise, the final commission – the Commission on the International Regime of Ports, Waterways, and Railways – was in particular considered the domain of scientists, lawyers, and engineers. At its first meeting, Albert Claveille of France opened the session by noting that France's second representative to the meeting would change depending on need: 'at one time an Engineer, at another a Professor of Law, or any other qualified person according to the nature of the question' (Dockrill 1989: 68). Claveille's declaration reinforced the notion that the commission's outputs would be technocratic and fair rather than based on political considerations.

The 25 January meeting decided that, with the exception of the Reparations Commission, the other commissions would include two representatives from the five victorious powers – the Council of Four plus Japan – and five representatives elected by other states. In response, Belgium, followed by a number of smaller powers including Brazil, Serbia, Portugal, Czechoslovakia, Romania, China, Siam, and Poland, protested this unfair allocation of representation and requested positions on all four commissions (Finch 1919: 172–3). In response to these requests, the French prime minister Georges Clemenceau framed the commissions' membership as a technical rather than political decision. He pointed out that while it would be reasonable for the Great Powers responsible for winning the war to exclude all other states and consult solely among themselves, their fairmindedness had prevented this and invited the participation of other states to the conference. However, if every state had a seat on every commission, nothing would be accomplished. Hence, procedures were established to ensure that 'immediate and useful work' could be accomplished (Finch 1919: 173).[3] Clemenceau's response to the issue of representation suggests that practicality and efficiency more than politics limited the participation of smaller powers.

However, participation in the commission made a political difference. The absence of Germany and Austria-Hungary, the two major pre-war riparian powers along the Rhine and Danube, meant that there were no advocates for the rivers as private or shared property. Instead, the river as international commons won a clear victory. The Netherlands, which also did not sit on the Commission, sent a special delegation to argue for a return to the pre-war Central Commission of the Rhine comprised only of riparian states – a plea to maintain the Rhine as shared property. However, as the commission's president, the Italian representative Silvio Crespi, noted, while he recognized the Netherlands' protest, the commission 'had already come to the conclusion that an International Rhine Commission was necessary' (Dockrill 1989: 90). Such an international body would bypass the fractious politics that had paralyzed riparian-only commissions and contribute to the new liberal order. By starting with the Rhine and Danube rivers, the commission saw its work as building on 'concrete and old-established precedents' (Dockrill 1989: 82) to devise legal principles to govern all international rivers.[4] Framing the *international* river as a longstanding precedent allowed the commission to represent its work as an uncontroversial improvement on established principles and the consolidation of a century of progress.

Rather than merely upholding 'old-established precedents', the Treaty of Versailles actually adopted sweeping measures that streamlined the joint management of international rivers. On the Danube, the Treaty re-established the European Commission to manage the delta and expanded the temporary membership to include Britain, France, Italy, and Romania until a further conference could be held to determine the commission's future (Article 346). In addition, the Treaty established the International Danube Commission to manage the entire length of the navigable river from Ulm to Brăila.[5] This international commission included two German representatives, a representative of every riparian state, and one representative for each non-riparian state on the European Commission (Article 347). On the Rhine, the Treaty established a new international commission, with Strasbourg – newly reclaimed by the French – as its seat. This new body would maintain the 1868 Mannheim Act but would comprise two representatives each from the Netherlands, Switzerland, Britain, Italy, and Belgium, and four representatives from Germany and France (Article 355). Hence, with the 1919 Treaty of Versailles, British aims at Vienna in 1815 and Paris in 1856 were finally fulfilled – both the Rhine and Danube would be considered international rivers over their entire navigable length and would be governed by truly international commissions that included outside powers along with riparian states. These changes laid the groundwork for the 1921 Barcelona Convention which guaranteed the same freedoms for riparian states as for non-riparian states along all navigable rivers and lakes of international concern.

As I have maintained throughout this book, characterizing processes such as the 1919 commissions as technocratic, scientific, and uncontroversial obscures the political nature of their deliberations and decisions. As the American representative David Hunter Miller noted, Versailles had finally codified the freedom of international rivers which 'has been contended for since at least 1792' (1919: 675). For Miller, this outcome was a victory for liberal economic progress. Anticipating arguments for a more integrated Europe, Miller suggested that closer commercial integration would lead Europe to peace and prosperity just as the interstate commerce clause of the US constitution brought the American union together. To support his contention, Miller quoted a letter from Clemenceau:

> The Allied and Associated Powers believe that the arrangements which they propose are vital to the free life of the new inland states that are being established and that they are no derogation from the rights of the other riparian states. If viewed according to the discredited doctrine that every state is engaged in a desperate struggle for ascendancy over its neighbors, no doubt such an arrangement may be an impediment to the artificial strangling of a rival. But if it be the ideal that nations are to cooperate in the ways of commerce and peace, it is natural and right. The provision of the presence of representatives of non-riparian states on these river commissions is security that the general interest will be considered. (quoted in Miller 1919: 683)

Clemenceau's words echo arguments made throughout the nineteenth century in support of the river as an international economic highway by naturalizing the link between cooperation, commerce, and peace. For Clemenceau, the presence of non-riparian states on international river commissions would guard against the 'discredited' Machiavellian vision of international politics as a struggle for power and ascendancy. Here, international river commissions are designed to tame much more than just the physical river – a powerful international body could also tame international politics and help guide the river of history toward peace and progress. The danger, of course, is that such a framing ignores the historical and ongoing contestations and resistance to this liberal narrative and risks underestimating the not-so-liberal undercurrents that lurk just beneath the surface.

A not-so-impartial peace

Not all commentators accepted the 1919 agreement on international river governance as a neutral and impartial outcome. In *The Economic Consequences of the Peace*, John Maynard Keynes dismissed the agreement on river commissions as one of many treaty provisions designed to chastise and humiliate Germany. Keynes has harsh words for these provisions as 'pinpricks, interferences and vexations, not so much objectionable for their solid consequences, as dishonourable to the Allies in light of their professions' (1920: ch. IV, sect. ii). Here, Keynes notes that he does not dispute the laudable goal of achieving freedom of navigation along international rivers; rather, his criticism is over how the victors at Versailles wished to carry out this goal. On the newly established Rhine, Danube, and Elbe commissions, Germany would have a minority of votes while Britain and other non-riparian Allied states would have prominent positions. For Keynes, this did not reflect the creation of an impartial international institution to peaceably manage a contested geography. Instead, this reflected a victor's peace in which Germany's vital economic waterways were 'handed over to foreign bodies with the widest power' (1920: ch. IV, sect. iii). By framing the outcome of 1919 in this way, Keynes revealed these river commissions as overt political tools to control a dangerous Germany.

Other accounts described the treaty more favorably than Keynes, but also questioned whether the outcome really reflected the lofty principles that the Allies had outlined. Versailles extended freedom of navigation to an entire set of European rivers, and non-riparian states on these commissions would work to ensure that larger riparian states did not dominate smaller ones – what Zeitoun and Warner (2006) would later term 'hydro-hegemony'. However, even Joseph P. Chamberlain, whose works on the Rhine and Danube have been invaluable resources throughout this book and who lauded both commissions as part of a progressive liberal project, confessed that some treaty provisions 'look more like revenge than justice' (1923: 129). This is particularly stark in Article 332 which, after declaring that ships of all nations would be treated equally, also states:

> Nevertheless, German vessels shall not be entitled to carry passengers or goods by regular services between the ports of any Allied or Associated Power, without special authority from such Power.

Further, the new International Rhine Commission would have equal numbers of German and French commissioners, with a French president overseeing the commission, even though Germany's interests along the Rhine outweighed France's recently restored ones. As Chamberlain admitted, this could only be attributed to geopolitical rather than technical reasons (1923: 279). Worse, the European Commission of the Danube was re-established with only the Allied states of Britain, France, Italy, and Romania. Additional members could only be admitted by the unanimous agreement of all current members (Popper 1943: 243–4). Of the statute governing the Danube, Otto Popper, the first secretary of the International Danube Commission from 1920 to 1929, wrote:

> Unfortunately, this fundamental document was drafted during a period when much of the original spirit of Wilson's Fourteen Points was beginning to fade. As it stands the Statute is a somewhat unsatisfactory compromise between broad conceptions and narrow-mindedness. (1943: 244)

Even within the proceedings themselves, it was clear that the French and other victors saw the Commission on the International Regime of Ports, Waterways, and Railways as a political instrument against Germany. For example, at the commission's second meeting, the British delegation presented a draft convention on the general principle of freedom of transit. The French responded that while they supported the noble sentiments that inspired the draft, such general principles were outside the purview of the peace treaty, particularly as such a principle 'would apply equally to all nations, enemy as well as Allied and Associated'. To be clear, Claveille declared that he would 'take no part in anything which would give freedom of transit to enemies as well as to Allies' (Dockrill 1989: 70). Belgium supported the French objection, arguing that 'care must be taken not to lose the benefit of the victory which they had gained over the Germans' (Dockrill 1989: 70). For the French and their supporters, the 'technical' commissions at Versailles were avenues for imposing a peace settlement on a defeated Germany and its allies. Framing the new international river statues and commissions as a continuation of longstanding technocratic projects allowed the victors to act under the guise of an impartial progressive spirit that opened international rivers as a highway for all nations.

The German observers at Versailles strongly protested the addition of non-riparian states to the river commissions. However, the Allies responded that transboundary rivers had been international since the 1815 Congress of Vienna, and this status had been confirmed by international conventions ever since. In addition, the new commissions would only carry out the technical application of Articles 332–7 of the Versailles Treaty which conformed with all precedents since the 1815 Congress of Vienna. Finally, non-riparian states would make the commissions more impartial and effective by ensuring that the strongest riparian states did not dominate affairs (Temperley 1920: 107). Here, the Allied Powers not only secured a certain interpretation of the transboundary river as international commons but also smoothed over the historical record to create a seamless sense of continuity since 1815 – a seamless sense of historical progression that I have challenged from the beginning of this book. While perhaps the Commission on the International Regime of Ports, Waterways, and Railways was a small part of the Versailles settlement, even in this supposedly technical matter, legal history was rewritten in a way that naturalized a linear understanding of progress. In this way, the commission was emblematic of the larger peace process at Paris.

Success and failure: international rivers and organizations in the twentieth century

Standing at Versailles, one might believe that the ideal river as a rational international highway that promises to bring economic wealth and progress to all nations had finally won out. What had begun as an orphan of Napoleonic reforms had finally been recognized and enshrined in international law as a model of interstate cooperation. This sense of liberal inevitability, however, was a mirage. Within two decades, another world war would again destroy the Danube Commission. In the late 1930s, Hitler's power over the Danube states grew and he was allocated a seat on the European Commission in 1939. In 1940, Hitler called a meeting in Vienna to dissolve the International Commission, removing French, British, and American influence from the upper Danube (Campbell 1949: 317).

In the aftermath of World War II, at the 1946 diplomatic conference convened in Belgrade to reach a post-war settlement for the Danube, political control over the river had shifted. For the first time since 1856, the West no longer exercised authority over the Danube's mouth. While the USA, the UK, and France attended the conference, 'the three Western powers ... were an impotent minority at Belgrade', and the Soviet representative Andrey Vyshinsky, 'his manner overbearing and offensive', dominated the conference and pushed through Moscow's draft convention for the Danube (Campbell 1949: 315). The new regimes of eastern Europe sided with Vyshinsky against the West. The new Danube Convention did away with both the International and European commissions and returned to a single commission of solely riparian states to manage the river as private property. All riparian states would have one delegate each, with the exception of the Soviets who were allocated two (G. L. 1951: 424). In its first meeting in December 1951, the new Danube Commission's Romanian president Grigore Preoteasa thanked the Soviets for defeating fascism and removing 'the domination of imperialist Powers ... from the largest section of the Danube'. Now under Soviet guidance, the commission could finally work for the 'economic and social progress of the Danubian nations' rather than for 'international' navigation which only served the interest of western imperialist powers (G. L. 1951: 425).[6]

Standing at Belgrade, it would seem that almost a century of liberal progress to transform the Danube into an international commercial highway had ended in failure. Reflecting on this reversal in the pages of *Foreign Affairs*, the advisor to the US delegation John Campbell concluded that 'the Danube has always been a *political* question ... those Powers which have been concerned either with opening it or closing it have been more interested in their influence and control in the Danubian region than in navigation on the river itself' (1949: 316, emphasis in the original). As Campbell recognizes here, for all its confidence in the international rivers as a 'natural' conduit for global trade, this liberal vision of the ideal river had to be made and sustained by power. Perhaps what the West had forgotten in the long arc of its own history along the Danube is that power, like the river, can shift. Global policymakers might strive to tame the river of history with prudent laws and institutions – the canals and dikes Machiavelli had recommended centuries ago – but the river is full of undercurrents that we do not understand and it pushes back in ways that consistently surprise us. Even cooperative international institutions a century in the making can be quickly undone in one geopolitical moment.

Too much success: pollution and the by-products of liberal progress

While geopolitical tragedy befell the Danube, a different tragedy dominated post-World War II politics along the Rhine – a tragedy that was not only unimaginable to the founders of the Rhine Commission, but accelerated by the very success of their efforts to transform the Rhine into a reliable highway. In 1946, the Netherlands brought a complaint before the restored Rhine Commission concerning the polluted condition of the lower Rhine. At first, the dire condition of the river was attributed to wartime damage to Germany's waste disposal and sewage treatment infrastructure, but as the years passed, it became clear that the problem ran deeper. The Rhine Commission's efficiency in taming the river had blinded scientists and policy-makers to the fragility of other facets of the river's relationship with society. While environmental movements in the late nineteenth century had fought to safeguard 'pristine' nature through the creation of parks and reserves, engineers and policymakers believed in the Rhine's self-cleaning properties and neglected to conduct holistic analyses of the river's health (Lekan 2008: 112). The Rhine Commission had successfully tamed the river for global commerce – so much so that at the start of the twenty-first century, the Rhine remains the second busiest river in the world after the Mississippi in terms of shipping volume (Cioc 2002: 4) – but this single-mindedness meant it was unable to see the river as a habitat and source of clean water for human and animal populations.

The Rhine's environmental decline was the result of three transboundary problems: waste disposal, industrial pollution, and river-rectification schemes of the nineteenth century. In 1897, Mannheim began to dispose sewage into the Rhine. The downstream city of Worms brought a lawsuit against Mannheim and lost, hence opening the floodgates for other cities to dispose their untreated sewage into the Rhine. As late as 1956, 29 riverside cities lacked appropriate treatment facilities for wastewater before it flowed into the river (Cioc 2002: 139–40; Lekan 2008: 115–16). In addition to organic waste, industrial pollution also contributed to the river's decline, particularly in the Westphalia and Ruhr regions. Chemical factories upriver producing dyes, explosives, fertilizers, acids, alkalis, and paper all helped transform Germany into an industrial powerhouse but at a heavy price for the Rhine and its tributaries (Lekan 2008: 116). The Emscher was a case in point. In the late nineteenth century, mining activities divided Westphalia's three Rhine tributaries based on three functions: the Ruhr to provide clean water; the Lippe to serve as a transport canal; and the Emscher for sewage (Cioc 2002: 88). As a result, the Emscher became an oozing black sewer, and in 1901, bacteriologist Rudolph Emmerich wrote of the river: 'here we find a black, thick, swampy, rotten, and fermenting manure, which hardly moves: during summer, gas bubbles burst, poisoning the surrounding area' (quoted in Brüggemeier 1994: 38).[7] By 1920, a member of the Reichstag had dubbed the Emscher *Der Höllenfluss* or the River of Hell.

Finally, the Rhine rectification projects that Johann Tulla began and that Eduard Adolph Nobiling continued with the support of an ascendant Prussian state also contributed to its environmental decline. Nobiling went further than Tulla to straighten the river into a uniform transportation highway – he developed a new type of wing dam that funneled the flow of water toward the middle of the river to protect the shorelines from erosion and ensure adequate depth for navigation (Cioc 2002: 56). These projects contributed to pollution by ending seasonal floods. Without floods, the fluvial plains could no longer filter toxins, and floodwaters could no longer replenish groundwater tables, forcing riverside communities to rely increasingly on river water for daily use (Lekan 2008: 117). As pollution worsened, a visible sign of the Rhine's declining health was the number of poisoned fish that washed up on its shores. In the 1950s and 1960s, fish kills regularly blighted the river, prompting East Germany's Socialist Unity Party to label the Rhine the 'river of horrors'. A 1952 article in the *Düsseldorfer Nachrichten* summed up the Rhine's plight: 'the mighty river is ... no longer in a state where it can digest the dirt and masses of feces fed into it ... the weakened self-cleaning powers of the river, which has been transformed into a cesspool, are no longer able to master them' (quoted in Lekan 2008: 122). Standing on the banks of the Rhine in the 1950s, one might contemplate how a successful project to tame the river was also at the same time an unhappy failure.

While pollution along the Rhine in the mid-twentieth century was particularly evocative, the transformation of rivers into straight and reliable highways of industry also contributed to environmental degradation elsewhere. Communist-era heavy industries along the Danube and its tributaries led to chemical leaks and fish kills – even in the post-communist era, decaying industrial infrastructure on the river's banks remains a threat to the river's health (Thorpe 2013: 194). The sturgeon, whose caviar graces elite dining tables around the world, also calls the Danube home but has been made critically endangered due to pollution, overfishing, and habitat loss. Society's success at transforming 'wasted' nature into economic profit has consequences that ripple out. Equally, continued efforts to transform the Congo into a conduit for Western commerce and modernity have had harmful environmental side-effects as the river is polluted with the by-products of economic development. If the Cold War Danube Commission affirmed the international river as a political project underpinned by Western power, then the environmental degradation of transboundary rivers stresses the dangers of a political project that neglects the river as a vital character in our stories and fails to take the holistic river – along with the entangled wellbeing of nature and society – into consideration.

To leave the story there, as human tragedy, would also be incomplete. By the end of the twentieth century, the Cold War was won and the Danube had been restored as the connecting river seeking to unite the core and near periphery into a liberal and progressive European whole. In 1996, thanks to effective anti-pollution mobilization and policies, the Rhine was named the cleanest river in Europe and beluga whales were even sighted in the lower river (Kleemann 2018). To facilitate transnational cooperation over pollution control and water quality, the International Commission for the Protection of the Rhine against Pollution was established in 1963 and the International Commission for the Protection of the Danube River in 1994. Local environmental organizations along the Danube are even restoring oxbows and meanders to help fish populations recover – the very oxbows that nineteenth-century river-rectification projects sought to eliminate in the name of progress (Thorpe 2013: 239). By shifting our analytical lenses in this way, it becomes clear that narratives of success and failure depend not only on where in history we stand but also the thickness and orientation of our analytical blinders. However, adopting a historical sensibility that allows us to see from multiple standpoints at once helps curb any temptation to tell either a one-sided story of exuberant political progress, or one of hopeless tragedy.

Not enough success? Functionalism and global governance in the twentieth century

Despite the variable fortunes of the Rhine and Danube commissions, the nineteenth-century precedent they set as the first international organizations had lasting influence on twentieth-century global governance. In terms of global river governance, the 1919 Versailles Treaty and the 1921 Barcelona Convention on the Regime of Navigable Waterways of International Concern settled the legal question of whether transboundary rivers are international. In particular, Article 4 of the Barcelona Convention states: 'in the exercise of navigation referred to above, the nations, property and flags of all Contracting States shall be treated in all respects on a footing of perfect equality', with no distinction made between riparian and non-riparian countries. Hence, while few states acceded to the Barcelona Convention, these rivers' status as international commons remains in force as international law. In addition, the creation of international commissions to govern transboundary rivers also became a common political practice, with examples including the 1909 International Joint Commission between the USA and Canada, the 1994 Okavango River Basin Water Commission, the 1995 Mekong River Commission, and the 1998 Nile Basin Initiative. However, the Rhine and Danube commissions had greater implications than just river governance – in the early twentieth century, they were upheld as early examples of how functional organizations could advance global governance on a host of other issues.

In particular, the 1856 European Commission of the Danube was lauded as a prototype for future institutions because of two interrelated characteristics – its political independence from any state authority and its success as a functional body able to carry out scientific projects for the benefit of all humanity. The commission had remarkable independence, with 'quasi-sovereign powers' (Lyons 1963: 63) that allowed it to control its own judicial, policing, and financial affairs. Historian Glen Blackburn marvels at the commission as an independent actor in international politics despite its lack of territorial possessions and highlights the 1927 World Court advisory opinion that declared, 'the European Commission exercises its functions in complete independence of territorial authorities' (1930: 1154).[8]

A main reason for its success and independence, Lyons suggests, was its status as a functional body established to oversee scientific tasks. As the first secretary of the post-World War I Danube Commission Otto Popper noted, 'politics were banned from transport which was considered exclusively a Public Utility Undertaking' (1943: 242). In this affair, Popper mused, it was 'the spirit of modern technical science' that forged international cooperation under difficult circumstances (1943: 245). Blackburn commended the Danube Commission as a 'demonstration of the growing recognition of the futility of arbitrary political frontiers not based upon logical economic considerations' (1930: 1159). Hence, the commission gave a glimpse of what was possible if international cooperation was a logical human activity based on science. Together, these two distinguishing characteristics allowed the Danube Commission to stand out as an example of what political scientist Edward Krehbiel praised as 'an international joint agent' that is 'more effective for good because it offers an organ through which nations can approach one another on the basis of common or united action, instead of as rivals' (1918: 49). Writing on the eve of the 1919 Paris Conference, Krehbiel's suggestion here is that leaders take up this model on a global scale to offer states a forum for united action.

Leonard Woolf was another influential early twentieth-century commentator who described the Danube Commission as a model for global governance. In his *International Government*, he argued that to have effective international governance, states needed to devise 'general rules regulating the conduct of nations' (1916: 21). For Woolf, the 1815 Congress of Vienna's Final Act declaration on the freedom of navigation on international rivers was the first example of such a 'deliberate international legislation', which led to the creation of the Danube Commission as 'the first international Executive' (1916: 21). Furthermore, Woolf linked the Danube Commission model to the idea of international trusteeship and argued that the model might offer a solution to the 'African problem' (Wilson 2003: 102). Under this framing, political administration of Africa would be invested in an international commission with a specific functional mandate, 'the same way as the European Powers, with marked success, delegated their powers of administration over the Danube' (quoted in Wilson 2003: 102). While such trusteeship arrangements never came to fruition, Woolf's use of the Danube Commission as a shining example of what functional international bodies could achieve influenced later thinkers. Woolf's work is considered foundational for theories of international functionalism and greatly influenced David Mitrany, whose thinking shaped European integration (Murphy 1994: 16–17; Wilson 2003: 58). Through Woolf's work, the 1856 European Commission of the Danube as a successful example of international functionalism informed early arguments on the need for powerful and independent international bodies to forge cooperation and address pressing global challenges.

Proponents of functionalism might have seen decolonization in the mid-twentieth century as the international community's failure to implement Woolf's technocratic solution to the 'African problem'. After all, the 1856 Danube Commission had shown that an independent and outcome-focused body could effectively tackle international problems by giving weight to science and expertise over power politics. If only international diplomats had had the political will to devise such an arrangement to ensure colonies were 'ready' for self-rule, perhaps the developmental tragedies of the twentieth century could have been averted.

However, as the myriad examples in this book suggest, our confidence that technocratic international bodies are politically neutral and produce necessarily progressive outcomes is unfounded. Indeed, this premise ignores failed international efforts in the late nineteenth century to create a rational international commission on the Congo and the human tragedy that ensued – not just under Leopold II but subsequently under the Belgian colonial government and under Joseph-Desiré Mobutu, the dictator who held the Democratic Republic of the Congo in his iron grip after the CIA assassinated popular leader Patrice Lumumba in 1960. Echoing the technocratic logics of river engineers who formulated grand schemes to repair the unintended consequences created by previous attempts to 'fix' the river, such an approach to trusteeship seems to forget the ways in which the West was and continues to be intimately complicit in the creation of the 'African problem'. The idea that Western experts might be impartial technicians brought in as neutral and objective outsiders to solve the 'African problem' is a deliberate forgetting of Africa's complex histories as well as a distortion of the West's own histories. In this way, the trusteeship model continues the longstanding propensity to collapse time and terrestrial space into the same civilizational continuum in the Western geographical imagination.

Furthermore, the notion of trusteeship – and many subsequent international development frameworks – assumes that the Congo and other areas of the decolonized world are merely 'technical problems' to be tamed and rationalized for the liberal world order. Like what occurred at the Berlin Conference in the late nineteenth century, painting the Congo and other developing regions as a 'technical problem' empties the river basin and its peoples of political agency and historical context. Likewise, framing international organizations as functional and technocratic bodies participates in the forgetting of the West's own imperial histories as well as the agency of the peoples and places our technocratic projects seek to tame and control.

Megadams and concrete temples

Confidence in society's ability to tame nature for the benefit of human progress continued to shape international politics into the twentieth century. Taming the river continued to inform what it meant to be a legitimate modern state and underpinned the hierarchies built into global economic development and state progress. Policymakers looked to science and technology to transform irrational nature and society into economically productive and morally progressive units of governance. This faith that science and technology would lead to social progress was most evident in the popularity of large-scale infrastructure projects to tame, harness, and domesticate the river for economic development. Monumental dams began the century as tools of 'progressive' colonial control but continued even after decolonization as nationalistic symbols of modernity and self-sufficiency. The continued construction of megadams into the twenty-first century speaks to the staying power of their rhetorical attraction as a modern method of taming nature for the benefit of society.

'Hydroimperialism' and the taming of imperial rivers

At the end of the nineteenth century, French and German engineers embarked on large-scale dam projects to regulate water for storage, irrigation, and flood prevention. Despite Tulla's dream of eliminating floods along Germany's rivers, the combination of deforestation, river rectification that increased the river's speed, and increased human settlement and industry along the river's supposedly 'tamed' banks meant that flooding continued to be a serious threat to lives and property (Blackbourn 2006: 214). True to self-perpetuating technocratic logics, the unintended negative consequences of previous projects to control the river necessitated even grander future schemes. The language used to describe these new dams celebrated science's ability to 'force', 'compel', 'shackle', and 'tame' the river in the service of society. However, European states' determination to control water was not confined to the European continent but also encompassed taming the rivers of the periphery, with German writers dreaming of extending domestic river management schemes to its newly acquired colonies in Africa (Blackbourn 2006: 229). French hydraulic projects in North Africa aimed to solve the region's 'problem of water' and, to quote one colonial official, 'transform the uncultivated lands of this country into immense fields of grain' (quoted in Pritchard 2012: 595). Pritchard's scholarship on what she calls France's 'hydroimperialism'[9] in North Africa also questions the idea that hydraulic expertise unidirectionally emanated from Europe outward, and details how expertise developed in the Maghreb returned to France to inform water management in the imperial metropole.

But perhaps more than others, the British Empire's large-scale water-management projects showcased its imperial ambition for transforming desert wasteland into useful and productive colonial spaces by taming the river. In the late nineteenth century, this dream was key to British imperial ambitions in the Indus valley. When the British looked upon the Punjab, which translates to 'land of five rivers', they saw what imperial historian Jan Morris describes as 'a gloomy wasteland' populated by nomads 'who made a living from cattle-thieving'. To this wasteland, the British would bring 'the latest technology' to achieve 'orderly progress and human improvement, in the best traditions of philanthropic imperialism' (Morris 2010 [1968]: 429). Local populations have long constructed seasonal canals to divert the Indus and its tributaries for irrigation, but the British envisioned a system of barrages and perennial canals that would provide irrigation year-round and transform the Indus valley into an agricultural heartland. This 'largescale agricultural colonization' of the Punjab and Sind regions would not only increase colonial revenues but attest to the grandeur of the British Empire and enfold the Indus valley into a larger rationalized imperial system (Pearce 2006: 40; Gilmartin 2015: 145). David Gilmartin details how even British engineering terminology speaks to water control as a tool of empire – the term 'duty' was used to signify the relationship between a certain volume of water and the area of land it could sustain (2015: 419). While used as a technical term to measure water's capacity, the word 'duty' also implies a sense of the ideal river's moral responsibility to support Britain's civilizing mission and the economic development it promised to bring.

Along with control of water and the landscape, the British colonial government also used hydraulic science to reorder the 'natural' everyday politics of the local population. To ensure a productive Indus valley, the British displaced the nomadic populations. They were replaced with agriculturalists brought from elsewhere in the Indian subcontinent and given parcels of private land to farm. In addition, the British built planned cities in the newly agricultural valley, and perhaps the most radical example of this rational town planning was Lyallpur, now renamed Faisalabad. Built as a regional transport hub, a clock tower marks the city's center and eight streets radiate out to form the shape of a Union Jack. The streets clearly divided the city into sectors to differentiate ethnic groups and class hierarchies (Pearce 2006: 41; Javed and Qureshi 2019: 234). This social reconfiguration to make the Punjab into a model of British technocratic control also displaced existing pastoral economic relations (Agnihotri 1996), eroded traditional water-management practices, and created what Rohan D'Souza argues was a 'colonial hydrology' (2006) that reordered ecological relations between society and nature. By 1918, Britain had transformed more than 10,000 sq km along the Indus into productive land, but its imperial vision did not stop with the upper Indus river. Across the subcontinent, hydraulic engineers also went to work on the Indus delta in the south and the Ganges in the east. Perhaps the British Empire's favorite poet, Rudyard Kipling, captures the ethos best in his poem 'The Secret of the Machines':

> Do you wish to make the mountains bare their head
>   And lay their new-cut forests at your feet?
> Do you want to turn a river in its bed,
>   Or plant a barren wilderness with wheat?
> Shall we pipe aloft and bring you water down
>   From the never-failing cisterns of the snows,
> To work the mills and tramways in your town,
>   And irrigate your orchards as it flows?

> It is easy! Give us dynamite and drills!
> Watch the iron-shouldered rocks lie down and quake
> As the thirsty desert-level floods and fills,
> And the valley we have dammed becomes a lake. (1911: n.p.)

This optimistic vision of the ease with which British engineers could control water to transform barren wastelands into productive orchards and wheatfields also reflected British imperial ambitions along two other colonial river systems: Egypt along the Nile and Mesopotamia between the Tigris and Euphrates. In the British imagination, these two ancient civilizations were similar in many ways. As Priya Satia observes, each river was 'constituted as a geographical and political entity centered on the basic developmental "problem" of an ancient river system ringed by desert and a backwards population' (2007: 215). The Nile and its seasonal floods have long been the lifeblood of Egyptian civilization, but in the nineteenth century, the introduction of large-scale cotton cultivation in the lower Nile and the upsurge in global demand due to the American Civil War increased the need for more reliable irrigation in the summer months for ever more cotton fields (Owen 1969; Tvedt 2011).[10] Hence, after the British occupation in 1883, there was a constant sense that more water was needed to ensure no land went unused – as a former inspector-general of the Egyptian Irrigation Service noted in 1893, 'we have arrived at a stage in the summer irrigation of Egypt where the available natural supply has been completely exhausted, and there still remained more land to grow cotton' (quoted in Tvedt 2011: 178). During World War I when British troops landed at Basra and entered Mesopotamia, they expressed a similar sense that an ancient fertile Eden was now squandered, a 'treeless waste of swamp and desert' with 'only bleak emptiness to conquer' (war correspondent Edmund Candler, quoted in Satia 2007: 219). To address the wasted economic potential along these great rivers, British colonial officials brought in hydraulic engineers from India – and in Mesopotamia, from Egypt – to legitimate British control by delivering economic and moral progress through the taming of these ancient rivers.

Irrigation schemes on the Nile and the Tigris and Euphrates were not new, but the British projects were a departure from Egyptian and Ottoman schemes in their monumental technocratic scale and long-term political and ecological consequences. Completed in 1902, the Aswan Low Dam was the largest concrete reservoir in the world at the time. It would store the Nile's floodwaters and ensure adequate release to cotton crops during the dry summer. In addition, chief British engineer William Willcocks argued that the dam would reclaim more than 500,000 hectares of swampland in lower Egypt for agricultural use (Cookson-Hills 2013: 304–7). However, despite its size, growing water needs outstripped capacity, and larger projects at Aswan were eventually needed to meet water demand (Tvedt 2011: 179). These dams ended the Nile's annual floods, and the region's fecundity became reliant on chemical fertilizers rather than river silt with, as Timothy Mitchell (2002) vividly describes, serious knock-on consequences for the Nile valley's human politics and natural environment. Further, these projects demonstrated Egypt's geostrategic vulnerability to damming upstream in the Sudan and beyond. As the first British counsel-general Lord Cromer maintained in the late nineteenth century, 'if any civilised Power holds the waters of the Upper Nile it would be in a position to exercise a perilous influence on the fate of Egypt' (quoted in Marlow 1970: 197). Here, Cromer was referring to French control of the Sudan, but this fear that diverting the Nile upstream would bring Egypt to its knees would continue to inform Egyptian foreign policy. Most recently, Egyptian President Mohammed Morsi's 2013 response to Ethiopia's plans to build the Grand Ethiopian Renaissance Dam upriver echoed this fearful rhetoric.[11]

Prior to World War I, Ottoman authorities had brought William Willcocks to Mesopotamia to consult on the hydraulic situation. Willcocks argued that in order to 'restore' Babylon to a lush Eden full of agricultural potential, a large-scale project would be needed to drain the marshes (Guarasci 2015: 134). But it was another British engineer from the Indian administration, Frank Haigh, who wrote a report for the Iraq Irrigation Development

Commission on draining the Mesopotamian marshes that would have lasting consequences for the region. To prevent the water of the Tigris from going to waste, the 1951 Haigh report recommended a series of sluices to divert the Tigris and its tributaries before they entered the marshes. Instead, the water would be redirected into a single canal to be stored for irrigation (Pearce 1993). The project would not only transform the Mesopotamian marshes into useful agricultural land but would convert the 'wild' Marsh Arab societies into rational subjects (Moumin 2008: 506–7). Decades later, Saddam Hussain would adopt Haigh's initial concept for his own infrastructure project to reclaim swampland and punish the Marsh Arabs for their resistance against his regime. When completed, the system of canals and dams drained more than 90 percent of the marshlands.[12] Saddam's war against the river, the marshes, and the rebels who sheltered there reinforces the argument that large-scale efforts to tame nature also imply the taming of unruly elements of society – and that the technocratic logics behind these efforts are part of longstanding Western imperial hierarchies. Into the late twentieth and early twenty-first centuries, the continuation of large-scale dams and canals to tame the river attests to their power as a legitimating force behind the modern state.

The river as the temple of modernity

Alongside the control of rivers for drinking water, sanitation, and food production, the construction of megadams in the twentieth century promised another economic treasure – hydropower, or what Aristide Bergès referred to at the 1889 Paris International Expo as 'Houille Blanche' or 'white coal'. While mills have long been powered by water, technological advances in harnessing the river for electricity meant that the river was no longer simply an efficient economic highway or a repository for agricultural potential, but a path toward economic modernization and national wealth. Indeed, the rushing water that had once made rivers so dangerous as economic highways was now an untapped asset. And unlike coal, hydropower as a clean and endlessly renewable energy source evoked a sense of utopian promise in a technology that, for the cost of initial construction, promised to solve all of a nation's economic and social ills (Blackbourn 2006: 209). In addition, more than the canals and embankments of earlier projects, megadams focused visual attention on a solid and awe-inspiring embodiment of modernity – an aesthetic monument signifying modern technology's complete conquest of nature for the benefit of society. The continued popularity of megadams as a panacea for development challenges around the world shows how, despite the end of formal empire in the mid-twentieth century, confidence in science's ability to harness the river for economic and moral progress continued to be adopted and to inform discourses on the modern state's responsibilities toward its own people and territory.

On a late September day in 1935, US president Franklin D. Roosevelt stood before an expectant crowd in the Arizona desert to dedicate the Hoover Dam, then known as the Boulder Dam. In his speech, Roosevelt celebrated the dam as a response to 'the greatest problem of law and of administration to be found in any government' – the question of how to manage the resources of the great Colorado river and its tributaries for the benefit of the people. The dam would provide irrigation and electricity, which in turn would boost food production, power mines and factories, and bring modern home comforts to everyday Americans. But bound up with the dam's economic utility was a moral argument – the dam would transform what had been 'an unpeopled, forbidding desert in the bottom of a gloomy canyon ... a cactus-covered waste' into a modern, productive site of wealth and progress. Floods and droughts alike would be nightmares of the past while the future held only prosperity. Hence, pacifying the river was both a moral and economic victory that reinforced longstanding ideas about the modern state's role in protecting the population and providing for their welfare through the taming of nature.

The Hoover Dam, as an engineering marvel and a sublime symbol of modernity and progress, would be emulated by engineers from the Volga to the Nile to the Niger and Zambezi to the Yangtze and Yellow rivers. At the turn of the twentieth century, not a single dam in the world exceeded 15 meters, but by century's end, 36,562 dams towered higher (Nixon 2011: 166–7). For many leaders in the 'Global South', megadams were the building blocks of post-independence nationhood. Egyptian leader Gamel Abdel Nasser celebrated the new Aswan High Dam project as a vehicle for 'everlasting property' for the new nation, while Indian prime minister Jawaharlal Nehru referred to hydroelectric dams as the 'new temples of India, where I worship' (Bell 2012: 113).[13] Here, there is a sense of wonder that the new states of the global periphery could also build technological marvels that showcased their mastery over the natural world. In the 1950s, Chinese leader Mao Zedong composed a poem called 'Swimming' in support of a project to build a monumental hydroelectric dam across the Yangtze:

> We will make a stone wall
> Against the upper river to the west
> And hold back steamy clouds and rain of Wu peaks
> Over tall chasms will be a calm lake
> And if the goddess of these mountains is not dead
> She will marvel at the changed world. (Mao 1972)

In the same decade as the Hoover Dam, the Roosevelt administration created the Tennessee Valley Authority (TVA) as part of Roosevelt's New Deal program to bring economic development to a traditionally impoverished region of the USA. In his famous bestselling book on the TVA published a decade later in 1944, one of the project's heads David Lilienthal describes the TVA as an unprecedented project that 'applied grassroots democracy to the job of rebuilding the land' (1944: 78). Lilienthal and the TVA's supporters saw the project as 'for the people' and 'by the people', with the goal of taming the river not just for wealth generation but for human emancipation. However, Lilienthal's *Democracy on the March* drew on longstanding rhetorical tropes about the 'destructive' and 'lazy' river that stood in the way of human progress. He begins his book by harkening back to the ideal river as a reliable economic highway and describes the story of the TVA as how 'a wandering and inconsistent river now became a chain of broad and lovely lakes' that people could use 'for the movement of the barges of commerce that now nourish their business enterprises' (1944: 1). Lilienthal evokes a sense that the river is a lazy worker finally being put to good use: 'how waters once wasted and destructive have been controlled and now work, night and day, creating energy to lighten the burdens of human drudgery' (1944: 1). Like many river engineers before him, Lilienthal paints the Tennessee as an irrational river in need of scientific correction. Once corrected, the river would enrich and enlighten human society.

But perhaps what is most startling about Lilienthal's book is the totality of his vision and the conscious way in which he upholds the TVA as a development model for river valleys everywhere. He argues that people might differ in language and race, but they are united by the problem of unruly rivers: 'rivers that in the violence of flood menace the land and the people, then sulk in idleness and drought – rivers all over the world waiting to be controlled by men' (1944: 2). Lilienthal makes it clear that his argument about the potential of river control to revitalize democratic societies is not confined to the Tennessee valley but is a call to societies everywhere. In the decades that followed, the TVA was indeed elevated as a model for regional economic development elsewhere, with foreign experts traveling to the USA to learn from the TVA and US experts going abroad as technical advisors.[14] Early TVA-inspired projects included the 1948 Damodar Valley Corporation in India, the 1947 Papaloapan Commission in Mexico, the 1955 Cauca Regional Cooperation in Colombia, and the 1960 Khuzistan Water and Power Authority in Iran (Neuse 1983: 492).

However, it would be simplistic to maintain that developing countries merely copied the TVA without question. These countries often adopted the TVA ideology as a shorthand for modern progress to both consolidate domestic legitimacy by generating economic growth and to gain international legitimacy as modern, self-sufficient states that could effectively exploit their own resources. In this respect, Daniel Klingensmith's work on the Damodar Valley Corporation (DVC), touted as 'India's TVA', is telling. Klingensmith details how, despite the glowing rhetoric, there were few actual on-the-ground similarities between the TVA and DVC. However, policymakers were committed to maintaining the link between the DVC and TVA in that the TVA model helped both Indian and American officials make claims to political authority and legitimacy 'all in the name of development' (Klingensmith 2003: 128). In other words, the TVA model was politically useful because it allowed states to claim proximity to an imagined standard of modernity based on the ability to master nature through technology. This was the same imagined standard of modernity that shaped projects to create the ideal river throughout this book. It is an imagined standard that continues to inform megadams into the twenty-first century – for example, the Grand Ethiopian Renaissance Dam, unveiled in April 2011, that promises to bring domestic economic wealth as well as international prestige to the East African state.

Conclusion: the battle against nature

The popularity of large-scale hydroelectric dams as transnational tools for economic development and human progress represents the success of James Dunbar's call to 'wage war with the elements, not with our own kind'. In the twentieth century, engineers and policymakers alike continued to draw on martial metaphors in the battle against both the natural world and irrational elements of society. In 1902, German engineer Otto Intze declared that to tame the river required presenting 'the water with a battleground so chosen that the human comes out the victor. This battleground against the forces of nature should be the creation of large dams' (quoted in Blackbourn 2006: 213). Hence, the war against nature continued to be fought by using science and technology to 'solve' the problem of the river. Society would transform the natural river into an ideal river cured of its uselessness, laziness, and waste. Instead, the ideal river would bring economic wealth and social progress to peoples everywhere.

However, as I have suggested in this book, the weapons mobilized in this war did not end with scientific and technological innovations, but also included the international laws and organizations pioneered in the nineteenth century to control the transboundary river. In the twentieth century, these international organizations grew in number, scale, and complexity and were accepted as central pillars of global governance to ensure that the flow of human affairs remained contained, manageable, and progressive. These organizations, framed as functional tools to maintain global order, might even be considered technologies that furthered Dunbar's vision to facilitate cooperation between human societies in order to better exploit and profit from the natural resources at our disposal.

Framing society's interaction with nature as one of our eventual domination over nature is fraught with dangers. It assumes that the campaign leads either to victory or defeat, but as the history of the Rhine and the Danube throughout the twentieth century has shown, narratives of success and failure do not fully capture the complexities of entangled human–river histories and the unseen eddies that lurk just around the river bend. In addition, the martial metaphor assumes a stark dichotomy between human civilization and nature that does not reflect how human and nonhuman forces are entwined – the scientists and engineers who seek to tame nature do not stand outside of and separate from nature, just as large-scale schemes to tame nature necessarily imply a political project to tame irrational elements of human society. The megadam projects of the twentieth century sought not only to tame the rivers but also to modernize the backward populations of the river valleys. The two are entangled and inseparable.

The adverse effects of large-scale projects such as megadams are also entwined. Dams disrupt seasonal floods and sedimentation, destroy wildlife habitats and ecosystems, and degrade the quality of scarce freshwater resources. But in harming the environment, dams also displace human communities, and in many cases such as the Narmada Project in India and the Aswan Dam in Egypt, reservoirs created by dams submerge places of cultural and spiritual significance and destroy the communities that depend on them. Rob Nixon describes the affected communities as 'unimagined communities' – an imposed absence that erases the visibility of populations that stand in the way of progress (2011: 154). Alongside natural ecosystems, human communities alongside the river that stand in the path of the ideal river are also sacrificed on the altar of progress. Resistance to and redress of the harmful effects of large-scale technocratic projects such as megadams must also account for the entwined and inseparable human and nonhuman relations along the river.

Notes

1 Also known as the Revised Rhine Navigation Act of 1868, the Mannheim Act was concluded after the consolidation of the German states, reiterated freedom of navigation along the river for all states, and transformed the Rhine Commission into a largely German-Dutch body, as the Treaty of Frankfurt in 1871 excluded France as a member.

2 In 1908, Leopold II was forced to 'sell' the Congo Free State to the Belgian government.

3 Eventually, after persistent petitions, Czechoslovakia, Poland, Portugal, and Romania were also given seats on the Commission on Ports, Waterways, and Railways.

4 Rivers were designated 'international' to include 'all navigable parts of these river systems which naturally provide more than one state with access to the sea, with or without transhipment from one vessel to another; together with lateral canals and channels constructed either to duplicate or to improve naturally navigable section of the specific river' (Miller 1919: 676). The 1919 Treaty of Versailles also established international commissions on the Elbe, the Oder, and the Niemen rivers.

5 See Chapter 5 for more on the division of the Danube between management of the navigable river between Ulm in Germany and Brăila right before the Danube delta, and the management of the river's seagoing section as it meanders through the Danube delta. This latter was the purview of the European Commission of the Danube.

6 For the most part, the Danube states fell in line with Soviet dictates. However, in an interesting example of political willfulness, when Yugoslavian dictator Josip Tito broke with Moscow, Tito refused to cooperate on the Danube Commission and remained a minority of one on all subsequent votes (G. L. 1951: 426).

7 Even the Ruhr, which was used to provide clean water, suffered environmental devastation. Industry removed large quantities of water for use, lowering the water tables and slowing the flow of the river. In 1911, August Thienemann described the lower Ruhr as a 'yellow soup with foam' and 'milk grey mud' (quoted in Cioc 2013: 92).

8 The 1927 World Court case emerged from a dispute between Romania and Britain over the commission's jurisdiction over the Danube between Galatz and Brăila. Romania argued that the commission possessed only 'technical' and not 'jurisdictional' competence – in particular, Romania protested against the commission exercising policing and jurisdictional powers after a 1921 collision on this stretch of the river. In the 1927 World Court decision, Romania lost its argument on all counts.

9 Pritchard defines 'hydroimperialism' as 'the ways that water, hydraulic knowledge, and water management practices both reveal and reproduce unequal power relations predicated upon an expansionist *mentalité*, whether political or economic in orientation' (2012: 592).

10 For the British, the health of the Egyptian cotton industry was of great concern, as Egyptian foreign debt was held largely by Britain and the servicing of that debt depended on the success of cotton crops. This concern was reflected in regular reports in *The Times* of London on the Nile's water levels and discharges (Tvedt 2011: 177).

11 In response to plans to build the Grand Ethiopian Renaissance Dam, Morsi gave a speech that stated: 'Egypt's water security cannot be violated at all. As president of the state, I confirm to you that all options are open ... if Egypt is

the Nile's gift, then the Nile is a gift to Egypt ... if it diminishes by one drop then our blood is the alternative' (BBC News 2013).

12 Saddam Hussain even named the canals 'Saddam River', 'Glory Canal', and 'Loyalty to the Leader Channel' (Yao 2013).

13 Nehru would later rethink his enthusiasm for megadams. In 1958, in an address to the Central Board of Irrigation and Power, he mused: 'for some time past, I have been beginning to think that we are suffering from what we call "the disease of gigantism". We want to show that we can build big dams and do big things. This is a dangerous outlook...' (quoted in Nixon 2011: 168).

14 US funding and technical assistance for large-scale hydroelectric dams in the mid-twentieth century was also part of the Cold War political calculus. In India in particular, David Engerman writes of an 'informal division of labour' between the USA, which funded hydroelectric power, and the Soviets who funded coal-based power plants (2018: ii).

Conclusion
The strong brown god of the Anthropocene

> I do not know much about gods; but I think that the river
> Is a strong brown god – sullen, untamed and intractable,
> Patient to some degree, at first recognised as a frontier;
> Useful, untrustworthy, as a conveyor of commerce;
> Then only a problem confronting the builder of bridges.
> The problem once solved, the brown god is almost forgotten
> By the dwellers in cities – ever, however, implacable.
>
> T. S. Eliot, 1941

In his 1941 poem *The Dry Salvages*, the third in his *Four Quartets* series, T. S. Eliot considers the taming of rivers and the transformation of a 'strong brown god – sullen, untamed and intractable' into something more useful, 'a conveyor of commerce' and 'only a problem confronting the builders of bridges'. It is then forgotten by modern society, the 'worshippers of the machine', but the river remains as an unnoticed presence in people's lives. Although he begins with the river, Eliot seems to abandon the tamed river for the richer metaphorical waters of the untamed and expansive oceans. However, the river remains a constant presence in the poem through the repeated theme of time and the flow of water always to the sea. In this poem, Eliot situates the river in the late twentieth-century geographical imagination as a mythical god of ancient civilizations that modern society has tamed and largely forgotten. But the river is also a constant presence that permeates local, national, and international politics as a reminder of modern society's faith in the taming of nature and the economic and moral progress that this act of domination promises to bring. And for those who dare look beneath its placid surface into the fluid mysteries that modern science has not yet conquered, the river also reminds us of the fragility of our confidence in that progress.

Perhaps we might make a similar observation about the river in the study of global governance and international organizations, which began in the nineteenth century along Europe's transboundary rivers. Since then, these rivers have been tamed and straightened as conveyors of commerce and sites of international policy collaboration, and our scholarly attention has turned toward the ocean as a more fruitful geography for theorizing the international. The Atlantic Ocean has long been a focus of scholarship, from Anglo-Saxon alliances to the Revolutionary and Black Atlantic (Gilroy 1993; Whelan 2004; Vucetic 2011; Linebaugh and Rediker 2000), but the Pacific and Indian Oceans have recently garnered more analytical attention (Shilliam 2015; Philips and Sharman 2015; Bowman and Clark 2019 [1981]). However, the river remains as an unnoticed presence in the research questions we ask of the ocean – as a geography that at once separates and connects societies, as a neoliberal maritime highway that ensures that goods efficiently reach global markets, as a mobility that shapes the migration of populations, as the promise of untapped natural resources, and as a clarion call that condemns our worst environmental excesses. This book suggests that paying attention to rivers offers insights into these questions and more. It foregrounds how the first international efforts to tame the river remain a presence in IR in the way we understand the sovereign territorial state, in the way we conceptualize economic development, and in the way we trust in the promise of IOs to resolve the dilemmas of global governance. The quest to tame the river may have been forgotten by the students of modern International Relations, but its influence continues to flow through and shape the global politics of the twenty-first century.

The taming of nature as a twenty-first-century Standard of Civilization

Into the twenty-first century, the control of nature continues to operate as a standard of legitimate governance that informs our understanding of what makes a legitimate actor in international politics. One of the hallmarks of modern statehood is territoriality, which John Ruggie describes as a system of political rule that 'differentiated its subjects collectively into territorially defined, fixed, and mutually exclusive enclaves of legitimate dominion' (1993: 151). Statehood, then, implies the ability to fix boundaries, to control affairs within those boundaries, and to articulate and defend those boundaries to international society. This book has argued that in order to present legitimate territoriality, a state must demonstrate its control over nature – in measuring and mapping the natural environment, in harvesting the natural bounty of the territory to improve state wealth, in making natural highways such as rivers safe for commerce, and in controlling and improving backward societies that are too close to nature.

These indicators still factor into our judgment of what makes a successful state rather than a failed one. The perennially failed states of early twenty-first-century international politics, from Somalia to Afghanistan, have failed to tame nature within their borders and therefore allowed instability to spill out and threaten international society. Like Russian failures to tame the Danube delta in the mid-nineteenth century, Somalia's inability to maintain control over its territorial waters and protect international shipping from piracy delegitimized its authority. The Afghan regime's inability to control its hostile terrain and the dangerous terrorists who flourish there also delegitimized its rule in the eyes of international society. These failures of statehood required intervention from more advanced international agents to establish law, order, and institutions to tame the unruly environment and the untamed politics such environments bred. When we imagine underdeveloped and often violent societies on the fringes of modernity, images of unyielding landscapes are rarely far behind.

Conversely, states wishing to reinforce their legitimate status in the eyes of international society continue to showcase control of nature as a demonstration of legitimate territorial control. Ambitious projects such as China's Three Gorges Dam, opened in 2003, and Ethiopia's Grand Renaissance Dam, begun in 2011, are designed to persuade domestic and international audiences of these states' rapid economic development, civilizational greatness, and international prestige by taming the river for the benefit of society. Like megadam projects before it, China's Three Gorges Dam, the largest hydroelectric dam in the world, has three aims – flood control, electricity generation, and navigation improvement along the Yangtze for commercial shipping and tourist cruises (Gleick 2009; *Engineering and Technology Online* 2019). More than eighty years in the making, the dam's history is entwined with that of modern China. The dam's success despite domestic and international criticism reinforces China's self-proclaimed image as a development marvel that consistently challenges and undermines Western expectations.

Speaking in support of Ethiopia's Grand Renaissance Dam, Ethiopian-Canadian and UNICEF ambassador Hannah Godefa praised the project's potential: 'With the success of the dam, many local and international investors will also come. Just imagine, with the building of the dam will come roads, railroads, homes, and more industries … Ethiopia has a chance to prove to the world that it can rise in challenging times' (quoted in Yao 2013). Godefa's words echo longstanding utopian dreams that megadams can cure all of a nation's ills and that harnessing the Nile will elevate Ethiopia's economic development alongside its international prestige. Globally, successful projects to tame the river and transform useless deserts and swamps into useful and productive land continue to be a marker of good governance, and states continue to showcase the success of these projects as evidence of their legitimate control over a fixed territorial space.

Territorial ownership and indigenous politics

Elevating land ownership, linear territoriality, and control over nature as the primary internationally accepted forms of legitimate authority has consequences for societies with different relationships to nature as they struggle to gain recognition as international actors. Indigenous communities from around the world have confronted this challenge. They are still often portrayed as primitive or backward and therefore must operate under the protection and tutelage of more sophisticated states that can effectively translate natural resources into economic wealth and social progress.

The United States' standoff with native groups over the Dakota Access Pipeline illustrates this inequality. The US government's position rests in the firm conviction that it has the legitimate right, and even duty, as the sovereign power over US territories to control and exploit natural resources in a way that enriches its citizens and benefits global commerce. Unrecognized groups such as the Standing Rock encampment have limited legitimate basis on which to challenge the US government's right to build the pipeline – forgetting that this 'right' was usurped from the Native Americans in the first place, based on arguments relegating certain types of land use as less civilized and therefore less legitimate. For Native American activists at Standing Rock, sacrificing the Missouri river for economic profit is nonsensical. Nick Estes explains that for the Lakota and Dakota, the river is a nonhuman relative and 'nothing owns her, and therefore she cannot be sold or alienated like a piece of property ... how do you sell a relative?' (2019: 15). A world of difference lies between these two understandings of society's relationship to nature and the meaning of the river. However, the international history of state territoriality and control over nature privileges the US view over the Standing Rock one.

This unequal legitimacy in the eyes of international society not only informs domestic affairs but also reflects indigenous groups' position in the institutions of global governance. Within these institutions, statehood remains a prerequisite for full participation. Hence, while actors without statehood have fought for and gained the right to participate in a number of United Nations bodies and organizations such as the Arctic Council, full voting rights remain out of reach (McIver 1997; Koivurova 2011; Tomaselli 2016). Furthermore, to gain epistemic legitimacy and therefore a voice in such global forums, indigenous peoples have relied on increasingly influential ideas about their status as 'savage ecologists' who possess a closer relationship to nature. Here, longstanding discourses about the primitive savage are flipped to make indigenous populations the torchbearers of environmental sustainability. However, in addition to enabling indigenous agency, these discourses can also 'essentialize indigenousness' (Lindroth and Sinevaara-Niskanen 2013: 286) and lock indigenous actors into what Jeffrey Sissons (2005) calls 'oppressive authenticity'. Framing all indigenous peoples as virtuous environmental warriors risks placing them on a pedestal and unfairly making them the key bearers of responsibility for saving the destructive modern world from itself (Rutherford 2007).

In recent decades, indigenous groups have also turned to international law to challenge domestic injustices by advocating for indigenous peoples as nations whose sovereign rights have been usurped. However, this approach must confront international law's complicity, particularly in the nineteenth century, in barring indigenous peoples from claiming legitimate authority over their lands and conferring that right instead on European states and their settler colonies (Anaya 1996; Anghie 2005). Other indigenous advocates have turned to international human rights law that recognizes the legal competency of individuals. In particular, groups from the Inuk in Canada to Pacific Islanders have used human rights institutions to challenge states for their inaction against climate change. However, as Inuk leader Shelia Watt-Cloutier's failed 2005 petition to the Inter-American Commission against the United States shows, powerful states such as the USA continue to hold the upper hand in the creation, interpretation, and enforcement of international law (Koivurova et al. 2012; Watt-Cloutier 2015).

However, legal norms evolve, and on the horizon radical developments may go further in challenging state-centric legal principles and the colonial relationships they embody. In 2008, Ecuador's Constituent Assembly adopted a new constitution that recognizes the legal rights of nature as the 'right to integral respect for its existence and for the maintenance and regeneration of its life cycles, structure, functions, and evolutionary processes' (quoted in Youatt 2017: 47).[1] Bolivia followed by adopting the Law of Mother Earth in 2010 that grants legal rights to nature or *Pachamama*. In addition to these general statements of principle, legal personhood has been granted to a number of nonhuman entities: the Whanganui river in New Zealand in 2017; the Ganges and Yamuna rivers in India in 2017 (later rescinded); the Colombian section of the Amazon rainforest in 2018; all of Bangladesh's rivers in 2019; Lake Erie by Toledo, Ohio, in 2019; and the Muteshekau-shipu (Magpie) river in Quebec, Canada, in 2021.

Some have challenged these innovations as simply legal greenwashing that plays on the heartstrings of an increasingly environmentally conscious global public but that in reality continues to subjugate nature under anthropocentric and patronizing legal frameworks (Haraway 2008). However, others see this as a first step to address both a normative and a practical gap – legal personhood grants nature intrinsic moral value separate from its usefulness to human society, and it gives natural environments and the societies that depend on them increased legal standing to fight for their interests in the court of law. Indeed, the Maori communities that advocated for granting legal personhood to the Whanganui river saw this legal innovation as an explicit 'unthinking' and 'unlearning' of the ideational legacies of colonialism and its legal emphasis on territorial ownership (Dentice 2018). As Ruth Barcan argues in her work on the campaign for legal personhood for the Great Barrier Reef, this first step 'attempts to rattle some of the foundations of the House that Modernism Built such as anthropocentrism and Western conceptions of autonomy, separability and property' (2020: 813; see also Andreotti et al. 2018). This innovation highlights practical challenges such as who should speak for the river and where does the river begin and end, but these challenges push us to think about the river from a different perspective. While the full implications of a river with legal personhood are not yet known, this growing international legal norm offers new possibilities to think beyond the longstanding narrative of society's conquest of nature and assumptions about who or what might act as political agents in international society.

Transboundary cooperation into the twenty-first century

The centrality of state sovereignty in international society also informs transboundary water cooperation in post-Cold War commissions established to manage some of the world's most contested waterways. For example, the 1995 Mekong River Commission includes Cambodia, Laos, Thailand, and Vietnam, and the 1999 Nile Basin Initiative comprises ten countries – Burundi, Democratic Republic of the Congo, Egypt, Ethiopia, Kenya, Rwanda, South Sudan, Sudan, Tanzania, and Uganda. While these bodies uphold the legal principles of equitable distribution and utilization, that equality pertains only to sovereign states and largely to harnessing the river for economic benefit. The 1995 Mekong River Agreement promises to 'optimize the multiple-use and mutual benefits of all riparians' by developing the river's full potential and 'the prevention of wasteful use of the Mekong River Basin waters'. The 1999 Agreement on the Nile River Basin Cooperative Framework recognizes the Nile's natural bounty as 'assets of immense value to all the riparian countries' and affirms that priority should be given 'to its most economic use'. Hence cooperation is essential to 'attain optimal utilization and adequate protection and conservation' of the Nile basin. Here, the language of waste, use, and value reflects international society's attitude toward rivers as demonstrated throughout this book, and stresses the ideal river as an economic resource that should not be wasted but controlled and harnessed to create economic wealth and social progress. Like previous river commissions, the Mekong and Nile frameworks envisioned the transboundary river as the joint property of its state owners who have come together to cooperate in order to optimize the river's uses. However, framing the river as a shared economic asset between states often ignores sustainable development within states and the distributional concerns of local human and nonhuman communities along the river, whose voices are sidelined in favor of state development (Furlong 2006; Sneddon and Fox 2006).

Indeed, while interstate cooperation is more desirable than armed violence over water, celebrating these cooperative agreements as unmitigated successes of global governance can conceal a multitude of sins. One example is interstate cooperation in the Aral basin. Arid central Asia has few sources of freshwater aside from its two major rivers – the Amu Darya and the Syr Darya – which flow through five states – Kazakhstan, Kyrgyzstan, Tajikistan, Turkmenistan, and Uzbekistan. To transform the dry steppes into lush and productive land, the Soviets constructed 20,000 miles of canals and 45 dams (Howard 2014) and had even formulated plans to divert water from Siberia and the Volga to satisfy water needs (Elhance 1997). The breakup of the Soviet Union threatened to throw the central Asian states into conflict over water. Turkmenistan and Uzbekistan are downstream and use large quantities of water for irrigating cotton during the dry summer months. Upstream on the Syr Darya, Kyrgyzstan needs its hydroelectric power station to release water during the winter months to generate electricity for heating.

With the mediation of the European Union, the central Asian states reached a barter arrangement that largely restored Soviet-era practices. During the summer, Kyrgyzstan would guarantee water for cotton irrigation, while in the winter months, the downstream states agreed to supply Kyrgyzstan with energy (Elhance 1997; Allouche 2007). The Interstate Commission for Water Coordination of Central Asia was created to oversee this renewed cooperation. However, like the success of the Rhine Commission which transformed the river into an efficient economic commodity at the expense of its ecological health, successful interstate cooperation in the Soviet and post-Soviet era have contributed to the ecological degradation of the Aral Sea. Once the fourth largest freshwater lake in the world, it has shrunk to a fraction of its previous size and seen the disappearance of four-fifths of its fish species.

In addition to ecological challenges, focus on 'successful' interstate cooperation can paper over existing inequalities. For example, Jan Selby (2003) argues that successful cooperation between Israelis and Palestinians over water use in the Oslo Process was only window dressing that 'repackaged' longstanding politics of domination. Oslo II established a joint water committee to oversee the collective management of water and sewerage systems and agreed that Palestinian authorities would have day-to-day control over water systems that only affected Palestinians. While this seemed fair on paper, in the 1980s the Israeli national water company Mekorot integrated West Bank water systems so that few water systems only affected Palestinians. Hence, Oslo II's promise of Palestinian autonomy translated to few real changes, and Israelis continued to benefit from cheap subsidized water while Palestinian communities continued to experience shortages. The international agreement merely legitimized and institutionalized longstanding inequalities. Similarly, upstream states along the Nile have argued that new international frameworks only maintain colonial-era water privileges that the British conferred on Egypt at the expense of its southern neighbors (Waterbury 1979; Hussein and Grandi 2017). Hence, as these examples illustrate, historical, and often imperial, legacies impact transboundary water cooperation into the twenty-first century through the continuation of longstanding power relationships as well as norms of cooperation and the ecological blinders they bring to bear.

These historical legacies underpin not only transboundary water cooperation but other institutions of global governance that draw their legitimacy from interstate cooperation's contribution to the neoliberal sense of ever-upward economic progress. To secure that progress brings us back to James Dunbar's call to wage war on the elements and not our own kind. International organizations in the twenty-first century have united international society in our quest to control the untamed nature that threatens us, and to maximize benefits from the underutilized nature that promises to enrich and ennoble us. The nineteenth-century fear that uncontrolled geographies bred illegality, piracy, and instability still haunts the transnational conduits that enable the growth of twenty-first-century global commerce – whether that conduit is a transboundary river, a global shipping lane, a key logistical network, or the dark digital corners of cyberspace. If, following Blaise Pascal, a river is a road that takes us where we wish to go, then today's transnational commercial routes are very much twenty-first-century rivers that must be controlled and tamed to achieve our ever-loftier economic objectives. Taming these at once productive and dangerous highways remains an important mission for today's institutions of global governance.

Confronting the great derangement

This book has argued that the creation of the world's first IOs to manage and tame transboundary rivers in the nineteenth century arose from Enlightenment confidence in science and technology's ability to control, order, and improve nature. This prevailing faith in society's ability to tame the river for economic wealth and social progress, however, met with resistance from the unintended consequences of these large-scale technocratic projects, from local populations whose livelihoods were erased by the march toward modernity, and from the undercurrents of the river itself that repeatedly thwarted efforts to tame it. In the more than two centuries since the Rhine Commission, has international society learned to moderate its unshakable faith in the taming of nature and the ever-upward liberal progress it will bring? In some sense, yes, there is increasing recognition that monoculture forests, sweeping river rectification, and megadams have caused untold social and ecological destruction, both intended and unintended. Indeed, along rivers including the Rhine and Danube, engineers and policymakers are making efforts to 'restore' riverbeds, floodplains, and meanders to rehabilitate river ecosystems and the local populations that depend on them.[2] Globally, international and local movements that include indigenous populations and environmentalists have successfully campaigned against megadams and other large-scale projects that focus solely on economic extraction from nature. Furthermore, there is increasing recognition that local context is important, and that small-scale interventions and the centering of local stakeholders are essential in order to even begin to tackle the environmental challenges confronting the world.

However, international society remains under the spell of European Enlightenment thinking in the way we value nature almost exclusively as an economic object, in our faith in technological innovation to resolve our troubled relationship with nature, and in our firm expectation of constant upward economic progress despite our growing realization that such progress is materially unsustainable. In *The Great Derangement*, Amitav Ghosh argues that modern India's economic development unmasks the fragility of modernity: 'every family in the world cannot have two cars, a washing machine, and a refrigerator – not because of technical or economic limitations but because humanity would asphyxiate in the process' (2016: 92–3). Here Ghosh pinpoints the realization that our faith in neoliberal progress prevents us from fully grasping that it is not ecologically possible for all the world's population to achieve the Western bourgeois standard of living. This is a consequence of the civilizational continuum as it confronts the Anthropocene – our duty as advanced and wealthy members of international society to help underdeveloped societies progress to our current standard is impossible because it would exhaust the earth's finite resources. The climate crisis has highlighted for us the catastrophic disconnect between the dream of Western modernity and the nightmare of ecological collapse, but this collision course has been centuries in the making.

Ghosh's writing shows us a glimpse of the derangement that shapes our economic desires and political expectations. Echoing Bruno Latour, he charts modernity's linear and irreversible conception of time and our fear of being, to quote Barack Obama, 'on the wrong side of history' (Ghosh 2016: 123).

To remain on the right side of history, then, modern society engages in the relentless pursuit of progress that drives us to derangement. At one point, Ghosh explains his book's title by contemplating why sought-after residential properties in South and Southeast Asia are situated on the water's edge, where they are most vulnerable to devastating cyclones and tsunamis. While indigenous populations have long settled on highlands to avoid storms and floods, the middle-class and upwardly mobile compete to live next to the water – the closer to the edge, the more prestigious the location. For Ghosh, this pattern exemplifies how 'the bourgeois belief in the regularity of the world has been carried to the point of derangement' (2016: 36). This derangement refers to our ironclad confidence that modern civilization has pacified nature, that rivers and tides submit to the regularity imposed by bourgeois life, and that modern technology can relegate cataclysmic events such as floods and tsunamis to the pages of science and dystopian fiction. Our firm belief that humankind sits in control of and separate from nature makes modern society believe it is not subject to the dynamics of nature – that despite rising oceans and accelerating biodiversity loss, we can invent our way out of environmental collapse. In this quest to control nature, Ghosh sees 'a colonial vision of the world, in which proximity to the water represented power and security, mastery and conquest' – a vision of the world embedded in the economic and social desires of the middle classes everywhere from New York to Mumbai (2016: 36–7).

Recognition that the standards and desires of modern life emerged from a global history of entanglement between international society and the natural world allows us to recognize the power and politics behind the creation of these modern standards. It allows us to dispel the myth that such standards are somehow natural and unmovable. Instead, it allows us to see that they are manufactured through centuries of intellectual, social, and political processes, and this denaturing perhaps allows us to imagine how they might be unmade and reconstructed otherwise. Ironically, the term 'denature' assumes that nature is 'written in stone' and cannot be changed, but the process of delinking progress from our conception of the good life also shifts our view of nature as the inflexible force that stands in the way of human attainment. As Anna Tsing (2015: 21) insightfully writes, 'we learn over and over that humans are different from the rest of the living world because we look forward … we imagine that humans are *made* through progress', relegating those who do not conform to the timeline of progress as less human and less worthy of normative attention. However, if we dim the relentless 'driving beat' of progress, 'we might notice other temporal patterns' (Tsing 2015: 21) and learn to value those patterns. What would happen if international society stopped looking for linear and ever-upward economic and social progress toward some universal standard of achievement? Is there another way to imagine value and mutual coexistence? In order to confront the looming challenges of the Anthropocene, perhaps this act of imagination must be the first step.

Further, climate change is eroding another longstanding myth of modern progress – that increasingly sophisticated science and technology will necessarily lead to a solution to all the world's ills. This myth is embedded in the notion of 'ecomodernism' that celebrates the idea of a 'good Anthropocene' in which humanity can finally rise above its greedy past to save the day, and 'climate change is a trial to be met and won with technology' (Hamilton 2016: 99). However, the historical narrative this book weaves suggests that technocratic overconfidence and hubris is a recurring theme of Western modernity. The scale and complexity of the climate crisis disrupts the simplistic dream that better technical solutions will be enough, and our global paralysis in the face of this crisis illustrates how all the scientific information in the world cannot account for the lack of political will. Increasingly, we have become disenchanted with the politics of climate change precisely because we are losing faith in the Enlightenment confidence that human society, through its command of science, can ruin or save a passive natural world that waits for our commands. Sweeping political promises to fix or prevent climate change seem to ring with the tinsel sound of wishful thinking.

Perhaps confronting the failings of our Enlightenment assumptions can reorient our thinking away from an empty commitment to wholly 'solve' climate change, as if the world were a Rubik's cube that could be restored to some pristine, color-coded perfection. Instead, we must ask how we might live – most justly and more compassionately – with the kaleidoscopic changes that are already sweeping the globe. This is not to suggest that we should abandon political battles to address fossil fuel consumption, combat consumerism, and prevent the wanton destruction of natural resources, but that we should think differently about our relationship with the natural world and how we should live with the political and social upheavals that climate processes have already brought into being. While environmental justice is a long road, grappling with the global history of why that road is so steep is a necessary first step.

Notes

1 Youatt cautions against a simplistic interpretation (often perpetuated by Western environmentalists) of the 2008 Ecuadorian constitution as the first step to healing society's relationship with nature. Instead, he highlights how this move should

be seen in the context of both indigenous groups' powerlessness in bringing Chevron-Texaco to justice for environmental damages and also the rest of the constitution which affirms the centrality of the Ecuadorian state.

2 Of course, the idea of river 'restoration' raises the question: restoration to what state at what point in time for whom? As human and nonhuman societies have always intervened to shape the river's bends, it is impossible to return the river to an idealized 'natural' state. Anne Rademacher's ethnographic work on river restoration efforts in Kathmandu (2011) reveals how contested histories and identities shape different actors with differing visions of how to restore the river.

Bibliography

Adas, M. (1989), *Machines as the Measure of Men: Science, Technology, and Ideologies of Western Dominance*, Ithaca, NY: Cornell University Press.

Adler, E. (1997), 'Seizing the middle ground: constructivism in world politics', *European Journal of International Relations* 3(3): 319–63.

ADM 123/86 (1882–85), 'The Southern Division and Congo', British National Archives, Kew, UK.

ADM 123/87 (1883–85), 'The Gold Coast Protectorate, the Oil and Niger Rivers and other territories', British National Archives, Kew, UK.

Agnew, J. (1982), 'Sociologizing the geographical imagination: spatial concepts in the world systems perspective', *Political Geography Quarterly* 1(2): 159–66.

— (1996), 'Time into space: the myth of "backward" Italy in modern Europe', *Time & Society* 5(1): 27–45.

Agnihotri, I. (1996), 'Ecology, land use and colonisation: the canal colonies of Punjab', *The Indian Economic & Social History Review* 33(1): 37–58.

Allan, B. (2018), *Scientific Cosmology and International Orders*, Cambridge: Cambridge University Press.

Allouche, J. (2007), 'The governance of Central Asian waters: national interests versus regional cooperation', *Disarmament Forum* 4: 45–56.

Anaya, S. J. (1996), *Indigenous Peoples in International Law*, Oxford: Oxford University Press.

Andreotti, V., et al. (2018), 'Mobilising different conversations about global justice in education: towards alternative futures in uncertain times', *Policy & Practice: A Development Education Review* 26: 9–41.

Anghie, A. (1999), 'Finding the peripheries: sovereignty and colonialism in nineteenth century international law', *Harvard International Law Journal* 40(1): 1–71.

— (2005), *Imperialism, Sovereignty and the Making of International Law*, Cambridge: Cambridge University Press.

— (2007), 'The evolution of international law: colonial and postcolonial realities', *Third World Quarterly* 27(5): 739–53.

Anstey, R. (1962), *Britain and the Congo in the Nineteenth Century*, Oxford: Clarendon Press.

Ardeleanu, C. (2010), 'Russian–British rivalry regarding Danube navigation and the origins of the Crimean War (1846–1853)', *Journal of Mediterranean Studies* 19(2): 165–86.

— (2014), *International Trade and Diplomacy at the Lower Danube, 1829–1853*, Brăila, Romania: Istros.

Arnold, E. (ed.) (2000), *Conversations with Leslie Marmon Silko*, Jackson, MS: University Press of Mississippi.

Atwood, M. (2011), *In Other Worlds: SF and the Human Imagination*, New York: Knopf Doubleday.

Austensen, R. (1973), 'Count Buol and the Metternich tradition', *Austrian History Yearbook* 9: 173–93.

Baicoianu, C. (1917), *Le Danube. Aperçu historique, économique et politique*, Paris: Librairie de la Société Recueil Sirey.

Banning, E. (1927), *Mémoires, politiques et diplomatiques: comment fut fondé le Congo belge*, Paris: La Renaissance du livre.

Barcan, R. (2020), 'The campaign for legal personhood for the Great Barrier Reef: finding political and pedagogical value in a spectacular failure of care', *EPE: Nature and Space* 3(3): 810–32.

Barrell, J. (1980), *The Dark Side of the Landscape: The Rural Poor in English Painting 1730–1840*, Cambridge: Cambridge University Press.

Barnett, M., and M. Finnemore (2004), *Rules for the World: International Organizations in Global Politics*, Ithaca, NY: Cornell University Press.

Basset, T. J. (1994), 'Cartography and empire building in nineteenth-century West Africa', *Geographical Review* 84(3): 316–35.

Bauer, J. (2012), *Lives of the Brothers Humboldt*, Bremen: Outlook Verlagsgesellschaft.

Bauman, Z. (1989), *Modernity and the Holocaust*, Cambridge: Polity.

— (1991), *Modernity and Ambivalence*, Cambridge: Polity.

Baumgart, W. (1981), *Peace of Paris, 1856: Studies in War, Diplomacy and Peacemaking*, Santa Barbara, CA: ABC-CLIO.

Bayly, C. A. (2004), *The Birth of the Modern World, 1780–1914: Global Connections and Comparisons*, Oxford: Blackwell.

BBC News (2013), 'Egyptian warning over Ethiopia Nile dam', 10 June, https://www.bbc.co.uk/news/world-africa-22850124 (accessed 30 August 2020).

Beattie, A. (2010), *The Danube: A Cultural History*, Oxford: Oxford University Press.

Beattie, W. (1843), *The Danube: Its History, Scenery, and Topography*, London: G. Virtue.

Bell, A. (2012), *Peak Water: How We Built Civilisation on Water and Drained the World Dry*, Edinburgh: Luath Press.

Bellone, E. (1980), *A World on Paper: Studies on the Second Scientific Revolution*, Cambridge, MA: MIT Press.

Benton, L. (2010), *A Search for Sovereignty: Law and Geography in European Empires, 1400–1900*, Cambridge: Cambridge University Press.

Benton, L., and L. Ford (2018), *Rage for Order: The British Empire and the Origins of International Law, 1800–1850*, Cambridge, MA: Harvard University Press.

Benton, L., and B. Straumann (2010), 'Acquiring empire by law: from Roman doctrine to early modern European practice', *Law and History Review* 28(1): 1–38.

Berlin, I. (1996), *The Sense of Reality: Studies in Ideas and Their History*, London: Chatto and Windus.

Bermingham, A. (1994), 'System, order, and abstraction: the politics of English landscape drawing around 1795', in W. J. T. Mitchell (ed.), *Landscape and Power*, Chicago: University of Chicago Press, 77–102.

Best, J. J. (1842), *Excursions in Albania: comprising a description of the wild boar, deer, and woodcock shooting in that country: and a journey from thence to Thessalonica & Constantinople and up the Danube to Pest*, London: Wm. H. Allen.

Bispham, E. (ed.) (2008), *Roman Europe*, Oxford: Oxford University Press.

Blackbourn, D. (2006), *The Conquest of Nature: Water, Landscape and the Making of Modern Germany*, London: Random House.

— (2008), 'Time is a violent torrent: constructing and reconstructing rivers in modern German history', in C. Mauch and T. Zeller (eds.), *Rivers in History: Perspectives on Waterways in Europe and North America*, Pittsburgh, PA: University of Pittsburgh Press, 11–25.

Blackburn, G. (1930), 'International control of the River Danube', *Current History* 32(6): 1154–9.

Bowden, B. (2009), *The Empire of Civilization: The Evolution of an Imperial Idea*, Chicago: University of Chicago Press.

— (2014), 'To rethink standards of civilisation, start with the end', *Millennium* 42(3): 614–31.

Bowman, L., and I. Clark (eds.) (2019 [1981]), *The Indian Ocean in Global Politics*, Abingdon: Routledge.

Branch, J. (2011), 'Mapping the sovereign state: technology, authority and systemic change', *International Organization* 65(1): 1–36.

— (2014), *The Cartographic State: Maps, Territory, and the Origins of Sovereignty*, Cambridge: Cambridge University Press.

Breuilly, J. (1993), *Nationalism and the State*, Manchester: Manchester University Press.

Brockway, L. (1979), 'Science and colonial expansion: the role of the British Royal Botanic Gardens', *American Ethnologist* 6(3): 449–65.

Brüggemeier, F. J. (1994), 'A nature fit for industry: the environmental history of the Ruhr basin, 1840–1990', *Environmental History Review* 18(1): 35–54.

Bukovansky, M. (2002), *Legitimacy and Power Politics: The American and French Revolutions in International Political Culture*, Princeton, NJ: Princeton University Press.

Butler, E. (2010), *The Metamorphoses of the Vampire in Literature and Film*, Rochester, NY: Camden House.

Buzan, B., and G. Lawson (2015), *The Global Transformation: History, Modernity and the Making of International Relations*, Cambridge: Cambridge University Press.

Byron, G. G., 6th Lord (1812–18), 'The Rhine', https://www.bartleby.com/270/8/131.html (accessed September 2016).

Campbell, J. (1949), 'Diplomacy on the Danube', *Foreign Affairs* XXVII: 317.

Capoccia, G., and R. D. Kelemen (2007), 'The study of critical junctures: theory, narrative, and counterfactuals in historical institutionalism', *World Politics* 59(3): 341–69.

Carlyle, T., and R. W. Emerson (1888), *The Correspondence of Thomas Carlyle and Ralph Waldo Emerson*, vol. 2, Boston, MA: Ticknor, https://www.gutenberg.org/cache/epub/13660/pg13660.html (accessed 9 September 2021).

Central Commission for the Navigation of the Rhine (1918), *Rheinurkunden Sammlung zwischenstaatlicher Vereinbarungen, landesrechtlicher Ausführungsverordnungen und sonstiger wichtiger Urkunden über die Rheinschiffahrt seit 1803*, vol. 1, *1803–1860*, Nijhoff: Gravenhage.

Cernovodeanu, P. (1986), *Relaţiile comerciale româno–engleze în contextul politicii orientale a Marii Britanii (1803–1878)*, Cluj: Napoca.

Chakrabarty, D. (2008), *Provincializing Europe: Postcolonial Thought and Historical Difference*, Princeton, NJ: Princeton University Press.

Chamberlain, J. P. (1923), *The Regime of the International Rivers: Danube and Rhine*, New York: Columbia University Press.

— (1974 [1918]), *The Danube. In Five Parts*, Wilmington, DE: Scholarly Resources, https://trove.nla.gov.au/work/757051 (accessed 9 September 2021).

Chandler, A. (2006). 'Empire of autumn: the French *Exposition Universelle* of 1867', http://www.arthurchandler.com/paris-1867-exposition (accessed August 2020).

Chapman, T. (1998), *The Congress of Vienna: Origins, Processes, and Results*, London: Routledge.

Charnovitz, S. (1997), 'Two centuries of participation: NGOs and international governance', *Michigan Journal of International Law* 183(2): 183–286.

Cioc, M. (2002), *The Rhine: An Eco-Biography, 1815–2000*, Seattle, WA: University of Washington Press.

— (2013), 'Europe's river: the Rhine as a prelude to transnational cooperation and the Common Market', in E. Bsumek, D. Kinkela and M. Lawrence (eds.), *Nation-States and the Global Environment: New Approaches to International History*, Oxford: Oxford University Press, 25–42.

Clapp, E. J. (1911), *The Navigable Rhine: The Development of Its Shipping, the Basis of the Prosperity of its Commerce and Its Traffic in 1907*, New York: Houghton Mifflin.

Clapp, J., and P. Dauvergne (2016), 'Researching global environmental politics in the 21st century', *Global Environmental Politics* 16(1): 1–12.

Claridge, R. T. (1837), *A guide along the Danube, from Vienna to Constantinople, Smyrna, Athens, the Morea, the Ionian Islands, and Venice*, London: F. C. Westley.

Coates, P. (2013), *A Story of Six Rivers, History, Culture and Ecology*, London: Reaktion.

Cobden, R. (1908 [1846]), *Speeches on Questions of Public Policy by Richard Cobden, M.P.*, ed. J. Bright and J. E. T. Rogers, London: T. Fisher Unwin.

Cogan, T. (1794), *The Rhine: Or, A Journey from Utrecht to Francfort; Chiefly by the Borders of the Rhine and the Passage Down the River from Mentz to Bonn*, vol. 2, London: G. Woodfall.

Coleridge, S. T. (1828), 'Cologne', https://www.blueridgejournal.com/poems/stc-koln.htm (accessed January 2016).

Conacher, J. B. (1987), *Britain and the Crimea, 1855–56: Problems of War and Peace*, London: Macmillan.

Conrad, J. (1899), *Heart of Darkness*, https://www.gutenberg.org/files/219/219-h/219-h.htm (accessed 1 June 2017).

Cookson-Hills, C. (2013), 'The Aswan Dam and Egyptian water control policy, 1882–1902', *Radical History Review* 116: 59–85.

Correspondence with the Russian Government Respecting Obstructions to the Navigation of the Sulina Channel of the Danube (1853), London: Harrison and Son.

Cosgrove, D. (1979), 'John Ruskin and the geographical imagination', *Geographical Review* 69(1): 43–62.

— (2006), 'Modernity, community and the landscape idea', *Journal of Material Culture* 11(1): 49–66.

Crankshaw, E. (1981), *Bismarck*, London: Bloomsbury.

Craven, M. (2015), 'Between law and history: the Berlin Conference of 1884–1885 and the logic of free trade', *London Review of International Law* 3(1): 31–59.

Crowe, S. (1942), *The Berlin West African Conference, 1884–1885*, New York: Longmans Green.

Crozier, M. (1996), 'The garden metaphor in modernity', in M. Crozier and P. Murphy (eds.), *The Left in Search of a Center*, Chicago: University of Illinois Press, 65–85.

Dalby, S., and G. Ó'Tuathail (eds.) (1998), *Rethinking Geopolitics*, London: Routledge.

Daniels, S. (1992), 'Place and the geographical imagination', *Geography* 77(4): 310–22.

— (2011), 'Geographical imagination', *Transactions of the Institute of British Geographers* 36(2): 182–7.

Davies, P. (1997), 'The politics of perpetuation: Trajan's Column and the art of commemoration', *American Journal of Archaeology* 101(1): 41–65.

Dentice, K. (2018), 'Granting legal personhood to natural systems: Kara Dentice – episode 17', *Blue Frontiers Podcast*, https://podcasts.apple.com/us/podcast/granting-legal-personhood-to-natural-systems-kara-dentice/id1336234557?i=1000414325665 (accessed May 2021).

Diehl, P. (2005), *The Politics of Global Governance: International Organizations in an Interdependent World*, 3rd ed., Boulder, CO: Lynne Riener.

Dockrill, M. L. (1989), *British documents on foreign affairs – reports and papers from the Foreign Office confidential print / Part II, From the first to the second world war. Series I, The Paris Peace Conference of 1919*, Frederick, MD: University Publications of America.

Dodds K., M. Kuus and J. Sharp (eds.) (2013), *The Ashgate Research Companion to Critical Geopolitics*, Farnham: Ashgate.

Dollinger, P. (1964), *The German Hansa*, London: Macmillan.

Donovan, S. (2006), 'Touring in extremis: travel and adventure in the Congo', in T. Youngs (ed.), *Travel Writing in the Nineteenth Century*, London: Anthem Press.

Drayton, R. (2000), *Nature's Government: Science, Imperial Britain, and the 'Improvement' of the World*, New Haven, CT: Yale University Press.

D'Souza, R. (2006), 'Water in British India: the making of a "colonial hydrology"', *History Compass* 4(4): 621–8.

Duffield, J. (2007), 'What are international institutions?', *International Studies Review* 9(1): 1–22.

Dumas, A. (1842), *Excursions sur les bords du Rhin*, vol. 2, Brussels: Hauman.

Dunbar, J. (1780), *Essays on the History of Mankind in Rude and Cultivated Ages*, London: W. Strahan.

Dunne, T., and C. Reus-Smit (eds.) (2017), *The Globalization of International Society*, Oxford: Oxford University Press.

East, W. G. (1932), 'The Danube route-way in history', *Economica* 37: 321–45.

Eastwood, J. (2005), 'The role of ideas in Weber's theory of interests', *Critical Review* 17(1–2): 89–100.

Eckersley, R. (2004), *The Green State: Rethinking Democracy and Sovereignty*, Cambridge, MA: MIT Press.

Elhance, A. (1997), 'Conflict and cooperation over water in the Aral Sea basin', *Studies in Conflict & Terrorism* 20(2): 207–18.

Eliot, T. S. (1941), *Four Quartets*, London: Faber and Faber.

Engelhardt, E. (1879), *Du regime conventionnel des fleuves internationaux*, Paris: Libraires du Conseil d'État.

Engerman, D. (2018), *The Price of Aid: The Economic Cold War in India*, Cambridge, MA: Harvard University Press.

Engineering and Technology Online (2020), 'China officials insist Three Gorges Dam is safe, as online rumours of collapse rise', https://eandt.theiet.org/content/articles/2019/07/china-officials-insist-three-gorges-dam-is-safe-as-online-rumours-of-collapse-rise/ (accessed 30 August 2020).

Epstein, C. (2008), *The Power of Words in International Relations: Birth of an Anti-Whaling Discourse*, Cambridge, MA: MIT Press.

Eyck, E. (1964), *Bismarck and the German Empire*, New York: W. W. Norton.

Estes, N. (2019), *Our History Is the Future: Standing Rock Versus the Dakota Access Pipeline, and the Long Tradition of Indigenous Resistance*, London: Verso.

Fabian, J. (1983), *Time and the Other: How Anthropology Makes Its Object*, Ithaca, NY: Cornell University Press.

Falkner, R. (2017), *Business Power and Conflict in International Environmental Politics*, Basingstoke: Palgrave Macmillan.

Ferkiss, V. (1993), *Nature, Technology and Society: Cultural Roots of the Current Environmental Crisis*, New York: New York University Press.

Figes, O. (2012), *Crimea*, London: Penguin.

Finch, G. (1919), 'The Peace Conference of Paris, 1919', *The American Journal of International Law* 13(2): 159–86

Findling, J. (ed.) (1990), *Historical Dictionary of World's Fairs and Expositions, 1851–1988*, Westport, CT: Greenwood Press.

Fitzmaurice, A. (2007), 'The genealogy of *terra nullius*', *Austrian Historical Studies* 38(129): 1–15.

— (2009), 'The resilience of natural law in the writings of Sir Travers Twiss', in I. Hall and L. Hill (eds.), *British International Thinkers from Hobbes to Namier*, Basingstoke: Palgrave Macmillan, 137–59.

— (2012), 'Liberalism and empire in nineteenth-century international law', *The American Historical Review* 117(1): 122–40.

Florescu, R. (1998), *The Struggle against Russia in the Romanian Principalities, 1821–1854*, 2nd ed., Iași: Center for Romanian Studies.

FO 7/461 (1855), 'Lord J. Russell (Vienna Conference). Drafts', British National Archives, Kew, UK.

FO 27/1168 (1856), 'Paris Conference, Archives, Lord Clarendon to Lord Palmerston, Drafts', British National Archives, Kew, UK.

FO 27/1169 (1856), 'Paris Conference, Archives, Lord Clarendon to Lord Palmerston, Drafts', British National Archives, Kew, UK.

FO 78/977 (1835–53), 'Navigation of Soulina, Mouth of the Danube', letters, British National Archives, Kew, UK.

FO 78/3724 (1844), 'Danube Navigation Commission. Mr. Sanderson', letters, British National Archives, Kew, UK.

FO 92/17 (1815), 'From Earl of Clancarty (to Earl Bathurst, Viscount Castlereagh and W. R. Hamilton). Vienna', letters, British National Archives, Kew, UK.

FO 97/402 (1828–30), 'Reports from E. L. Butte and Others on the Proceedings of the Russians in Moldavia and Wallachia', British National Archives, Kew, UK.

FO 97/403 (1830–32), 'Reports from E. L. Butte and Others on the Proceedings of the Russians in Moldavia and Wallachia', British National Archives, Kew, UK.

FO 403/46 (1884), 'West African Conference. Further Correspondence', British National Archives, Kew, UK.

FO 403/47 (1884), 'West African Conference. Further Correspondence', British National Archives, Kew, UK.

FO 403/48 (1884), 'West African Conference. Further Correspondence', British National Archives, Kew, UK.

Forrester, K., and S. Smith (2018), *Nature, Action and the Future: Political Thought and the Environment*, Cambridge: Cambridge University Press.

Franey, L. (2001), 'Ethnographic collecting and travel: blurring boundaries, forming a discipline', *Victorian Literature and Culture* 29(1): 219–39.

Fromby, H. (1843), *A Visit to the East; Comprising Germany and the Danube, Constantinople, Asia Minor, Egypt, and Idumea*, London: James Burns.

Furlong, K. (2006), 'Hidden theories, troubled waters: international relations, the "territorial trap", and the South African development community's transboundary waters', *Political Geography* 25: 438–58.

G. L. (1951), 'Europe's international waterways', *World Today* 7(10): 419–29.

Gavin, R. J., and J. A. Betley (1973), *The Scramble for Africa: Documents on the Berlin West African Conference and Related Subjects*, Ibadan: Ibadan University Press.

Geffcken, F. (1883), *La Question du Danube*, Berlin: H. W. Müller.

Gellner, E. (1983), *Nations and Nationalism*, Ithaca, NY: Cornell University Press.

Getachew, A. (2019), *Worldmaking After Empire: The Rise and Fall of Self-Determination*, Princeton, NJ: Princeton University Press.

Ghosh, A. (2016), *The Great Derangement: Climate Change and the Unthinkable*, Chicago: University of Chicago Press.

Gibson, M. (2006), *Dracula and the Eastern Question: British and French Vampire Narratives of the Nineteenth-Century Near East*, Basingstoke: Palgrave Macmillan.

Gilmartin, D. (2015), *Blood and Water: The Indus River Basin in Modern History*, Oakland, CA: University of California Press.

Gilroy, P. (1993), *The Black Atlantic: Modernity and Double Consciousness*, London: Verso.

Gleason, J. H. (1950), *The Genesis of Russophobia in Great Britain 1815–1841*, Cambridge, MA: Harvard University Press.

Gleick, P. (2009), 'Water brief 3: Three Gorges Dam project, Yangtze River, China', in P. Gleick, H. Cooley, M. Cohen, M. Morikawa, J. Morrison, and M. Palaniappan (eds.), *The World's Water 2008–2009*, The Biennial Report on Freshwater Resources, London, 139–50

Goldstein, J., and R. Keohane (1993), *Ideas and Foreign Policy: Beliefs, Institutions, and Political Change*, Ithaca, NY: Cornell University Press.

Goldsworthy, V. (1998), *Inventing Ruritania: The Imperialism of the Imagination*, New Haven, CT: Yale University Press.

Gong, G. (1984), *The Standard of 'Civilization' in International Society*, Oxford: Oxford University Press.

Gordon, C. (1884), *General Gordon's Letters from the Crimea, the Danube, and Armenia: August 18, 1854 to November 1858*, London: Chapman and Hall.

Grattan, T. C. (ed.) (1847), *Lays and Legends of the Rhine: To Which are Added Translations of German Poems and Songs, and a Selection from Gattan's Rhenish Legends*, Frankfurt: Charles Jugel.

Grove, R. (1995), *Green Imperialism: Colonial Expansion, Tropical Island Edens and the Origins of Environmentalism, 1600–1860*, Cambridge: Cambridge University Press.

Gruffudd, P. (1995), 'Remaking Wales: nation-building and the geographical imagination, 1925–1950', *Political Geography* 14(3): 219–39.

Gruffydd Jones, B. (2013), '"Good governance" and "state failure": genealogies of imperial discourse', *Cambridge Review of International Affairs* 26(1): 49–70.

Guarasci, B. (2015), 'The National Park: reviving Eden in Iraq's marshes', *The Arab Studies Journal* 23(1): 128–53.

Haas, P. M. (2015), *Epistemic Communities, Constructivism, and International Environmental Politics*, Abingdon: Routledge.

Hacking, I. (1990), *The Taming of Chance*, Cambridge: Cambridge University Press.

— (2002), *Historical Ontology*, Cambridge, MA: Harvard University Press.

Haggard, H. R. (2002 [1887]), *She: A History of Adventure*, New York: Random House.

Hajnal, H. (1920), *The Danube: Its Historical, Political and Economic Importance*, The Hague: Martinus Nijhoff.

Hamilton, C. (2016), 'The Anthropocene as rupture', *The Anthropocene Review* 3(2): 93–106.

Hammond, A. (2008), 'Typologies of the East: on distinguishing Balkanism and Orientalism', *Nineteenth-Century Contexts* 29(2–3): 201–18.

Hansen, L. (2006), *Security as Practice: Discourse Analysis and the Bosnian War*, London: Routledge.

Haraway, D. (2008), *When Species Meet*, Minneapolis, MN: University of Minnesota Press.

Harley, J. B. (1988), 'Maps, knowledge, and power', in D. Cosgrove and S. Daniels (eds.), *The Iconography of Landscape*, Cambridge: Cambridge University Press, 277–312.

Harvey, D. (1973), *Social Justice and the City*, Baltimore, MD: Johns Hopkins University Press.

— (2006), 'The sociological and geographical imaginations', *International Journal of Politics, Culture, and Society* 18: 211–55.

Hawkins, H. (2010), 'Turn your trash into… Rubbish, art and politics. Richard Wentworth's geographical imagination', *Social & Cultural Geography* 11(8): 805–27.

Heckscher, E. (1994 [1931]), *Mercantilism, Volume 1*, London: Routledge.

Hegel, G. W. F. (2007 [1899]), *The Philosophy of History*, trans. J. Sibree, New York: Cosimo.

Helmreich, A. (1997), 'Re-presenting nature: ideology, art and science in William Robinson's "Wild Garden"', in J. Wolschke-Bulmahn (ed.), *Nature and Ideology: Natural Garden Design in the Twentieth Century*, Washington, DC: Dumbarton Oaks Research Library and Collection, 81–112.

HL Deb (16 February 1842), vol. 60, cols. 538-625, https://api.parliament.uk/historic-hansard/commons/1842/feb/16/corn-laws-ministerial-plan-adjourned (accessed August 2015).

HL Deb (31 March 1854), vol. 132, cols. 140-98, https://api.parliament.uk/historic-hansard/lords/1854/mar/31/war-with-russia-her-majestys-message (accessed August 2015).

Hobson, J. (2007), 'Reconstructing international relations through world history: oriental globalization and the global-dialogic conception of inter-civilizational relations', *International Politics* 44(4): 414–30.

Hochschild, A. (1998), *King Leopold's Ghost: A Story of Greed, Terror, and Heroism in Colonial Africa*, New York: Mariner Books.

Hohensinner, S., C. Sonnlechner, M. Schmid, and V. Winiwarter (2013), 'Two steps back, one step forward: reconstructing the dynamic Danube riverscape under human influence in Vienna', *Water History* 5: 121–43.

Holbrooke, R. (1999), 'Conflict in Africa and the search for peace in Congo', speech, 14 December, https://www.africa.upenn.edu/Urgent_Action/apic_121499.html (accessed 9 August 2021).

Hölderlin, F. (1801–02), 'Der Rhein; the Rhine', trans. S. Ranson, https://sites.google.com/site/germanliterature/19th-century/hoelderlin/der-rhein-the-rhine (accessed June 2020)

Holmes, R. (2008), *Age of Wonder: How the Romantic Generation Discovered the Beauty and Terror of Science*, London: Harper.

Holmqvist, C. (2014), *Policing Wars: On Military Intervention in the Twenty-First Century*, Basingstoke: Palgrave Macmillan.

Holsti, K. (2016), 'Governance without government: polyarchy in nineteenth-century European international politics', in *Kalevi Holsti: Major Texts on War, the State, Peace, and International Order*, Cham: Springer, 149–71.

Howard, B. (2014), 'Aral Sea's eastern basin is dry for the first time in 6000 years', *National Geographic*, https://www.nationalgeographic.com/news/2014/10/141001-aral-sea-shrinking-drought-water-environment/ (accessed 15 August 2020).

Howse, R. (2006), 'Montesquieu on commerce, conquest, war, and peace', *Brooklyn Journal of International Law* 31(3): 693–708.

Hugo, V. (1843), *The Rhine*, trans. David Mitchell Aird, London: D. Aird.

Humboldt, W. (1910), *Wilhelm und Caroline von Humboldt in ihren Briefen 1812–1915*, Berlin: E. S. Mittler.

Hume, D. (1994), *Political Writings*, ed. S. Warner and D. Livingston, Indianapolis, IN: Hackett.

Hunt, A. (2010), *The Geographical Imagination of Annie Proulx: Rethinking Regionalism*, Lanham, MD: Lexington Books.

Hurd, E. S. (2004), 'The political authority of secularism in international relations', *European Journal of International Relations* 10(2): 235–62.

Hussein, H., and M. Grandi (2017), 'Dynamic political contexts and power asymmetries: the case of the Blue Nile and the Yarmouk Rivers', *International Environmental Agreements: Politics, Law and Economics* 17: 795–814.

Hutchings, K. (2008), *Time and World Politics*, Manchester: Manchester University Press.

— (2018), 'Time and the study of world politics', *Millennium* 46(3): 253–8.

Ikenberry, G. J. (2001), *After Victory: Institutions, Strategic Restraint, and the Rebuilding of Order After Major War*, Princeton, NJ: Princeton University Press.

Israel, J. (2010), *A Revolution of the Mind: Radical Enlightenment and the Intellectual Origins of Modern Democracy*, Princeton, NJ: Princeton University Press.

Jabri, V. (2007), *War and the Transformation of Global Politics*, Basingstoke: Palgrave Macmillan.

Jahn, B. (1999), 'IR and the state of nature: the cultural origins of a ruling ideology', *Review of International Studies* 25(3): 411–34.

— (2000), *The Cultural Construction of International Relations: The Invention of the State of Nature*, Basingstoke: Palgrave.

— (2005), 'Barbarian thoughts: imperialism in the philosophy of John Stuart Mill', *Review of International Studies* 31(3): 599–618.

Jahn, J. (1961), *Muntu: African Culture and the Western World*, New York: Grove Press.

Jarrett, M. (2013), *The Congress of Vienna and Its Legacy: War and Great Power Diplomacy after Napoleon*, London: I.B. Tauris.

Jasanoff, M. (2017), *The Dawn Watch: Joseph Conrad in a Global World*, London: William Collins.

Javed, N., and N. Qureshi (2019), 'City profile: Faisalabad, Pakistan', *Environment and Urbanization ASIA* 10(2): 233–54.

Jay, M. (2007), 'No state of grace: violence in the garden', in D. Harris and D. Fairchild Ruggles (eds.), *Sites Unseen: Landscape and Vision*, Pittsburgh, PA: University of Pittsburgh Press, 45–60.

Jervis, R. (1985), 'From balance to concert: a study of international security cooperation', *World Politics* 38(1): 58–79.

Johnson, P. (1991), *The Birth of the Modern: World Society, 1815–1830*, London: Weidenfeld and Nicolson.

Jones, R. (1976), *The British Diplomatic Service: 1815–1914*, Waterloo, Ont.: Wilfrid Laurier University Press.

Kaeckenbeeck, G. (1918), *International Rivers: A Monograph Based on Diplomatic Documents*, London: Published for the Grotius Society by Sweet and Maxwell.

Kagan, K. (1998), 'The myth of the European Concert: the realist-institutionalist debate and Great Power behavior in the Eastern Question, 1821–41', *Security Studies* 7(2): 1–57.

Kaiser, W., and J. W. Schot (2014), *Writing the Rules for Europe: Experts, Cartels, and International Organizations*, Basingstoke: Palgrave Macmillan.

Kant, I. (1795), *Perpetual Peace*, London: George Allen and Unwin.

Kaplan, F. (2013 [1983]), *Carlyle: A Biography*, New York: Open Road Integrated Media.

Karns, M., and K. Mingst (2010), *International Organizations: The Politics and Process of Global Governance*, 2nd ed., Boulder, CO: Lynne Rienner.

Keynes, J. M. (1920), *The Economic Consequences of the Peace*, New York: Harcourt, Brace and Howe, https://www.gutenberg.org/files/15776/15776-h/15776-h.htm (accessed 9 September 2021).

Kieran, B. (2019), 'The legal personality of rivers', *EMA Human Rights Blog*, http://www.emahumanrights.org/2019/01/16/the-legal-personality-of-rivers/ (accessed 30 August 2020).

Kipling, R. (1911), 'The Secret of the Machines', https://www.poetryfoundation.org/poems/46786/the-secret-of-the-machines (accessed July 2020).

Kleemann, K. (2018), '"Moby Dick" in the Rhine: how a beluga whale raised awareness of water pollution in West Germany', Environment & Society Portal, *Arcadia*, no. 6, Rachel Carson Center for Environment and Society, doi.org/10.5282/rcc/8222.

Klingensmith, D. (2003), 'Building India's "modern temples": Indians and Americans in the Damodar Valley Corporation, 1945–60', in K. Sivaramakrishnan and A. Agarwal (eds.), *Regional Modernities: The Cultural Politics of Development in India*, Stanford, CA: Stanford University Press, 122–42.

Klüber, J. L. (1819–36), *Acten des Wiener Congresses, in den Jahren 1814 und 1815*, vol. III, Erlangen: J. J. Palm und E. Enke.

Koivurova, T. (2011), 'Jurisprudence of the European Court of Human Rights regarding indigenous peoples: retrospect and prospects', *International Journal on Minority and Group Rights* 18(1): 1–37.

Koivurova, T., S. Duyck, and L. Heinämäki (2012), 'Climate change and human rights', in E. Hollo, K. Kulovesi, and M. Mehling (eds.), *Climate Change and the Law*, Dordrecht: Springer, 287–325.

Krehbiel, E. (1918), 'The European Commission of the Danube: an experiment in international administration', *Political Science Quarterly* XXXIII: 38–55.

Kubalkova, V. (2006), 'Towards an international political theology', *The Brown Journal of World Affairs* 12(2): 139–50.

Lambert, A. (2011), *The Crimean War: British Grand Strategy Against Russia, 1853–56*, 2nd ed., Abingdon: Routledge.

Latour, B. (1993), *We Have Never Been Modern*, Cambridge, MA: Harvard University Press.

Lawson, G. (2006), 'The promise of historical sociology in international relations', *International Studies Review* 8(3): 397–423.

— (2012), 'The eternal divide? History and international relations', *European Journal of International Relations* 18(2): 203–26.

Lee, L. (1991), 'Baden between revolutions: state-building and citizenship, 1800–1848', *CEH* 24: 248–67.

Lekan, T. (2008), 'Saving the Rhine: water, ecology and *Heimat* in post-World War II Germany', in C. Mauch and T. Zeller (eds.), *Rivers in History: Perspectives on Waterways in Europe and North America*, Pittsburgh, PA: University of Pittsburgh Press, 110–26.

Lengyel, E. (1940), *The Danube*, London: Gollancz.

Lilienthal, D. (1944), *TVA: Democracy on the March*, New York: Harper and Brothers.

Lindley, D. (2004), 'Avoiding tragedy in power politics: the Concert of Europe, transparency, and crisis management', *Security Studies* 7(2): 1–57.

Lindroth, M., and H. Sinevaara-Niskanen (2013), 'At the crossroads of autonomy and essentialism: indigenous peoples in international environmental politics', *International Political Sociology* 7(3): 275–93.

Linebaugh, P., and M. Rediker (2000), *The Many-Headed Hydra: Sailors, Slaves, Commoners, and the Hidden History of the Revolutionary Atlantic*, London: Verso.

Loiseaux, O. (2016), 'Regnauld de Lannoy's nineteenth century map of Africa at a scale of 1:2,000,000', *The Cartographic Journal* 84(3): 316–35.

Longfellow, H. W. (1857), *Prose Works, Complete in Two Volumes*, Cambridge, MA: Houghton and Co., https://www.ebooksread.com/authors-eng/henry-wadsworth-longfellow/prose-works-of-henry-wadsworth-longfellow–complete-in-two-volumes-volume-2-hci/1-prose-works-of-henry-wadsworth-longfellow–complete-in-two-volumes-volume-2-hci.shtml (accessed August 2020).

Loucks, D. P., and J. Gladwell (eds.) (1999), *Sustainability Criteria for Water Resource Systems*, Cambridge: Cambridge University Press.

Lyons, F. S. (1963), *Internationalism in Europe: 1815–1914*, Leiden: A. W. Sythoff.

Machiavelli, N. (1998 [1532]), *The Prince*, trans. H. C. Mansfield, 2nd ed., Chicago: University of Chicago Press.

MacKenzie, J. M. (1988), *The Empire of Nature: Hunting, Conservation, and British Imperialism*, Manchester: Manchester University Press.

Magris, C. (2001 [1986]), *Danube*, London: Harvill Panther.

Maluwa, T. (1982), 'The origins and development of international fluvial law in Africa: a study of the international legal regimes of the Congo and Niger rivers from 1885 to 1960', *Netherlands International Law Review* 29(3): 368–400.

Manchester Guardian (1853), 'Russian hostility to commerce navigation of the Danube', 28 December.

Mao Z. (1972 [1956]), 'Swimming', in *The Poems of Mao Zedong*, trans. W. Barnstone, Berkeley, CA: University of California Press, 83–5.

Marcus Aurelius (1749), *The Meditations of the Emperor Marcus Aurelius Antoninus*, vol. 1, Glasgow: Robert and Andrew Foulis.

Marlow, J. (1970), *Cromer in Egypt*, New York: Praeger.

Marx, K., and F. Engels (1848), *Communist Manifesto*, Moscow: Progress, https://www.marxists.org/archive/marx/works/1848/communist-manifesto/ (accessed 9 August 2021).

Masters, R. (1999), *Fortune is a River: Leonardo Da Vinci and Niccolò Machiavelli's Magnificent Dream to Change the Course of Florentine History*, London: Plume.

Mauch, C. (2004), *Nature in German History*, Oxford: Berghahn.

Mayall, J. (1990), *Nationalism and International Society*, Cambridge: Cambridge University Press.

Mazower. M. (2009), *No Enchanted Palace: The End of Empire and the Ideological Origins of the United Nations*, Princeton, NJ: Princeton University Press.

— (2012), *Governing the World: The History of an Idea, 1815 to the Present*, London: Penguin.

McClintock, A. (1995), *Imperial Leather: Race, Gender, and Sexuality in the Colonial Context*, London: Routledge.

McIver, J. (1997), 'Environmental protection, indigenous rights and the Arctic Council: rock, paper, scissors on the ice?', *Georgetown International Environmental Law Review* 10: 147–68.

Mellor, R. E. (1983), *The Rhine: A Study in the Geography of Water Transport*, Aberdeen: Department of Geography, University of Aberdeen.

Mill, J. S. (1836), 'Civilization', *London and Westminster Review*, April, https://www.laits.utexas.edu/poltheory/jsmill/diss-disc/civilization/civilization.html (accessed March 2016).

Miller, D. H. (1919), 'The international regime of ports, waterways and railways', *The American Journal of International Law* 13(4): 669–86.

Mitchell, T. (2002), *Rule by Experts: Egypt, Techno-politics, Modernity*, Berkeley, CA: University of California Press.

Mitchell, W. J. T. (1994), 'Imperial landscape', in W. J. T. Mitchell (ed.), *Landscape and Power*, Chicago: University of Chicago Press, 5–34.

Mitzen, J. (2013), *Power in Concert: The Nineteenth-Century Origins of Global Governance*, Chicago: University of Chicago Press.

Montesquieu, C. (1989 [1748]), *Spirit of the Laws*, ed. A. Cohler, B. Miller, and H. Stone, Cambridge: Cambridge University Press.

Morgenthau, H. (1946), *Scientific Man vs. Power Politics*, Chicago: University of Chicago Press.

Morris, J. (2010 [1968]), *Pax Britannica: The Climax of an Empire*, London: Faber and Faber.

Mosse, G. L. (1978), *Toward the Final Solution: A History of European Racism*, London: J. M. Dent.

Moumin, M. (2008), 'Mesopotamian marshlands: an ecocide case', *Georgetown International Environmental Law Review* 20: 499–519.

Mukerji, C. (1997), *Territorial Ambitions and the Gardens of Versailles*, Cambridge: Cambridge University Press.

— (2007), 'The Great Forestry Survey of 1669–1671: the use of archives for political reform', *Social Studies of Science* 37(2): 227–53.

— (2010), 'The territorial state as figured world of power: strategics, logistics, and impersonal rule', *Sociological Theory* 28(4): 402–24.

Münster, G. H. (2013 [1868]), *Political Sketches of the State of Europe, from Count Ernst Count Dispatches to the Prince, Regent, from the Congress of Vienna*, London: Forgotten Books.

Munteanu, M. (2015), 'The Danube Question during the period of the Vienna Peace Conference and Congress of Paris (1855–1856)', *Hiperboreea* 2(1): 108–32.

Murphy, C. (1994), *International Organization and Industrial Change: Global Governance Since 1850*, Oxford: Oxford University Press.

Murphy, C., and J. Yates (2019), *Engineering Rules: Global Standard Setting since 1880*, Baltimore, MD: Johns Hopkins University Press.

Neumann, I. (2008), 'Russia as a Great Power, 1815–2007', *Journal of International Relations and Development* 11(2): 128–51.

Neuse, S. (1983), 'TVA at age fifty – reflections and retrospect', *Public Administration Review* 43(6): 491–9.

Nicolai, H. (1993), '*Le Mouvement Géographique*, un journal et un géographie au service de la colonisation du Congo', *Civilisations* 41(1/2): 257–77.

Nicolson, H. (1946), *The Congress of Vienna: A Study in Allied Unity, 1812–1822*, London: Methuen.

Nixon, R. (2011), *Slow Violence and the Environmentalism of the Poor*, Cambridge, MA: Harvard University Press.

Norton, W. (2007), 'Human geography and the geographical imagination', *Journal of Geography* 88(5): 186–92.

O'Neill, K. (2017), *The Environment and International Relations*, 2nd ed., Cambridge: Cambridge University Press.

Ó'Tuathail, G. (1994), '(Dis)placing geopolitics: writing on the maps of global politics', *Environment and Planning D: Society and Space* 12: 525–46.

— (1996), *Critical Geopolitics: The Politics of Writing Global Space*, London: Routledge.

— (2003), 'Back to the regions? Geographic illiteracy and political geography', *Political Geography* 22(6): 653–6.

Osiander, A. (2001), 'Sovereignty, international relations, and the Westphalian myth', *International Organizations* 55(2): 251–87.

Owen, R. (1969), *Cotton and the Egyptian Economy, 1820–1914: A Study in Trade and Development*, Oxford: Clarendon Press.

Pakenham, T. (1991), *The Scramble for Africa: White Man's Conquest of the Dark Continent from 1876 to 1912*, New York: Avon Books.

Palmer, A. (1972), *Metternich*, London: Weidenfeld and Nicolson.

Pardoe, J. (1854 [1837]), *The City of the Sultan, and Domestic Manners of the Turks: With a Steam Voyage Up the Danube*, London: Routledge.

Pascal, B. (1670), *Pensées*, trans. W. F. Trotter, Grand Rapids, MI: Christian Classics Ethereal Library, https://www.taugh.com/wormfarm/pensees.pdf (accessed July 2020).

Pearce, F. (1993), 'Draining life from Iraq's marshes: Saddam Hussein is using an old idea to force the Marsh Arabs from their home', *New Scientist* 1869, 16 April, https://www.newscientist.com/article/mg13818691-800-draining-life-from-iraqs-marshes-saddam-hussein-is-using-an-old-idea-to-force-the-marsh-arabs-from-their-home/ (accessed August 2020).

— (2006), *When the Rivers Run Dry: Water, the Defining Crisis of the Twenty-First Century*, Boston, MA: Beacon Press.

Pevehouse, J., T. Nordstrom, and K. Warnke (2004), 'The Correlates of War 2 International Governmental Organizations Data Version 2.0', *Conflict Management and Peace Science* 21(2): 101–19.

Philips, A., and J. Sharman (2015), *International Order in Diversity: War, Trade and Rules in the Indian Ocean*, Cambridge: Cambridge University Press.

Phillimore, R. (1879), *Commentaries upon International Law, Volume 1*, London: Butterworths.

Pišút, P. (2009), *Cartographic Evidence of the Disastrous Ice Flood of 1809 and its Aftermath*, Vienna: EGU General Assembly.

Pitts, J. (2012), 'Empire and legal universalism in the eighteenth century', *American Historical Review* 117(1): 92–121.

— (2018), *Boundaries of the International: Law and Empire*, Cambridge, MA: Harvard University Press.

Planché, J. R. (1827), *Descent of the Danube, from Ratisbon to Vienna, during the autumn of 1827. With anecdotes and recollections, historical and legendary, of the towns, castles, monasteries, &c., upon the banks of the river, and their inhabitants and proprietors, ancient and modern*, London: J. Duncan.

Plonien, K. (2000), '"Germany's river, but not Germany's border" – the Rhine as a national myth in early 19th century German literature', *National Identities* 2(1): 81–6.

Popper, O. (1943), 'The international regime of the Danube', *Geographical Journal* 102(5/6): 240–53.

Porter, C. (1996), *The Rhine as Musical Metaphor: Cultural Identity in German Romantic Music*, Lebanon, NH: Northeastern University Press.

Pred, A. (1997), 'Somebody else, somewhere else: racism, racialized spaces and the popular imagination in Sweden', *Antipode* 29(4): 383–416.

Pritchard, S. (2011), *Confluence: The Nature of Technology and the Remaking of the Rhone*, Cambridge, MA: Harvard University Press.

— (2012), 'From hydroimperialism to hydrocapitalism: "French" hydraulics in France, North Africa, and beyond', *Social Studies of Science* 42(4): 591–615.

PRO 30/22/18/4 (1855), 'Pack 4 Numbered Despatches 21-40 and Enclosures from Clarendon to J.R', British National Archives, Kew, UK.

PRO 30/22/18/8 (1855), 'Pack 8 Numbered Despatches 21-40 and Enclosures from Clarendon to J.R', British National Archives, Kew, UK.

PRO 30/29/198 (1880–85), 'Belgium, Netherlands, Denmark, Portugal, Spain, Sweden and Hawaii', British National Archives, Kew, UK.

Puryear, V. (1931), *England, Russia and the Straits Question, 1844–1856*, Berkeley, CA: University of California Press.

Quijano, A. (2000), 'Coloniality of power and Eurocentrism in Latin America', *International Sociology* 5(2): 215–32.

Quin, M. J. (1836), *A Steam Voyage down the Danube. With Sketches of Hungary, Wallachia, Servia, Turkey*, New York: T. Foster.

Radcliffe, A. (2009 [1794]), *A Journey Made in the Summer of 1794, through Holland and the Western Frontier of Germany*, Ann Arbor, MI: University of Michigan Library.

Rademacher, A. (2011), *Reigning the River: Urban Ecologies and Political Transformation in Kathmandu*, Durham, NC: Duke University Press.

Rao, R. (2020), *Out of Time: The Queer Politics of Postcoloniality*, Oxford: Oxford University Press.

Ravndal, E. (2020), 'Colonies, semi-sovereigns, and great powers: IGO membership debates and the transition of the international system', *Review of International Studies* 46(2): 278–98.

Rejai, M., and C. Enloe (1969), 'Nation-states and state-nations', *International Studies Quarterly* 13(2): 140–58.

Reinalda, B. (2009), *Routledge Handbook of International Organization*, Abingdon: Routledge.

Reinsch, P. (1911), *Public International Unions, Their Work and Organization: A Study in International Administrative Law*, Boston, MA: World Peace Foundation.

Reus-Smit, C. (1999), *The Moral Purpose of the State*, Princeton, NJ: Princeton University Press.

Richardson, J. (1994), *Crisis Diplomacy: The Great Powers since the Mid-Nineteenth Century*, Cambridge: Cambridge University Press.

Richter, W. (1965), *Bismarck*, New York: Putnam.

Rittberger, V., B. Zangl, A. Kruck, and H. Dijkstra (2019), *International Organization*, 3rd ed., London: Red Globe Press.

Robert, C. (1852), *Le monde slave: son passé, son état présent et son avenir*, Paris: Passard.

Robinson, R., J. Gallagher, and A. Denny (1978 [1961]), *Africa and the Victorians: The Official Mind of Imperialism*, Basingstoke: Palgrave Macmillan.

Roosevelt, F. D. (1959), 'Speech by Roosevelt at the Dedication of Boulder Dam, September 30, 1935', in E. Nixon (ed.), *Franklin D. Roosevelt and Conservation, 1911–1945*, 2 vols., New York: Franklin D. Roosevelt Library.

Rosenau, J. (1992), *The United Nations in a Turbulent World*, Boulder, CO: Lynne Rienner.

Rosenberg, J. (1994), *The Empire of Civil Society: A Critique of the Realist Theory of International Relations*, London: Verso.

Ruggie, J. (1993), 'Territoriality and beyond: problematizing modernity in international relations', *International Organizations* 47(1): 139–74.

Ruland, W. (1908), *Legends of the Rhine*, Cologne: Hoursch & Bechstedt.

Rutherford, S. (2007), 'Green governmentality: insights and opportunities in the study of nature's rule', *Progress in Human Geography* 31(3): 291–307.

Rydell, R. (1984), *All the World's a Fair: Visions of Empire at American International Expositions*, Chicago: University of Chicago Press.

Sahlins, P. (1990), 'Natural frontiers revisited: France's boundaries since the seventeenth century', *AHR* 95: 1423–51.

Said, E. (1978), *Orientalism*, New York: Pantheon.

Salzman, J. (2012), *Drinking Water: A History*, London: Overlook Duckworth.

Satia, P. (2007), 'Developing Iraq: Britain, India and the redemption of empire and technology in the First World War', *Past & Present* 197(1): 211–55.

Schama, S. (2004 [1995]), *Landscape and Memory*, London: Harper Perennial.

Schenk, J. (2020), *The Rhine and European Security in the Long Nineteenth Century: Making Lifelines from Frontlines*, Abingdon: Routledge.

Schiller, F. von (1972 [1789]), 'The nature and value of universal history: an inaugural lecture', *History and Theory* 11(3): 321–34.

Schmitt, H. (1983), 'Germany without Prussia: a closer look at the Confederation of the Rhine', *GSR* 6: 9–39.

Schneider, L. (2007), 'High on modernity? Explaining the failings of Tanzanian villagisation', *African Studies* 66(1): 9–38.

Schreiber, A. W. (1825), *The Traveller's Guide to the Rhine, Exhibiting the Course of that River from Scahffhausen to Holland, and describing the Moselle from Coblentz to Treves*, Paris: A. and W. Galignani.

Schroeder, P. (1968), 'Bruck versus Buol: the dispute over Austrian eastern policy, 1853–1855', *The Journal of Modern History* 40(2): 193–217.

— (1972), *Austria, Great Britain, and the Crimean War: The Destruction of the European Concert*, Ithaca, NY: Cornell University Press.

Schroeder, P. W. (1994), *The Transformation of European Politics 1763–1848*, Oxford: Clarendon.

Schumpeter, J. (1994 [1942]), *Capitalism, Socialism and Democracy*, London: Routledge.

Scott, J. C. (1998), *Seeing Like A State: How Certain Schemes to Improve the Human Condition Have Failed*, New Haven, CT: Yale University Press.

Scott, T. (2012), *The City-State in Europe, 1000–1600*, Oxford: Oxford University Press.

Selby, J. (2003), 'Dressing up domination as "cooperation": the case of Israeli–Palestinian water relations', *Review of International Studies* 29: 121–38.

Senf, C. (1988), *The Vampire in Nineteenth Century English Literature*, Bowling Green, OH: The Popular Press.

Shelley, M. W. (1818), *Frankenstein*, Planet Ebooks, http://www.planetebook.com/ebooks/Frankenstein.pdf (accessed 5 July 2016).

Shilliam, R. (2015), *The Black Pacific: Anti-Colonial Struggles and Oceanic Connections*, London: Bloomsbury.

Sissons, J. (2005), *First Peoples. Indigenous Cultures and Their Futures*, London: Reaktion.

Skene, F. (1847), *Wayfaring Sketches among the Greeks and Turks, and on the Shores of the Danube*, London: Chapman and Hall.

Slade, A. (1840), *Travels in Germany and Russia: including a steam voyage by the Danube and the Euxine from Vienna to Constantinople, in 1838–39*, London: Longman, Orme, Brown, Green and Longmans.

Slantchev, B. (2005), 'Territory and commitment: the Concert of Europe as self-enforcing equilibrium', *Security Studies* 14(4): 565–606.

Sluga, G. (2015), 'Women at the Congress of Vienna', *Eurozine*, http://www.eurozine.com/articles/2015-01-28-sluga-en.html (accessed 1 April 2016).

Smith, A. (1904 [1776]), *The Wealth of Nations*, London: Methuen.

Sneddon, C., and C. Fox (2006), 'Rethinking transboundary waters: a critical hydropolitics of the Mekong basin', *Political Geography* 25: 181–202.

Snow, R. (1842), *Journal of a steam voyage down the Danube to Constantinople, and thence by way of Malta and Marseilles to England*, London: Moyes and Barclay.

Snowe, J. (1839), *The Rhine: Legends, Traditions, History, from Cologne to Mainz*, London: Moyes and Barclay.

Souffrant, E. M. (2000), *Formal Transgression: John Stuart Mill's Philosophy of International Affairs*, Lanham, MD: Rowman and Littlefield.

Spaulding, R. M. (1999), 'Anarchy, hegemony, cooperation: international control of the Rhine River, 1789–1848', published online by the Central Commission for the Navigation of the Rhine, https://www.ccr-zkr.org/files/histoireCCNR/21_anarchy-hegemony-cooperation.pdf (accessed 9 September 2021).

— (2007), 'The modern bequest of a dying empire: the rise of joint management of the Rhine River', published online by the Central Commission for the Navigation of the Rhine, https://www.ccr-zkr.org/files/histoireCCNR/22_the-modern-request-of-a-dying-empire.pdf (accessed 9 September 2021).

— (2011), 'Revolutionary France and the transformation of the Rhine', *Central European History* 44: 203–26.

Spencer, E. (1837), *Travels in Circassia, Krim-Tartary, [etc.]: including a steam voyage down the Danube, from Vienna to Constantinople, and round the Black Sea*, London: Colburn.

Spencer, H. (1868), *Social Statics: Or, The Conditions Essential to Human Happiness Specified, and the First of Them Developed*, London: Williams and Norgate.

Stanley, H. M. (1878), *Through the Dark Continent: or, The Sources of the Nile Around the Great Lakes of equatorial Africa, and down the Livingstone River to the Atlantic Ocean*, 2 vols., New York: Harper.

— (1885), *The Congo and the Founding of Its Free State*, 2 vols., New York: Harper and Brothers.

— (1896), 'Africa and powers: the partition of the Dark Continent', *The Logansport Reporter*, 27 February.

Stengers, J. (1971), 'King Leopold and the Anglo-French rivalry, 1882–1884', in P. Gifford and W. R. Louis (eds.), *France and Britain in Africa*, New Haven, CT: Yale University Press, 121–66.

Stock, P. (2019), *Europe and the British Geographical Imagination*, Oxford: Oxford University Press.

Stoker, B. (1897), *Dracula*, Project Gutenberg, http://www.gutenberg.org/ebooks/345 (accessed 5 February 2016).

Suganami, H. (1978), 'A note on the origin of the word "international"', *British Journal of International Studies* 4(3): 226–32.

Suzuki, S. (2009), *Civilization and Empire: China and Japan's Encounter with European International Society*, Abingdon: Routledge.

Sylvest, C. (2008), '"Our passion for legality": international law and imperialism in late nineteenth century Britain', *Review of International Studies* 4(3): 403–23.

Talleyrand, C. (1881), *The Correspondence of Prince Talleyrand and King Louis XVIII during the Congress of Vienna (hitherto unpublished)*, vol. II, New York: Harper.

Taylor, A. J. P. (1955), *Bismarck: The Man and Statesman*, London: Hamish Hamilton.

— (1961), *The Origins of the Second World War*, London: Hamish Hamilton.

Taylor, R. (1998), *The Castles of the Rhine: Recreating the Middle Ages in Modern Germany*, Waterloo, Ont.: Wilfrid Laurier University Press.

Temperley, H. W. (ed.) (1920), *A History of the Peace Conference of Paris, Vol 2*, London: Hodder and Stoughton.

Teschke, B. (2003), *The Myth of 1648: Class, Geopolitics, and the Making of Modern International Relations*, London: Verso.

Thacker, C. (1979), *The History of the Gardens*, London: Croom Helm.

Thayer, W. (1917), 'The Congress of Paris', in *Three Peace Congresses of the Nineteenth Century*, Cambridge, MA: Harvard University Press, 23–44.

Thill, E. W. (2010), 'Civilization under construction: depictions of architecture on the Column of Trajan', *American Journal of Archaeology* 114(1): 27–43.

Thompson, C. W. (2012), *French Romantic Travel Writing: Chateaubriand to Nerval*, Oxford: Oxford University Press.

Thornton, J. (1993), '"I am the subject of the King of Congo": African political ideology and the Haitian Revolution', *Journal of World History* 4(2): 181–214.

Thorpe, N. (2013), *The Danube*, New Haven, CT: Yale University Press.

Todorov, T. (1984), *The Conquest of America: The Question of the Other*, New York: Harper and Row.

Todorova, M. (1997), *Imagining the Balkans*, New York: Oxford University Press.

Tomaselli, A. (2016), 'Exploring indigenous self-government and forms of autonomy', in C. Lennox and D. Short (eds.), *Handbook of Indigenous Peoples' Rights*, Abingdon: Routledge, 83–100.

Torday, E. (1913), *Camp and Tramp in African Wilds*, London: Seeley, Service and Co.

Townsend, M. (1930), *The Rise and Fall of the German Colonial Empire, 1884–1918*, London: Macmillan.

Tshimanga, R. (2009), 'Traditional values and uses of water along the upper Congo River', in T. Oestigaard (ed.), *Water, Culture and Identity: Comparing Past and Present Traditions in the Nile Basin Region*, Bergen: BRIC Press, 23–54.

Tsing, A. (2015), *The Mushroom at the End of the World: On the Possibility of Life in Capitalist Ruin*, Princeton, NJ: Princeton University Press.

Tvedt, T. (2011), 'Hydrology and empire: the Nile, water imperialism and the partition of Africa', *The Journal of Imperial and Commonwealth History* 39(2): 173–94.

Twiss, T. (1884), *The Law of Nations Considered as Independent Political Communities; On the rights and Duties of Nations in Time of Peace*, Oxford: Clarendon Press.

Urquhart, D. (1833), *Turkey and its Resources: Its Municipal Organization and Free Trade: the State and Prospects of English Commerce in the East: the New Administration of Greece: Its Revenue and National Possessions*, London: Saunders and Otley.

— (1851), *The Mystery of the Danube: Showing How Through Secret Diplomacy, that River has Been Closed, Exportation from Turkey Arrested, and the Re-Opening of the Isthmus of Suez Prevented*, London: Bradbury and Evans.

— (1853), *Progress of Russia in the West, North, and South, by opening the sources of opinion and appropriating the channels of wealth and power*, London: Trübner.

Van Eysinga, W. J. M. (1935), *La Commission Centrale pour la Navigation du Rhin: Historique*, Leyde: Société d'éditions A. W. Sijthoff.

Van Reybrouck, D. (2014), *Congo: The Epic History of a People*, Amsterdam: De Bezige Bij.

Vattel, E. (2008 [1797]), *The Law of Nations, Or, Principles of the Law of Nature, Applied to the Conduct and Affairs of Nations and Sovereigns, with Three Early Essays on the Origin and Nature of Natural Law and on Luxury*, ed. B. Kapossy and R. Whitmore, Indianapolis, IN: Liberty Fund.

Vucetic, S. (2011), *The Anglosphere: A Genealogy of a Racialized Identity in International Relations*, Stanford, CA: Stanford University Press.

Waterbury, J. (1979), *Hydropolitics of the Nile Valley*, Syracuse, NY: Syracuse University Press.

Watson, P. (2010), *The German Genius: Europe's Third Renaissance, the Second Scientific Revolution, and the Twentieth Century*, London: Simon and Schuster.

Watt-Cloutier, S. (2015), *The Right to be Cold: One Woman's Fight to Protect the Arctic and Save the Planet from Climate Change*, Toronto: Penguin Canada.

Weber, M. (1946), *From Max Weber: Essays in Sociology*, ed. H. Gerth and C. W. Mills, Oxford: Oxford University Press.

Webster, C. K. (1919), *The Congress of Vienna 1814–1815*, London: G. Bell.

Wehler, H. U. (1970), 'Bismarck's imperialism 1862–1890', *Past & Present* 48: 119–55.

Weiss, T., and R. C. Thakur (2010), *Global Governance and the UN: An Unfinished Journey*, Indianapolis, IN: Indiana University Press.

Wells, P. (2003), *The Battle that Stopped Rome: Emperor Augustus, Arminius, and the Slaughter of the Legions in the Teutoburg Forest*, New York: W. W. Norton.

Wendt, A. (2001), 'Driving with the rearview mirror: on the rational science of institutional design', *International Organization* 55(4): 1019–49.

Whaley, J. (2012), *Germany and the Holy Roman Empire, c 1490–1806*, 2 vols., Cambridge: Cambridge University Press.

Wheaton, H. (1864), *Elements of International Law*, annotated by W. Lawrence, London: Sampson Low, Son and Co.

Whelan, K. (2004), 'The green Atlantic: radical reciprocities between Ireland and America in the long eighteenth century', in K Wilson (ed.), *A New Imperial History: Culture, Identity and Modernity in Britain and the Empire 1660–1840*, Cambridge: Cambridge University Press, 216–38.

Wilson, A. (2012), 'Water, power and culture in the Roman and Byzantine worlds: an introduction', *Water History* 4(1): 1–9.

Wilson, P. (2003), *The International Theory of Leonard Woolf: A Study in Twentieth Century Idealism*, Basingstoke: Palgrave Macmillan.

Windelspecht, M. (2003), *Groundbreaking Scientific Experiments, Inventions and Discoveries of the 19th Century*, London: Greenwood Press.

Wittfogel, K. (1956), 'Hydraulic civilization', in T. William (ed.), *Man's Role in Changing the Face of the Earth*, Chicago: University of Chicago Press, 152–64.

Wolff, L. (1994), *Inventing Eastern Europe: The Map of Civilization on the Mind of the Enlightenment*, Stanford, CA: Stanford University Press.

Wood, A. (1964), *Europe, 1815–1945*, London: Longmans.

Woolf, L. (1916), *International Government: Two Reports*, London: Fabian Society.

Wright, G. (1995 [1974]), *France in Modern Times*, New York: W. W. Norton.

Wright Mills, C. (1959), *The Sociological Imagination*, New York: Oxford University Press.

Wulf, A. (2008), *The Brother Gardeners: Botany, Empires and the Birth of an Obsession*, London: Windmill Books.

— (2015), *The Invention of Nature: The Adventures of Alexander von Humboldt, the Lost Hero of Science*, London: John Murray.

Yao, J. (2013), 'Super dam: Egyptian concern for Nile water security spurs cooperation over Ethiopia's new dam', Circle of Blue, http://www.circleofblue.org/2013/world/super-dam-egyptian-concern-for-nile-water-security-spurs-cooperation-over-ethiopias-new-dam/ (accessed 1 October 2013).

— (2019), '"Conquest from barbarism": the Danube Commission, international order and the control of nature as a Standard of Civilization', *European Journal of International Relations* 25(2): 335–59.

Youatt, R. (2017), 'Personhood and the rights of nature: the new subjects of contemporary earth politics', *International Political Sociology* 11(1): 39–54.

Young, O. (1994), *International Governance: Protecting the Environment in a Stateless Society*, Ithaca, NY: Cornell University Press.

— (2016), *On Environmental Governance; Sustainability, Efficiency, and Equity*, Abingdon: Routledge.

Youngs, T. (1994), *Travellers in Africa: British Travelogues, 1850–1900*, Manchester: Manchester University Press.

— (2006), 'Introduction: filling the blank spaces', in T. Youngs (ed.), *Travel Writing in the Nineteenth Century*, London: Anthem Press, 1–18.

Zahm, J. A. (1922), *From Berlin to Bagdad and Babylon*, New York: D. Appleton.

Zeitoun, M., and J. Warner (2006), 'Hydro-hegemony – a framework for analysis of trans-boundary water conflicts', *Water Policy* 8(5): 435–60.

Index

9 781526 154385